HAUNTED BASEBALL

GHOSTS,

CURSES,

LEGENDS, AND

EERIE EVENTS

MICKEY BRADLEY

AND DAN GORDON

THE LYONS PRESS
Guilford, Connecticut
An imprint of The Globe Pequot Press

The Lyons Press is an imprint of The Globe Pequot Press.

10 9 8 7 6 5 4

Printed in the United States of America

Library of Congress Cataloging-in-Publication Data

Bradley, Mickey.
  Haunted baseball : ghosts, curses, legends, and eerie events / Mickey Bradley and Dan Gordon.
    p. cm.
  Includes bibliographical references.
  ISBN-13: 978-1-59921-022-3
  1. Baseball--United States--Anecdotes. 2. Baseball--United States--History. 3. Baseball players--United States--Anecdotes. 4. Supernatural--Anecdotes. I. Gordon, Dan, 1965- II. Title.
  GV873.B66 2007
  796.3570973--dc22

                                                              2007014418

To our fathers,
whose own love of baseball haunts this book

CONTENTS

Curses

INTRODUCTION

Baseball is a sport that honors its past.

From long-standing records still talked about today, to retro-style parks, to retired uniform numbers, players and fans are vividly aware that they are part of a baseball continuum. The greatest names of the past—Ted Williams, Ty Cobb, Lou Gehrig, Hank Greenberg, Jackie Robinson—never leave us entirely. In fact, there's nothing dusty or archaic about these names: They are as familiar and relevant to most baseball fans as Ken Griffey Jr., Albert Pujols, David Ortiz, or Derek Jeter. Babe Ruth has been dead for nearly sixty years and remains the best-known name in baseball.

There are many reasons for the continuing presence of the baseball giants of the past: the sport's wealth of statistics, which put contemporary players in competition with those from earlier eras; the adoration of childhood heroes, which fans take into their adult years; the many books and movies that are still being created about these men. But perhaps the biggest reason is simply baseball's deep history and hallowed traditions. The sport dates back well over a hundred years and is a national treasure.

Given that, it is not surprising that folklore has developed around it. Superstar athletes are regarded as "baseball heroes," and heroes inspire myths. On top of that, baseball culture seems tailor-made for wide-eyed tales. Players sit around clubhouses, on team buses, and in hotel rooms on the road swapping stories. Parents pass down to their children memories of larger-than-life moments from the past. Beat reporters one-up each other with tales that were too tall to print in their columns. In some ways, these are modern-day versions of the tribal elders telling stories around the fire.

In embarking on this book we set out to capture these magical stories and legends. While a few are well known, such as Boston's Curse of the Bambino, most have never before appeared in print. (Even W. P. Kinsella, author of *Shoeless Joe*, the book upon which the film *Field of Dreams* is based, told us he'd never heard of an actual baseball ghost story.)

Take, for example, the visiting team hotel for the Devil Rays in St. Petersburg, Florida. Numerous players who have stayed there in the past ten years have heard of or experienced the many ghost stories associated with the hotel—we heard them from dozens upon dozens of major leaguers. But most fans have never had access to these tales before.

The "underground" nature of some of these stories made researching them a bit challenging. We spent a year and a half scouring clubhouses, interviewing professional players and managers (over 800), searching out fans, contacting retired athletes, and working any angle we could find to track down leads. The hunt took us not only to major-league ballparks and Spring Training camps, but to places we would not have predicted, like Chinatown in Los Angeles, a medical office in Champaign, Illinois, and a firehouse in Queens, New York.

And then there were those serendipitous moments when the baseball gods seemed to smile on us. A casual mention of the project at an unrelated business meeting resulted in a colleague approaching to say that his brother once lived in a house owned by Hall of Famer Sam Rice, and there was some kind of ghost story there. A cold call to a former Spring Training ballpark in St. Petersburg, not especially likely to unearth any nuggets, surprisingly yielded a goldmine. The result is "Field of Legends," the opening chapter of this book.

While the road to these stories could be circuitous and we encountered many puzzled faces along the way, we never doubted that tales were out there waiting to be recorded. Ghost stories are among the oldest and most popular narratives. They capture the imagination, challenge our beliefs, and—most of all—illuminate our heritage. They evoke history, tradition, and passion, and keep the past alive *figuratively* by keeping it alive *literally*. A beloved, time-honored game steeped in nostalgia, we felt, must have accumulated haunted lore.

Something similar goes on with team curse stories. They provide a lens through which to view a team's past—usually a heartbreaking past—that connects disappointment to tradition and legacy. Everyone knows the famous hexes said to befuddle the Cubs and Red Sox, but we were surprised to discover a number of other alleged curses that both confound and delight fans.

Then there are stories that simply capture the behind-the-scenes fun of professional baseball: life on the road, superstitious rituals, the camaraderie of the clubhouse. As well as those that illuminate the special—and sometimes quite personal—meaning the sport has for devout fans. (Indeed, we found some faithful who want to be buried at their favorite ballparks—see Chapter 15: Coming Home to Rest.) This book, like baseball itself, is full of colorful and memorable characters. And those are just the ones who are *living*.

For us, writing *Haunted Baseball* was a chance to pay homage to the great American pastime by exploring these untold myths and legends. On a personal level, it also provided an opportunity for two old college buddies to work together again. (If all Yankees and Red Sox fans got along this well, the world would be a more harmonious place.) And we got to indulge the twelve-year-old fan inside each of us, navigating the behind-the-scenes world of professional baseball and chatting up players in dugouts, on the field, and at their lockers. The lineup included up-and-coming phenoms (David Wright, Jeff Francoeur, Conor Jackson), established superstars (Jim Thome, Johnny Damon, Ken Griffey Jr.), and legendary Hall of Famers (Willie Mays, Dave

Winfield, Yogi Berra). Our unusual line of questioning generated some blank looks from players used to standard interviews and cliched queries. But it also allowed these media-weary athletes to open up in new ways, taking the conversation in unpredictable directions. This could range from religious beliefs to childhood memories to the odd thing that happened to them on the field years ago that they'd never talked about publicly. Questions they'd never been asked before led to answers and stories they'd never shared before.

In talking about history and tradition, many spoke from the heart about their love of the game and the thrill of being in the big leagues. Fans, too, told touching stories about the role baseball and its heroes have played in their lives. Not all of the tales and tidbits and remembrances and accounts we heard could be used in the book, but we always felt privileged that so many people—both famous and unknown—were willing to relate their stories to us.

A few of the anecdotes collected here are shared widely among the baseball faithful. Others are joked about in the privacy of team locker rooms. And some are whispered about nervously by stadium workers who can't believe their eyes. Our goal is not to prove or disprove the fantastical tales we were told by players, ballpark employees, and fans. Rather, we present their accounts to give readers a fresh take on the sport they love and an insider's view of the stories those in the game share with each other. As for their literal truth, we'll let you decide. More than anything, we aim to entertain. The soulful stories here run the gamut from the spooky to the humorous to the inspirational—from haunted ballparks to folks visited by departed players to the healing role of baseball after the 9/11 tragedy.

In these pages, the faithful tell their tales; along the way, skeptics have their say too. But whether you're a believer or not, haunted stories are a fun way to examine the romance of baseball, the history of a great team, and the magical place that is The Ballpark.

GHOSTS, SPIRITS, AND UNEXPLAINED EVENTS

CHAPTER 1

FIELD OF
LEGENDS

On a sunny, temperate day, Crescent Lake Park gives every appearance of heaven on earth. Nestled in a cozy suburban community in St. Petersburg, the picturesque park is an oblong stretch of green wrapped around a spring-fed lake. A distinctive giant banyan tree anchors one end of the lake, its signature image for many local residents. Just about any time of day, the joggers, the dog walkers, and the babysitters are out, circling the landscaped lake in easy laps.

Attached to the park on the southeast end is an old-style baseball field. Its dugouts are primitive wooden lean-tos that evoke a simpler era, an impression reinforced by the lack of lights on the field. The ballpark is an inviting expanse of verdant green that seems to stretch out into infinity.

Charlie Lockett has been the groundskeeper for the ball field for the last seven years. Most mornings he's out there early, trimming the grass, raking the dirt, and painting the lines. "I love this job," he says. "This is a beautiful place to come to work every day."

Lockett loves his job so much that he doesn't even mind the ghosts.

Charlie Lockett was taking his lunch break one day, sitting on a bench in front of the grounds-keeping shed, with the field in front of him. "I was looking out at the sky and out of the corner of my eye, I saw this gray entity come out of the building." He describes what he saw as "a large, bulky figure"—a person, dressed in a gray uniform. The vision was "profound enough that it made me jump," says Lockett. But when he turned his head toward the figure, it had vanished.

Some time later, Lockett was watching TV when *The Babe* came on, a movie starring John Goodman as Babe Ruth. The celebrated Yankee was wearing a gray uniform "and something went click," says Lockett. He determined that the figure he'd seen was none other than the Bambino.

Maybe the Babe was looking for the Old Perfessor. When Lockett began at the park in 2000, he was working alone in centerfield one morning when he glimpsed "a short figure sitting in the visitor's dugout in a white baseball uniform," he says. He stared at the apparition for a while before it disappeared.

The image looked familiar to him. On Lockett's desk inside the storage shed sits a photo of a small man in a white uniform. His name is Casey Stengel.

Lockett's sightings of famous ballplayers might be dismissed as the wishful delusions of a lonely groundskeeper spending a little too much time under the Florida sun, except for one thing: Both Babe Ruth and Casey Stengel spent years at this field. So did Lou Gehrig, Joe DiMaggio, Bill Dickey, Yogi Berra, Mickey Mantle, Whitey Ford, Nolan Ryan, Gary Carter, Doc Gooden, Wade Boggs, and countless other baseball legends.

Welcome to Huggins-Stengel Field, one of the oldest ballparks in the United States, with perhaps the richest history.

The site began life as Crescent Lake Field, shortly after Crescent Lake Park came into being, in the mid-1920s. It quickly became the Spring Training facility for the New York Yankees, who were looking to relocate to Florida. The story goes that Yankee ownership was tired of Babe Ruth going wild in New Orleans, where the Yankees had been holding Spring Training. They decided to bring the team to what was then a sleepy retirement community with no nightlife. "When Ruth got here, St. Petersburg was born, because the Babe tore this town up," says one local resident.

The Yankees made the field their pre-season home for most of the next four decades (they spent a few years at other sites), leaving for good after the 1961 season; the very next year, an expansion team, the New York Mets, took over. They used the field until 1988. After them, the Baltimore Orioles and then the Tampa Bay Devil Rays called the ballpark home. (Throughout much of that time, the field was actually owned by the Cardinals, who leased its use to the other clubs while occasionally playing there too.)

In addition to its illustrious Spring Training denizens, the park has also been home to winter instructional leagues, visiting international teams, and other professional groups. Along the way its name changed, first to Miller Huggins Field in 1931, two years after the legendary Yankee manager's death, and then to Huggins-Stengel Field in 1963, to honor another great manager, who helmed both the Yankees and Mets at the park. Monuments to both Huggins and Stengel currently stand in front of the two small buildings at the field.

With nearly seventy-five years of use as a major-league training field, the list of great players who have dug in at this friendly, accessible community ballpark is mind-boggling. All-Star pitcher Matt Morris occasionally used the field when training with the Cardinals and remembers the stories Hall of Famer Red Schoendienst would tell the young players. "He talked about all the games that used to be played there and all the people that stepped on that field, and it was kind of amazing to me," he says. "The history's unbelievable."

Morris also found that the low-tech, uncluttered feel of Huggins-Stengel Field gives it the sense of a place out of time, and the simplicity of a park that is pure baseball. "It seemed like that field was stuck back in that era, of when those players played."

An old photograph captures what the small clubhouse was like back then. Twenty-eight uniformed Yankees are seen sitting and standing around the cramped locker room, smiling and laughing, holding bats, and punching gloves. In the middle stands Casey Stengel next to an old potbellied stove that provided primitive heat for the space. The presence of certain players (Joe DiMaggio, Ralph Houk, Bobby Brown, Johnny Lindell, Phil Rizzuto) dates the picture from either 1949 or 1950.

That clubhouse no longer stands; a new one was built in the early 1960s when the Mets came in. Next to it is another small building formerly used as the Mets administrative offices, which currently houses the city's athletics department.

And it's the site of another Huggins-Stengel ghost story.

Pete Samsoe—known as "Big Pete" to his friends—was groundskeeper at Huggins-Stengel Field before Lockett took the job. One day Samsoe was sitting by the field at 6:30 A.M. drinking his morning coffee. He looked across the grass and saw someone standing there. "I thought, nah—that ain't nobody. I must be dreaming," he says. "Then it started to walk toward me." The image passed in front of him and "walked right into the building—right through the wall.

"I thought, 'That's crazy! I must be seeing things.'" The ghostly figure wore a uniform bearing the number 3. "It looked like the Babe to me," says Samsoe. "And here's the kicker. My boss came out later and we were walking around the field. He said, 'What the heck is this over here?'" The pair discovered footprints burned into the grass. The impressions followed the path the apparition had taken, stopping right by the wall it had walked through.

Samsoe vowed never to tell anyone the story. But he felt vindicated when, some time later, he and a coworker were sitting by the field and she suddenly turned to him. "You won't believe what I see," she said. "It's something like a ghost." She described the vision as she was having it, pointing to the spot where she saw the figure. Samsoe saw nothing. "It's walking now," she said, and described the figure approaching the building and penetrating the same wall Samsoe saw the Babe pass through.

"She basically described to me what I had seen," says Big Pete. "She was really nervous. I said don't worry about it—this place is *nice* haunted."

Whom did she see? She didn't identify him, but Samsoe says that in the office there's a picture of Lou Gehrig on the wall, standing in the same spot that she described.

Big Pete had heard these stories before. A former Devil Rays pitching coach once confided that every time he walked through the gate and onto the field, his watch stopped. "But when I leave, it starts again," he told Samsoe.

And then there are the two clubbies who spent a night in the clubhouse, to catch up on last-minute work. "What a night!" they told Samsoe the next morning. "We heard card games—the Yankees were having a big card game. We smelled cigar smoke and we heard them drinking—the glasses and the bottles. We kept peeking out and there was no one there! All night long!"

Workers at Huggins-Stengel, like Lockett and Samsoe, come to take such stories in stride, mere manifestations of the field's rich history. As a lifelong baseball fan, Samsoe knows this is hallowed ground. "I always felt that it was a special place," he says. "I thought of it as a museum."

Accordingly, Samsoe saw himself as curator. For instance, when Mickey Mantle—who spent a number of Spring Trainings at Huggins-Stengel—died in 1995, "I went out and put a big '7' in centerfield," he recalls. Painting Mantle's number on the spot he occupied was a private tribute to the great player. Later that day Samsoe mowed the field, but found something odd happening. "Every time I went into centerfield, the mower would stop," he says. "It just wouldn't work." He eventually put it away for the day, leaving Mantle's spot untouched.

When Joe DiMaggio died four years later, the same thing happened. "I put a '5' out in centerfield." When Samsoe tried to cut the grass there, the mower again conked out—it simply shut down whenever he approached it.

Those were the only two times the mower ever failed, claims Samsoe, though there were other occasions when he wrote numbers in the grass to honor players. "I used to do that for players that were part of the field at one time—I used to paint their numbers on the field for that day. Not many people knew I did it. A lot of people never saw it. But I knew I did it."

Samsoe is not the only person who regards the field with reverence. He says it is not uncommon for big-name ballplayers to stop by the field while in town, to revisit a place that holds magical memories for them.

"Tom Seaver came by one day," he recalls. "He said, 'Gee, I'd just like to come back and see it. This is where I started.'" Samsoe let him in the locker room and Seaver started reminiscing. "He said, 'I remember my first day. When Casey Stengel came out, I was so intrigued and nervous.' I said, 'Tom, you just have your own time and relax,' and I went outside."

When Seaver came out, he had tears in his eyes—and seemed to have visited his own ghosts of the past. "So many great things happened to me in there," he told Samsoe. "I felt like I saw people I enjoyed back then."

Though he's no ballplayer himself, Samsoe could relate. At the end of a work day, he would often sit by the field with a cool drink, watching the sun set beyond the outfield and imagining the baseball greats who had raced around the bases. "When you stop and think about who played there, it just totally amazes you.

"That was a special job. Like you were put there to preserve this holy ground. That's the way I look at it." For Samsoe, the ghosts just made the place all the more special. "I always felt like Casey was there at all times," he says. And that was a comforting thought. "I was never scared."

If the specters Samsoe and others claim to have seen on this perfectly preserved field are relatively peaceful, the same cannot be said for what goes on in the adjacent building, the one-time clubhouse for the baseball teams who played there.

In December 1999, the Devil Rays gifted the ballpark to the city, having shifted most of their training activities to two other facilities. They had been letting others play on the field for a while; even so, in 1999, the ballpark was unused 216 days out of the year. Once they took it over, the city made the field available to community groups, like local high school squads and a six-team men's baseball league.

And they converted the old clubhouse into office space for an organization called TASCO (Teen Arts, Sports, and Cultural Opportunities), which runs a series of youth centers at spots around St. Petersburg.

The building was in disrepair. At first TASCO merely stored equipment there, setting up a trailer in the parking lot for offices. Then as money became available for renovations, the building's interior was drastically altered. Rows of old lockers were taken out, new bathrooms put in, and prefab walls inserted to divide the space into offices and cubicles.

It wasn't long before the TASCO team got the feeling that the previous tenants didn't like the changes.

"We've had lights flicker for no apparent reason, and the electricians have come and said the wiring is fine," reports Robert Norton, who works in the building. "We've had doors closing without any air-conditioning being on. [People] will just be sitting here at night working on flyers and a door will close."

"Oh, it's definitely haunted," says Bob Valenti, a supervisor for TASCO who has worked for the city for nearly thirty years. "I had an incident where I just about died—literally, just about died." Valenti had just participated in a teen program called Mud Wars. He was showering after hours at the facility when the near-fatal event occurred.

"The shower has a light sunken into the ceiling that's spring-loaded. Normally you have to pull hard on it to get it out. I was in the shower and the light suddenly popped out and dropped down about twelve inches and started swinging." The exposed wires were about eight inches from the running water, directly over his head. Valenti quickly jumped out.

"That was really scary," he says. "I left it hanging and took off." Since then, he has never been alone in the building at night. Valenti has also heard coworkers talk about seeing a man on the field, usually assumed to be Casey Stengel. They have approached him . . . only to find he's disappeared. And Valenti has experienced the slamming doors and on-and-off lights. Steve Sergent who worked as a batboy for the Devil Rays and then with TASCO recalls the time "we were doing some late night work and this light kept going on and off. Nobody ever went near the switch. We kind of freaked out and said 'forget this!' and left."

Sergent had abandoned the building once before. He arrived one morning to discover the alarm was off. "I know we had set the alarm and nobody came through the building in the night." He and a coworker started searching the building to see if someone else might be there. "We were looking around and we heard a door shut," he says. "We ran out! It took us about half an hour to come back into the building because we were out there watching, and nobody came out."

The odd, inexplicable moments got to a point where the office crew wanted to know just what was going on. They brought in Ian Beck, a teen supervisor at one of TASCO's recreation centers in St. Petersburg, who is an amateur ghost hunter on the side.

When Bob Valenti called, Beck was ready to investigate. "I had heard the different stories about stuff that goes on there. My interest was already piqued. It was a great chance to get into the building at night."

Beck arrived a little before 8:00 P.M. with a ghost hunting crew that included three other adults and two teens from the program. They spent two hours setting up some high-tech equipment. "We use everything from infrared video recorders to handheld camcorders to an infrared motion detector. We plug it into the computer and it records right to the hard drive."

The group also had highly sensitive microphones, which were placed strategically in the building, with audio recording to a separate hard drive. "If people say they're hearing things, we tend to put the audio there. If they've seen things or smelled things, we put the video in those areas." The staff walked around the building to get a feel for the place and to listen for environmental sounds (air-conditioning, water pipes, everyday creaks, etc.) so they could later distinguish these from more ghostly noises.

At 10:00 P.M., the investigation got under way. "We do what we call 'going black,' which is a process of eliminating lights and adjusting the camera. And then people go around and do mike checks, read the time that we officially start recording—that kind of thing."

Working in pairs to affirm anything one person might see or experience, the team spent from thirty to forty-five minutes roaming from room to room. As is usually the case, Beck then began interrogating any spirits that might be lurking around.

"It's just typical questions. *'What's your name?' 'How old are you?'* We try to set up a background foundation first," he says. "If we get something, we may do a little more research and come back at a later date with more in-depth questions." In "active environments," Beck says, some questions get immediate or delayed responses; on other stakeouts, there's nothing but silence all night.

Here the team recorded no audible responses to the questions. But in the first hour, microphones in the bathroom (where the shower stall light almost fell on Bob Valenti) picked up some noises. "It was very much like a tapping," says Beck, "and then you would hear what some people classified as a shuffling of the feet, like through the bathroom around the mike."

A few hours later, microphones in the back room recorded "very, very faint whispers—almost inaudible whispers," described Beck. "You couldn't really understand what they were saying, but it was definitely something." Bob Valenti, listening to the tapes afterward, claims he heard two beeping noises followed by a voice that distinctly said, "That was stupid."

In addition to noises, the team picked up other signs of a presence. "There was a definite temperature change and there was a definite feel of a presence in the room," Beck says. "Not necessarily next to you, but passing through almost."

An indication of this registered on the equipment. "At that point in our audio recordings we got a huge spike as if somebody was trying to say something. I could see it on my computer screen in front of me. It's like a heartbeat kind of thing. I thought, 'So if they can't speak to us directly, they're going to speak to us electronically.' "

The biggest piece of "evidence" the team collected that night, however, was not a sight or sound, but a smell. One of the most commonly experienced oddities in the no-smoking building had been the whiff of cigar smoke. "When you come into the building [in the morning] and there's a faint smell of cigar," says Valenti, "that's usually an indication we've been visited."

Beck says this was the one piece of information he withheld from his crew prior to their overnight investigation. He wanted to see if people would pick up on it on their own. "We did get the cigar smoke smell," he reports. "It started in the back bathroom and worked its way through the building. The way someone described it was that it was like somebody was walking through with a cigar."

The cigar smell is usually interpreted as evidence that the ghost in question is Miller Huggins. "Because he did smoke cigars," claims Beck. "If I could've gotten anything that night, [the cigar smell] was the one thing I wanted somebody to experience. It was good."

Could it be that someone was smoking on the field and the scent wafted in through a back door? Beck thinks not. "This was probably three or four in the morning," he says, adding that "we never felt any breeze come through the building."

The surveillance concluded some time after 6:00 A.M. Toward the end, while it was still dark out, one member of the team said she saw someone standing on the field, "a dark, shadowy figure." The group quickly headed out with an infrared camera. Beck had heard stories of Huggins or Babe Ruth rounding the bases. This apparition was described as being dressed in a fedora and old-style clothes (not a baseball uniform). The cameras picked up nothing, but a notation was made in the log. "Our hearts were saying it was [Huggins]," says Beck. "But we can't really give a definite yea or nay to it."

So what was Beck's official conclusion at the end of the stakeout?

"With my professional experience, I do feel there is something there." But he's quick to point out that the presence of a spirit is not necessarily cause for alarm. "When you say haunted, a lot of people think negative. I like to say that something is living. For me, he's living his plane, his time, and we just happen to be moving through it."

In other words, Miller Huggins (or Casey Stengel, or Babe Ruth, or Lou Gehrig, or Joe DiMaggio, or Mickey Mantle, or any of the other baseball legends rumored to haunt the field) might linger at the site simply because he is so used to it. At Huggins-Stengel Field, a place where they spent the prime years of their careers, players are eternally young and the game never ends.

And what about Bob Valenti's shower incident, in which he was nearly electrocuted?

"If there are negative responses," says Beck, "it may be because they are no longer in the environment that they remember and love. It's now a modern environment and they don't know how to fit into it anymore." In addition, they may not approve of the modern environment. "It went from a beloved locker room to a plain old blasé office," says Beck.

Valenti acknowledges that TASCO changed the building, but thinks that the organization's work would make any of the old-timers proud. The group has brought sports—and arts, and culture—to countless St. Petersburg teens who might otherwise never experience them. The organization runs eleven rec centers in the city, serving kids of all economic classes and backgrounds. Some 3,000 to 5,000 kids participate in sports programs each year, and tens of thousands take part in special events.

He also notes that renovations were done with respect for the past. "We tried to preserve as much of the history as possible."

In the entranceway, several historic photographs of the field line
the wall. Across from the photos an original locker is on display,
complete with old uniforms and equipment. There's talk of bringing more lockers out of storage and creating a larger "wall of
fame" to honor the site's incredible baseball history.

For Pete Samsoe that's no consolation. "I think what they did
to [the building] is a crying tragedy. Somebody should be ar-
rested for it." Samsoe says that when the renovation occurred,
maintenance crews found old letters to Whitey Ford and other
players behind the lockers. "It should've always been left a clubhouse," he says shaking his head. "It was sad to see that go."

According to Valenti, it could all come back some day. "Anything you see here is not permanent," he says, referring particularly to the freestanding walls. "Everything that's up can come
down. It was done like that on purpose. We still have the lockers; we can take down the existing walls and go right back to
what it was. Other than the restrooms, which were changed, all
the other stuff is free-fitting."

In the meantime, TASCO employees just try to be polite. "We
say, 'Thank you for letting us use your facility. We're keeping it
nice and clean,'" says Valenti. When Steve Sergent left for the
night he'd say, "'Good-bye Huggins, good-bye Casey.' Because
we don't want them to mess with us."

On a warm March afternoon, a large bus sits in the small parking lot adjacent to Huggins-Stengel Field. It is bright pink, with
Day-Glo blue playfully splotched along the side: colors that
scream "teen transport." It has brought the Northeast Vikings
high school team here for a game against the St. Petersburg
Green Devils, who use the ballpark for home games.

On the diamond where Babe Ruth and Lou Gehrig played a
style of baseball that would define the game, 15-, 16-, and 17-
year-olds are fielding grounders and dragging bunts. A street
cart vendor offers hot dogs and drinks. Parents yell out from the
stands, booing ump calls and cheering on their kids.

Lee Rogers is here to watch his friend's grandson pitch. It's a thrill to see him out on this field. "I started coming here when I was twelve years old, back in 1950," he recalls. "I used to come to Spring Training and watch the Yankees play." He rattles off the names of legendary Yankees he saw (DiMaggio, Mantle, Berra, Ford, Skowron) as well as others who used the field some seasons or came as visitors (Willie Mays, Sal "The Barber" Maglie, Roy Campanella) and marvels that you could often walk right up to these men for autographs, or just to say hi. "They were friendly. They would talk to you, especially if you were a kid."

Gene Haig came to the area as an adult in the mid-1960s, when the Mets trained here, and considered the ball field a terrific local attraction. "It was great being up against the fence with my kids, watching Casey Stengel teaching people how to lead off first base." In later years he would see stars like Cal Ripken Jr. jogging around the lake in the morning as part of their personal routine.

A lot has changed in Crescent Lake Park since then. The neighborhood, too, is undergoing something of an identity crisis, as older buildings are being replaced with condos and larger houses that stick out from the quainter, quieter homes. But Huggins-Stengel Field remains a throwback. "It looks today just like it did back in the 1950s," says Rogers.

Out on the field, the Vikings turn a double play, shutting down a potential home-team rally. Rogers says these kids have been playing together for years, which is one reason the team is ranked fourth in the state in their division.

Huggins-Stengel Field is daunting for high school players, with its seemingly endless outfield. (It's 340 feet to leftfield, 400 feet to straightaway center, and a dispiriting 430 feet down the rightfield line.) Only three kids in the last ten years have hit one out in game play. But in the next inning, a Northeast player wearing uniform number 4 smacks a long fly ball over the centerfielder's head and races around the bags for a two-run inside-the-park homer. The next batter—a lefty wearing number 3—draws a walk.

Most of the spectators here are parents in their forties. Few know much of the history of the field, beyond the oft-cited fact that Babe Ruth played here and supposedly once hit a ball into the lake, a distance of over 500 feet. Only a couple can identify who Miller Huggins was; more are familiar with Stengel's name. One woman says, incorrectly, that "Ruth's and Gehrig's and Stengel's lockers are still inside the building."

The kids are a little more savvy. On the St. Petersburg team, the coach says, "We talk about it a little bit. They know the names, but they can't put it in context of what it means."

Although the Northeast squad doesn't play home games here, they seem to be more aware of the field's majestic past. They haven't heard the numerous ghost stories, but they are well familiar with what the flesh-and-blood players did here in their prime. "They know the history about Babe Ruth and everybody that's been on this field," their coach reports. "They love it. These kids love everything that has to do with baseball."

After the game—a 4–0 Northeast victory—the St. Petersburg players grab their equipment and head to the stands to connect with family members and catch rides home. The Vikings excitedly congratulate each other around home plate; this is their first win against St. Petersburg in six years.

No one is more pumped up than number 4, who hit the home run. His name is Jose Ramos Jr., a sixteen-year-old who plays centerfield for the team and appreciates how famous that spot is at Huggins-Stengel Field.

"I felt good playing in center, right where Joe DiMaggio and them played," he says, still smiling from the victory. Though he's many generations removed from the heyday of the old-time greats, Ramos says he has "watched movies and read books on them."

For Ramos, these players aren't just archaic historical figures—or shadowy ghosts in a clubhouse. "They're role models," he says. "My goal is to make it, just like them—make it to the big leagues. Play like they did.

"To me, they made baseball. The game wouldn't be the same without them."

CHAPTER 2

THE BIRD
AND JIM THOME

Every major leaguer cherishes the memory of his first big-league hit. But for All-Star slugger Jim Thome, the night of September 4, 1991, packed something extra. It was day one of a meaningful friendship with Indians trainer Jimmy Warfield.

Called up that morning and inserted into the lineup, Thome collected two solid hits and knocked in a run. As he passed by the training room after the game, he shyly asked Warfield where rookies sit on the bus. The trainer smiled warmly and said, "I'm on bus number one. I ride in the back. I'll save you a seat." After Thome had dressed, he boarded the first bus and saw there were hardly any players on it. He thought to himself, "Man, oh man, here I am a rookie. I need to get on bus number two." As he turned to head off the bus, Warfield stepped on, led him to the back, handed him a beer, and said, "Hey, congratulations, Kid."

From that day forward, until Warfield passed away eleven years later, the pair would always ride together in the back seat of bus number one. Thome saw in Warfield a kind, honorable, generous man who looked people squarely in the eye, treated everyone with respect and dignity, and believed in the goodness of people—a role model for how to conduct oneself in the Big Leagues. Their friendship deepened in the off-season. Thome and Warfield both owned homes in Cleveland, and they'd often get together or make trips to Columbus for Ohio State football games. "Jimmy and I were friends more than just another relationship in baseball," says Thome. "That's what was so hurtful for me when he died. I lost a good friend."

Warfield touched countless lives during his thirty-year tenure with the Indians. He was beloved throughout baseball both for his devotion to his craft and his positive influence on all those around him, from parking attendants to front office brass.

"He was the kind of person that you wanted to be around all the time," says Omar Vizquel, "because you learn a lot from Jimmy Warfield. He was so kind with everybody. It doesn't matter what kind of person you are. He treats you the same, equally."

"He was the only guy I knew who read the Indians media guide and looked up something on the person, something good, and talked to the person about it," remembers Bob Wickman. "He knew what college you were from, what your home state was. He looked at you and remembered. He would never mix up names. That's pretty tough figuring all the guys that come in and out of the clubhouse. Knowing every single guy in our organization, whether the guy was coming into the training room or not—that was showing a lot of respect for guys."

"He made a point of it to know everybody, no matter if he ran across your path as an A-ball guy or if you were up there and just got drafted and went through the clubhouse," says Charles Nagy. "He just made a point to go out of his way and say hello to everybody."

Utility outfielder Karim García recalls that players occasionally would give Warfield a big hug when they greeted him in the training room. Dave Burba remembers his infectious smile, even after a tough loss or an exhausting road trip. Jaret Wright appreciated how Warfield treated everyone as people first, ballplayers second. "You never really felt like you were friends just because you played baseball," says Wright. "He was always there for you no matter what."

Sandy Alomar is forever grateful to Warfield for bringing him back from a number of injuries and, on top of that, caring deeply about his well-being. "The care he put into treating players was unbelievable," says Alomar. "I was young and I learned a lot of things about my body."

The deep affection players had toward their trainer made it all the more painful when he died from complications from an aneurysm. On the morning of July 15, 2002, at Jacob's Field, Jimmy was busy filling out training reports and preparing the training room for afternoon treatments before that night's game versus the White Sox. Centerfielder Matt Lawton remembers stopping through the clubhouse that morning to get a little extra batting in. Warfield came over to him and enthusiastically promised to introduce him to Ohio State head football coach Jim Tressel, who was scheduled to come through the clubhouse at four o'clock that afternoon. Warfield also mentioned that he wasn't feeling well, but added, "Ah, don't worry about me. I'll be all right." Shortly after Lawton left, Warfield suffered a brain hemorrhage.

Warfield was rushed to Cleveland Clinic where he underwent emergency surgery and then slipped into a coma. As players trickled into the clubhouse that afternoon, they were shocked by the news. Jim Thome was among several who thought that Warfield's situation wasn't as bad as it sounded and he would be back with the team shortly. Still, the mood in the pregame Indians clubhouse was subdued. Passing through the locker room and not being able to greet Warfield or joke around with him or have him help them get ready for the game that evening was difficult. Several players wrote "JW" in chalk or marker on their caps. As he took his position at the start of the game, Thome etched his close friend's initials in the dirt.

Then something odd happened on the field that served as a distraction. In the bottom half of the second inning, a lone seagull landed near the corner of the Indians dugout near where Warfield and fellow trainer, Paul Spicuzza, always sat. The bird seemed scruffier and smaller than most of the seagulls that circle the field and stands during games and scavenge the upper deck after fans depart. It was without the usual shading of gray on the wing tips and was in fact so small that some witnesses at first confused it for a dove. In the dugout, Milton Bradley turned to his teammates and said, "Anybody ever notice there was a bird here before?" Several on the bench shook their heads. For the rest of the game, those in the dugout and even some from the front office would be struck by what seemed to them as the bird's resolve to stay near the team even when players, grounds crew, and umpires attempted to shoo it off. It often hovered over the action, roamed in fair play along the third base line, and sometimes landed by the batter's circle or by the home dugout. It walked across home plate a couple of times while rookie Indians pitcher Jason Phillips was warming up. For at least a couple of innings while Thome fielded his position at third, the bird lingered only a few feet away.

From the White Sox bench Sandy Alomar Jr. said to a few of his teammates who knew Warfield, "Oh, that's Jimmy. He probably misses the game so bad that he's out there on the field watching everybody."

Phillips would go on to notch his first major-league victory that evening, and Vizquel became the first Indians shortstop in forty years to collect 11 home runs in a season. The team headed to the hospital early the next morning and players were heartbroken to learn that Warfield was in intensive care and fighting for his life. "Seeing him in that state really put things in perspective how serious it was," says Thome. "Prior to that no one wanted to believe what was going on or what had happened."

As they stretched sullenly on the field before batting practice, with the seagull from the previous night's game still lingering nearby, word came that their trainer had passed. Players from both benches broke out in tears and consoled one another.

Indians manager Joel Skinner ushered his players into the clubhouse and the squad prayed and shared their favorite Warfield stories. They also discussed the emotional challenge of playing a game that night. Before the meeting, Linda Warfield told general manager Mark Shapiro that her husband of thirty-four years would have preferred that the game go on that evening, rather than calling it off in his honor. After Skinner made the team aware of this, the players unanimously voted to take the field out of respect for Warfield's family and his relentless devotion to the team. Warfield had never missed a game during his thirty-two seasons with the Indians.

Not realizing that the decision came from the Indians locker room and not the front office, White Sox players were bothered when they learned that the game was still on. Less than four weeks earlier, a Cardinals–Cubs game had been called off after the sudden passing of St. Louis ace Darryl Kile. "We were all kind of like 'just because Kile was a player and Warfield a trainer, we're still in the same business, the same company, the same job,'" recalls White Sox first baseman Jeff Liefer. "We were kind of upset that they were canceling the game for one guy and not the other."

The sentiment that Warfield was as much a team member as any player was shared among all the players—particularly the scheduled starting pitcher C. C. Sabathia, who came out to the mound with tears in his eyes after a moment of silence in Warfield's honor. The big lefthander had first met Warfield his first year coming up through the minors and like most of his teammates regarded him as a nurturing father figure. Warfield would often call the farm club Sabathia was playing for and ask, "How's C. C. doing?" Upon his arrival on the major-league scene, Sabathia was struck by the small gestures Warfield would make that made players feel more comfortable. If someone was taking medicine and didn't come into the trainers room, Warfield would bring the medicine to that player's locker. Whenever Sabathia felt down and came into the trainers room, Warfield would say, "Don't worry. There will be a better day."

Sabathia found himself more down than ever this particular outing and battled to keep focus, although he still had command of his fastball most of the night. He held the White Sox to four runs over five and two-thirds innings. As gutsy as the big lefthander's performance was, he admitted after the game that it had been solely adrenaline that had got him through. "I can usually put things out of my mind when I'm out there, but I couldn't tonight," said the twenty-one-year old. "I couldn't tell you what I threw to anybody. I was just out there tonight."

Sabathia did, however, find comfort in the presence of the bird, which had returned to the field prior to game time and wandered in foul territory near the backstop, lingered on the third base side of the infield—often within steps of Thome—then eventually settled for the rest of the game in the leftfield corner. The pitcher was among several who assumed it was their trainer "saying his final good-byes and watching us." Among the telltale signs was that the bird was scruffy (players had often kidded Warfield about having that trait), that it wandered on the field as if it were involved with the game, that it seemed to be observing the Indians players, and that it was often following around Thome.

"The bird always hung out," recalls Omar Vizquel, "it didn't matter what we did. Always was like on a lookout. So you wonder is that a message from Jimmy Warfield, or if that was Jimmy Warfield's ghost walking around."

"You'd sit there and watch," says Matt Lawton. "Nobody could believe it. The bird followed Thome everywhere he went. And Thome had the first intuition. Because during the game everyone wanted to shoo the bird off the field, and Thome was like, 'No, leave this bird here.'"

Magglio Ordóñez's tie-breaking home run that evening in the top of the ninth lifted the White Sox to victory, dashing a hard-fought effort by the emotionally drained Indians. The pain of losing was made all the harder by Warfield's absence. For many of the players, the camaraderie of the team made the absence of Warfield slightly easier to handle, since they could swap Jimmy memories and share in their sadness. But Thome, the player who perhaps needed the most consoling, felt too far down to participate and could often be found sitting sullenly by his locker. His teammates showed respect and gave him more space. "When he passed it was very tough," recalls Thome. "It was almost like a family member passed. I felt that pain and I wondered why."

Thome hit a two-run homer the following evening in the first of a two-game series against the Twins. Rounding the bases, he pointed skyward, a gesture for Warfield. Moments before, the odd, loitering seagull had wandered onto the mound, and Twins starting pitcher Rick Reed had to step off the rubber and frighten it away.

For many on the Twins' bench that evening, the presence of the bird was nothing other than an oddity. Rightfielder Dustan Mohr was one of the few in the dugout who considered that it might be Warfield.

As a young prospect in the Indians farm system, Mohr had met Warfield in the winter development program. According to Mohr, Warfield had "the best set of guns I've ever seen," because he was often in the weight room doing curls. Mohr also recalls that Warfield had a calming effect on people. "He was a person that immediately the first time you met him, you feel totally comfortable with him right on the spot. It's not like there was an awkward moment, like with most people that you meet for the first time."

In the eyes of all those at the game who knew Warfield, the bird's presence on the field had a similar effect. "In hindsight, the bird was in the right place at the right time," says Mohr. "But it didn't seem like it was just coincidence. Even though he was not there physically, he was still there in spirit and watching over all the guys in the Indians organization, because I know he loved the Indians."

Following an 8–6 Tribe loss the next day, the team held a private memorial service for Warfield at the Terrace Club, a windowed restaurant high above third base. An overflow crowd of several hundred squeezed into the luxury box lounge, including the entire Indians team, former managers Mike Hargrove and Charlie Manuel, Hall of Famer Bob Feller, future Hall of Fame manager Tony La Russa, and former Indians players Paul Assenmacher, Buddy Bell, Bert Blyleven, Rick Manning, John Smiley, and Andre Thornton. The room was so crowded that many attendees were forced to line the back of the room against the window, which offered a sweeping view of the field.

Thornton, an ordained minister, presided over the tribute. Travis Fryman shared the story of how Warfield had been mugged and pistol-whipped on two separate occasions in Oakland but never spoke badly about his assailants. When pressed Warfield had said, "They probably needed the money more than I did."

"He would give you the shirt off his back," said Kenny Lofton. "And if you needed an extra arm, he'd take his off and give it to you."

The impact Warfield had on almost everyone in the room was summed up best by Milton Bradley. As a player who mostly kept to himself during his years in Cleveland, the young centerfielder surprised many in attendance by sharing his tender appreciation for Warfield and his heartache about his passing. He described how Warfield had taken him under his wing after he was traded from the Montréal Expos the previous year. The trainer had not only encouraged Bradley and praised his talents, but went out of his way to make Bradley feel like a veteran on the club. When Bradley walked into the trainers room, Warfield would embrace him and say, "Hey Kobe!" in playful reference to the marquee NBA shooting guard Kobe Bryant, whom Bradley worshiped as a basketball fan. "Everything happens for a reason," Bradley tearfully told his fellow mourners, "and I was brought here so I could meet Jimmy Warfield."

In the matinee game before the service, Bradley had launched a grand slam in the third inning and could only think of Warfield smiling down on him as he rounded the bases. Bradley says he had felt like something special was going to happen during that at-bat and describes his swing as "an out of body experience," a home run that had Warfield's blessing on it.

The lone seagull, which had been unanimously embraced by all those at the Jake who were close with Warfield as a symbol or manifestation of the late trainer, didn't show up for the game. Instead, it appeared by the Indians' dugout during the memorial service. Players standing against the Terrace Room window turned and saw the seagull and later commented among themselves that the bird took flight just as Thornton offered his closing remarks, seemingly rounding the bases and then flying by the Terrace Room windows and into the night.

The seagull never returned to Jacobs Field. But its memory has lingered. According to Jake Westbrook, the topic came up frequently during the remainder of the 2002 season and still comes up from time to time. "Me and C. C. [Sabathia] always talk about if that was Jimmy," says Westbrook, "and he's kind of looking over us and stuff like that. Now, every time we see a bird, C. C. and I just kind of look at each other."

Of course it doesn't take a bird sighting to prompt fond recollections of Warfield. "He's mentioned a lot when we go to different places and you have different stories about things that he said," says Westbrook. "He was such a big part of the organization and such a big part of each person's life. He touched each person's life. It's just kind of neat holding onto him a little longer, even if it's with a bird or things like that."

Jim Thome has no intention of ever letting go. Every year he hosts the Thome/Warfield Charity Golf Tournament. He had "JW" stitched under the tongue of his baseball cleats and still wears it to this day.

Asked whether he thinks the seagull that had followed him around Jacobs Field for four days was Warfield, Thome is wistful. "You never know with things like that," he says. "Whether that was coincidence or not, that was cool."

CHAPTER 3

THE GHOSTS OF
YANKEE STADIUM

The 2003 American League Championship Series between the New York Yankees and the Boston Red Sox was already a classic, even by the high-drama standards of their historic rivalry. In the first six games there had been fistfights, seesawing leads, improbable comebacks, demoralizing defeats. When the Yankees overcame a four-run deficit to tie Game 7 in the eighth inning—eventually sending the nail-biter into the extra innings that seemed inevitable all along—Aaron Boone got antsy on the bench. He asked Derek Jeter how he could be so calm, with all that was at stake. Jeter's reply was brief: "The ghosts will come eventually."

Three innings later, Boone—who was hitting .125 in the series—belted the walk-off home run that ended the legendary match-up.

To hear players tell it, the ghosts have been coming to Yankee Stadium for years. And they're not the only ones who think so. As early as 1947—when the Yankee lineup included some of the names that might now be said to haunt the field—Red Barber previewed the upcoming World Series by saying in his radio broadcast that "there will be some on the field at Yankee Stadium whom nobody will see. They'll be dim ghosts in the shadows . . .

Miller Huggins and Walter Johnson and Lou Gehrig, and some others. They'll be there." In 1962, a *New York Times* column talked about the "house of ghosts" and its effect on the team:

> There's something about playing in the Stadium that brings the heart out in every ballplayer. They know the ghosts are looking down on them . . . The Babe. The Iron Horse. The old Yankee Clipper himself sitting up there in the pressbox. Playing out there in the House that Ruth built. It gets a player right here.

If the ghosts were observers in 1962, they have since gained a reputation for more active participation. There is no shortage of major leaguers willing to attest to the strange goings-on that always seem to favor the Bronx Bombers.

"Stuff happens there," says Chipper Jones, whose Atlanta Braves lost the 1996 World Series to the Yankees after taking a 2–0 lead. "Like they are down four runs to a Hall of Fame pitcher with three outs left and come back. I don't know if it's Babe, Lou, or whoever. But it's not Derek Jeter coming to bat, but somebody else."

"I just know when you go into Yankee Stadium late in the game you got problems," says relief pitcher Ricky Bottalico. "If it's a one- or two- run game? Oh yeah. They're there."

Rickey Henderson, who played at the Stadium as both a home and visiting player, believes that "the ghosts take over on who is going to win the ball game. If [the Yankees] have their backs against the wall, the ghosts come out to give them a boost."

Bob Melvin was bench coach with the Arizona Diamondbacks when the Yankees staged remarkable late-inning comebacks to win Games 4 and 5 at home in the 2001 World Series (see Chapter 11: An Otherworldly World Series). As unlikely as those wins may have seemed—both nights, the Yanks were down two runs with two outs in the bottom of the ninth, and rallied to win—they didn't surprise Melvin. "I've seen a lot of games at Yankee Stadium where the ghosts have shown up," he says. "I was with the Yankees in '94 and they talk about those things, that Yankee Stadium has spirits."

Indeed, among current Yankees the notion of the team's legendary players chipping in by getting a ball to drop, or sneak over the outfield wall, or roll through the legs of an opposing infielder is commonly accepted.

"I've seen it firsthand," says Alex Rodriguez. "I believe it as a home player and I believed it as a visiting player. I think Yankee Stadium has one of the greatest home field advantages in all of sports. You just feel like the ghosts of Yankee Stadium are overlooking the guys in the pinstripes."

"Everybody believes in it," confirms Jason Giambi. "Everybody laughs about it and jokes about it, but I've seen some weird things happen there."

Rich Monteleone, the Yankees special pitching instructor, doesn't wait for the ghosts to come; he summons them, especially when a play-off game is on the line. "I look up and say, 'Okay guys, come on. We need some help. Come out and help us.' We just know they're looking down on us, the guys that have passed. It's just something that goes with Yankee Stadium."

Yankee Stadium opened for business on April 23, 1923. Prior to that, the team was essentially homeless.

The New York Highlanders—precursor to the modern-day Yankees—began their life playing in Hilltop Park in upper Manhattan, the current site of Columbia-Presbyterian Medical Center, from 1903 to 1912. The field's high altitude inspired not only the name of the park, but also the name of the team (though the franchise acquired the nickname "Yankees" almost immediately, reflecting their northern location).

From 1913 until the Stadium opened, the Yankees played their home games at the Polo Grounds, leasing the park from the Giants. When new owners Colonel Jacob Ruppert and Colonel Tillinghast L'Hommedieu Huston bought the team in 1915, they inherited what Ruppert described as "an orphan ball club, without a home of its own, without players of outstanding ability, without prestige."

The colonels set quickly to change all that, their biggest coup being the January 1920 acquisition of Babe Ruth from the Boston Red Sox. The hottest player in the game commanded a record cash price ($125,000) but paid immediate dividends at the gate. The Yankees set a league attendance record in Ruth's first season: 1,289,422, more than twice the league average and significantly more than the Giants pulled in at the same venue. New Giants owner Horace Stoneham resented the club—now a threat to his own team's dominance—and talked about kicking them out of the Polo Grounds.

But Ruppert and Huston were already eager to find their own park. After considering several locations in New York City and Long Island (nearly buying an asylum at one point), they finally chose a ten-acre site in the Bronx at 161st Street and River Avenue. It was purchased from the estate of William Waldorf Astor for $675,000.

The original design for the first park to be called a "stadium" was ambitious. Three decks would completely encircle the field and provide a seating capacity of 75,000 to 85,000. Even the scaled-back version that was eventually built accommodated 58,000, enough to earn the title of the biggest park in baseball.

The stadium was also characterized by its short rightfield porch (295 feet), making it especially friendly for lefty hitters like the Babe. In fact, the rightfield seats came to be known as "Ruthville," while the imposing distance to left-center (460 feet) that victimized many right-handers earned the nickname "Death Valley." These dimensions have changed over the years, but Yankee Stadium remains much more hospitable to left-handed batters than right-handed ones.

The $2.5 million stadium was a stunning attraction and opening day was full of fanfare. Politicians, generals, baseball bigwigs, and other dignitaries attended, along with more than 74,000 fans, a third of whom had to be turned away. In a pregame ceremony, John Philip Sousa led a marching band and both teams to the outfield where the American flag and the Yankees 1922 pennant were raised.

Prior to the first game, Babe Ruth said, "I'd give a year of my life if I could hit a home run on opening day of this great new park." In the third inning, with two men on, he deposited a 2–2 pitch from Boston's Howard Ehmke into the rightfield bleachers, the first homer in Yankee Stadium. Shortly thereafter, sportswriter Fred Lieb christened the park "The House That Ruth Built," acknowledging that it was funded by Ruth-based profits and forever associating the Babe with the Stadium.

But Ruth's incredible talent may not have been the only source of the park's good fortunes. Notes on the accounting records of White Construction, which helped build the great park, indicate that in late December of 1922, a subcontractor buried something at the site to give the team good luck. It is not known exactly what the laborer tossed into the water main pit just before it was graded over. But his stated goal was to confer success on the team that played there.

And maybe he helped. Yankee Stadium seemed to be the final piece in creating a championship team. The year the park opened, the Yankees won their first World Series title ever. Twenty-five more would follow.

"I think Joe DiMaggio's still in Yankee Stadium today," says Butch Wynegar, a catcher with the Yanks in the mid-1980s. "He's looking down on it. He's there all the time. I believe in that, I really do. Mickey and Roger and all the old-time Yankees."

Whether the great names of the past are still at Yankee Stadium or not, there's no denying the indelible mark they made there while alive.

DiMaggio won three MVP awards, still holds the record for the major league's longest hitting streak (56 consecutive games), and in the three decades prior to his death in 1999 was widely referred to as the "Greatest Living Baseball Player." Mantle, his centerfield successor, also won three MVP awards, as well as the 1956 Triple Crown. He maintains the record for most World Series home runs (18), but then he had plenty of chances, having appeared in the Fall Classic twelve times, with the Yankees winning seven of them. Other Yankee legends like Roger Maris, Elston Howard, Bill Dickey, Billy Martin, and Casey Stengel are fondly remembered and frequently mentioned by fans.

But the two Yankees most commonly said to still inhabit the Stadium are Babe Ruth and Lou Gehrig, American cultural icons whose renown is much bigger than the game of baseball. Their tenures overlapped for twelve seasons, from 1923 to 1934. They had vastly different personalities (Ruth was the showy party boy; Gehrig the quiet homebody) and sometimes clashed off the field. But hitting in the three and four spots in the lineup, Ruth and Gehrig were the most fearsome combo in baseball. They were the engine behind the 1927 Yankees, often cited as the best team ever. They set some of the most respected records in baseball—for home runs and consecutive games played—and even though some of their milestones have fallen, they remain among the most revered names in the sport.

Their energy and vitality are forever associated with Yankee Stadium; so too are their early deaths. It was here that Gehrig, dying of the disease that would bear his name, bid an emotional farewell to the fans, calling himself the luckiest man on the face of the earth. Here that Babe Ruth made a final appearance in 1948, his voice raspy from the throat cancer that would kill him two months later. When he died on August 16, 1948, his body lay in state at the Stadium for two days as more than 100,000 fans filed past his casket. (A public wake for manager Miller Huggins was held there too.)

Their legacies have been so strong it's no wonder baseball fans—and Yankee fans in particular—have never let go of their memory. Yankee players are no different.

"You always thought that ghosts were in the hallways," remembers former shortstop Mike Gallego of his days with the team. "When you were walking down to the old batting cages in the back, you always felt that. Guys would say, 'Watch the ghosts while you're walking down the halls.' And when you get toward rightfield you kinda peek over your shoulder and you wonder. And I swear you can hear some bats cracking in the background, when the machine's not on."

Buck Showalter, who managed the team from 1992 to 1995, would sometimes sleep in his office after a night game when there was a day game to follow. The nights were often restless ("As managing the Yankees lends to, there were some sleepless nights," he says) and being alone in the Stadium inevitably led to sensing some spirits.

"There were quite a few times where I'd get up at three o'clock, make some coffee, and go sit in the dugout and watch that ring of light around the top of [the Stadium] that's almost ethereal. You hear noises late at night there. I always thought it might be the Babe or Gehrig."

While that may sound eerie, Showalter wasn't fazed. "It wasn't something that scared me at all," he says. "I'd just think, 'That must be the Babe rustling around somewhere.' More than likely if it was two o'clock in the morning, he was just getting in."

If history feels "alive" at Yankee Stadium, it's no accident. The organization does a lot to bring the past into the present. The team maintains an active alumni association, and former players are often invited back for events and games. An annual highlight for many fans is Old-Timer's Day, when former Yankees play a three-inning exhibition game prior to that day's main event.

Players are also indoctrinated in Yankees history. Many former Yankees are invited to Spring Training, to give young players an awareness of and connection to the team's past. "Yogi is still in camp, [Guidry] was in camp for years before he started coaching here," says Don Mattingly. "Whitey Ford was always coming in, Graig Nettles is back in camp, Tommy John."

"And it's not just Spring Training," adds Rich Monteleone. "During the season these guys are showing up. They sit down and talk [to current players] and I think it's a big help."

With so many of the living former players playing a role with the team, it's not surprising that the departed ones are still felt so acutely. Walk the tunnels and corridors of Yankee Stadium and pictures and quotes from famous stars are everywhere. Enter the clubhouse and see a locker labeled "15"—a tribute to Thurman Munson, the gutsy and much beloved team captain who died tragically in a plane crash in the middle of the 1979 season. The locker has been left reverently and symbolically vacant ever since.

Out behind the leftfield wall, flanked by the bullpens, sits Monument Park, a small tract of land that pays tribute to the great players and events of Yankee Stadium. A walkway leading to it salutes the sixteen Yankee players and managers whose numbers have been retired, the most of any ball club. (The Yankees were the first team to bestow this honor, retiring Lou Gehrig's number 4 in 1939.)

In Monument Park itself, twenty-five people are honored with bronze plaques that line the inner wall. These are very similar to the plaques in the Cooperstown Hall of Fame Museum. The majority of the plaques are for players, though a few others, such as broadcaster Mel Allen and GM Ed Barrow, are also recognized. In addition, there are plaques commemorating the two papal masses said at the site, and a large plaque saluting the heroes of September 11, 2001.

But the centerpieces here are the monuments. Only five men have been immortalized this way: Miller Huggins, Lou Gehrig, Babe Ruth, Mickey Mantle, and Joe DiMaggio.

Monument Park adds to the notion of ghosts lurking in the Stadium. To many visitors, it has the air of a graveyard. The plaques on the wall give it the look of a mausoleum, while the monuments themselves resemble tombstones. (Indeed, some players commonly refer to the monuments as "headstones.") Monuments are only bestowed posthumously. Bob Costas recalls that as a child exiting the park through centerfield (where the monuments once stood, right on the field of play), he thought that the large granite slabs were actual gravestones, and that Huggins, Gehrig, and Ruth were buried in the outfield.

For modern-day players, the site has a special appeal. Roger Clemens, who won a Cy Young Award and two World

Series rings in his tenure with the Yankees, preceded every pitching start with a visit to Monument Park, where he ceremonially rubbed the Ruth monument before taking the mound. Teammates have brought champagne to the Park following post-season victories, to celebrate with the Yankees of the past and—for some players—thank the ghosts for their help.

"You have goose bumps when you walk through there," says Chris Chambliss, who was with the team as player or coach in each of its last six World Championship seasons. "What you're talking about is ghosts—you feel that as you're walking through there."

Visiting players also pilgrimage to Monument Park to pay their respects. Jeff Cirillo says that every rookie, on playing in New York for the first time, should "just take two minutes to see the headstones. You will definitely feel a surge by looking at all that."

All of Yankee Stadium—not just Monument Park—inspires that kind of reaction from visiting players. B. J. Upton recalls his first time there. "I'm a superstitious guy, so I think anything is possible. You walk through that place, man . . . Lou Gehrig . . . it's where it started. So many great players have been involved with that ball club and it has so much history."

That history is something few players can ignore when playing in Yankee Stadium, ghosts or not. "When you walk in, there is a mystique to it because of all the history that was made there," says Ron Guidry. "There is this aura and you're awed by it. It's like a shrine. You're trying to play so you can place your name with the names that will be mentioned years from now."

To most Yankee fans, the name most likely to be mentioned years from now as the continuation of the lineage that started with Ruth and Gehrig is shortstop Derek Jeter. On the road, he is the most booed Yankee; at home, the most cheered. In 2003, he was given one of the rarest and most cherished of Yankee honors, joining a short list of players named captain of the team.

It is virtually guaranteed that his uniform number 2 will one day be retired by the club, and highly likely that a monument—

the team's greatest valedictory for a beloved Yankee—will be erected in his honor.

For Jeter, Yankee Stadium is more than just a building. "It means tradition. It means winning. Excellence. You go in there, and you think about Babe Ruth, Mickey Mantle, Joe DiMaggio, Thurman Munson."

Jeter spent most of his childhood in Michigan, but was born in New Jersey and grew up following the Yankees and idolizing Dave Winfield. He also idolized the ballpark. "I went to Yankee Stadium on a couple of occasions growing up," he recalls. "Being a Yankee fan, going to Yankee Stadium everything seems larger than life."

Coming back as a player was even more awe-inspiring. Jeter vividly remembers the first time he took the field.

"I was eighteen years old, it was after my first year in rookie ball. The Yankees flew me up there just to have a workout on the field for a day. It was something that I don't really think you can put into words. I had been playing high-school ball with a couple of friends. Now I'm taking ground balls next to Don Mattingly."

Not long afterward, Jeter was playing in his first game, digging in at home plate, and hearing Bob Sheppard—the Yankee Stadium announcer since 1951—call his name and number.

"It's kind of a surreal situation when you go there to play for the first time. I got called up when I was twenty years old and my first game was in Seattle. Then we went home after that and played at Yankee Stadium and that was something that . . . I can't even remember who we played, or anything like that. I just know I was at Yankee Stadium.

"You're nervous. You're scared. This is what you've always dreamed of and now it's finally coming true. You're getting the opportunity to play shortstop and play for the Yankees in Yankee Stadium, and you're just really nervous."

Today, Jeter pretty much owns the place. "Now it's home," he says. "That's where I work. That's where I am every day. I feel most comfortable playing here."

The ghosts of the greats—whom Jeter believes inhabit Yankee Stadium, especially during the postseason—are part of that home. Even when they're not physically present, they are an inspiration.

"You feel a sense of pride. You feel like you're playing for all the old players, all the ex-players that played for the Yankees. You're out there and you're trying to make sure you make them proud."

The pride of heritage may be one of the strongest assets the Yankees have going for them. Perhaps this is the true power of the ghosts. "Other teams don't have the history and the connection that team does," says Dave Winfield. "Or the great players and the winning tradition. History plays a role."

"I think it elevates your game," says A-Rod. "You realize that when you step in Yankee Stadium, there's a great responsibility."

Some players are overwhelmed by the Yankee history. "I remember the first time I was ever there, to begin the season in '95," recalls John Wetteland, who won the World Series MVP award with the Yanks in 1996. "I said, 'I just can't walk out on this field.' I was coming out of the tunnel and I saw it kind of open up, and I got goose bumps. And I went up to the top step and I just *jumped* onto the field."

The field's magical history never intimidated David Wells; in fact, it elevated him to baseball perfection: The veteran pitcher threw a perfect game at the Stadium as a Yankee in 1998. Wells, who also had success there as a visitor, says the ghosts of Yankee legends helped inspire him. "I'm sure they're hovering in there. [They make] you want to pitch well."

Even visiting players feel that special vibe. "It occurs to me sometimes that you're in the same box that Mickey Mantle was in, or Joe DiMaggio, or whatever," says Chicago White Sox star Paul Konerko. "You're definitely conscious of it. It's cool as a player to play in the same place that the greats of the game played."

But that winning legacy can just as easily intimidate opponents. For those visitors, the "ghosts" aren't literal spirits, but mental hobgoblins that get in their heads and undo their confidence.

"You always hear stories of the ghosts of Yankee Stadium," says Alex S. González. "I think it's a psychological advantage that the Yankees have. As an opposing player you feel that against you. There's always the chance that they're going to come back or something in their favor is going to happen."

Johnny Damon, who credits some supernatural pinstripers for that Boone home run that ended the Red Sox's season in 2003 ("The ghost of Babe Ruth came back and helped them beat us in Game 7," he claims), felt it before joining the team in 2006. "As a visiting player going in, you always knew about it. You always took that walk by the monuments. You think about Babe Ruth playing rightfield there, you think about DiMaggio and Mantle, and Berra catching."

It's worth noting that not all Yankee players subscribe to the notion that the greats of the past still reside in the Bronx.

"Crazy stuff happens there, no doubt about it," says Don Mattingly. "But I don't believe in the whole ghost thing."

"I think it's amusing and it makes for a great story, and it's funny to think about things in those terms," says Bernie Williams. "I guess it's the way you choose to think about it." Alfonso Soriano, who came up with the Yankees as their second baseman, doesn't choose to think about it as ghostly. "I know that people think it's the greatest ballpark," he says. "I just go to the park every day and play my game." Jorge Posada is even more definitive: "There are no ghosts *anywhere*."

Even Aaron Boone has his doubts about supernatural assists in his pennant-clinching home run. "I don't know. It was a great night for us as a team to come back and win that. But I don't know. Chalk it up more to a lot of people doing a lot of different things." (Boone notes that the team ultimately lost the World Series that year. "There were no ghosts helping us out in Game 6," he says. "Where the heck were they then?")

Willie Randolph, who played with the team from 1976 to 1988, and served as a coach from 1994 to 2004, doesn't go for apparitions, "but I believe in a certain karma in a ballpark and the winning environment there. If the player feels and believes that,

I think he can translate it into a confidence that can work for him. But I didn't think that in the bottom of the ninth we were going to win because Babe Ruth is lurking in the crowd."

Of course, crediting big wins to supernatural forces can deprive current players of the credit they deserve. "As far as ghosts—the Bambino, or Gehrig, or Mantle—I didn't really see it that way," says Tim Raines, who was with the team from 1996 to 1998. "To me, Yankee Stadium was full of tradition and a lot of World Championships. But I just feel like I was a part of it."

Indeed, many great players have been a part of it. As the architect of the Yankees winning 1990s teams, former GM Bob Watson understandably stresses the role of *living* Yankees rather than dead ones. "Mr. Steinbrenner tries to get the best players available. When you have the best players, bad things happen to the visiting team."

Opposing pitchers know this well. Bronson Arroyo faced the team in the playoffs while with the Red Sox. "They talk about the ghosts coming out in the ninth inning, but with that heckuva lineup they've had for a long time, it's hard for teams to come in to close you out."

The antighost argument is bolstered by the fact that the Yankees have staged some impressive wins—including remarkable comebacks—in parks all around major-league baseball, not just in Yankee Stadium. If the ghosts are responsible, they must be traveling with the team.

On August 16, 2006—the fifty-eighth anniversary of the death of Babe Ruth—the Yankees broke ground on the new Yankee Stadium. For years, principal owner George Steinbrenner had expressed his desire for a new ballpark. In the 1980s, his argument was built around flagging attendance: People don't want to go to the Bronx, he said. But the team's 1990s resurgence was accompanied by record-breaking gate receipts, and the justification shifted to crumbling infrastructure and limited room. Steinbrenner tried to work with city officials on the issue, initially wanting to move the team into Manhattan, and eventually threatening to take them to New Jersey if no agreement could be reached. But in the end, the Yankees decided to stay right in the Bronx. In fact, the new park will be literally across the street from the current one.

The groundbreaking ceremony was held on a beautiful sunny day. Fourteen speakers addressed an invitation-only crowd, which included Yankee greats like Yogi Berra and famous fans such as Billy Crystal. City dignitaries and team representatives talked about the legacy of Yankee Stadium and the special memories it has created for millions of fans over the years, as well as the jobs and funds a new park will bring. Ceremonial shovels with Louisville Sluggers for handles were given to guests to commemorate the event.

Across the street, several dozen protesters were corralled into a space set aside by police for their demonstration. The new Yankee Stadium will occupy land formerly used for a neighborhood park and the loss of precious green space in New York has drawn the ire of some local residents. They formed a group called Save Our Parks and have filed a series of unsuccessful lawsuits to stop the project. Members picketed the groundbreaking with signs asking WHAT ABOUT OUR CHILDREN? and declaring that BRONX POLITICIANS ARE DIGGING THEIR OWN GRAVES.

Among the protesters was Nancy Veit, whose handwritten placard expressed a different sentiment. DON'T DESTROY YANKEES HISTORY AND TRADITION—RENOVATE. Veit is a member of Friends of Yankee Stadium, a group that opposes the new park not for its disruptive impact on the borough, but for the loss of what Veit calls "a piece of cultural history."

"The Yankees have a very special, unique, distinct product in this stadium," she says. "That creates an image and a mystique and an aura that won't be replicated in a new stadium." Like other fans, Veit notes that despite talk of greater fan amenities, the new park will actually contain fewer seats—but more lucrative luxury suites. Her group also believes that the current stadium "could be renovated to bring the quality and enhancements the Yankees want."

Though a Yankee fan, Veit is also a member of a similar coalition formed to save Fenway Park. Such groups have networked through a Web site called Field of Schemes, which monitors stadium economic developments around the country. The site attracts baseball purists who want to see historic ballparks preserved and restored, rather than razed.

"When I go to the Stadium, a chill goes up my spine," says Veit. "I'm doing the same thing that generations of New Yorkers did before me. I'm going to the same place that my great-grandfather went to, and all those Yankee greats. There's just so much history and it's a shame to lose it. It's not going to feel the same in a new stadium."

Veit says that only two former Yankees have publicly opposed the new stadium (Jim Bouton and Ron Blomberg). But others are at least wistful, if not conflicted about it. "The [current] stadium is baseball to me," says Paul O'Neill, who won four World Series rings with the team. "It's exciting to see a new Yankee Stadium and what it can bring to New York. But there's a loss of history and tradition. So in that sense, I'll miss it."

"I like the old stadiums," admits David Wells. "I was sad to see Tiger Stadium go. I was sad to see Comiskey go. When you have history like that, why mess with it?"

However, many associated with the team, from players to fans, anticipate the new park with excitement. Even Freddy "Sez" Schuman—an eighty-one-year-old Yankee Stadium institution who has attended nearly every home game since 1988 (passing around his trademark frying pan for Yankee fans to bang, cheering the team)—says he is mostly looking forward to the new venue. "There's always a sentimental feeling about Babe Ruth's stadium," he acknowledges. "But life continues. I'd rather have an optimistic feeling toward this than to be pessimistic."

Michael Kay, the longtime Yankees broadcaster who grew up going to the ballpark, says, "There's part of me that's going to feel

some modicum of sadness. Obviously it's hallowed real estate."
But he adds that the "real Yankee Stadium" was already destroyed
in the mid-1970s renovation. "If this stadium had not been refur-
bished, then I think there would be a deeper meaning."

Certainly the reconstruction that began after the Stadium's
fiftieth anniversary season in 1973 was extensive. Much of the
building's innards were gutted and rebuilt. The upper decks were
expanded and cantilevered, obstructive steel columns were removed throughout the stands, the unique exterior was drastically
remodeled. Today a replica of the famous façade is preserved in a
stretch that spans the top outfield edge of the park. (The distinctive scalloped frieze was erected only at the urging of Cary Grant,
who attended a game with George Steinbrenner shortly before
the renovation and told the Boss, "Don't let them take that down.
Preserve it and put it back up. To me, that is the Yankees.")

Tony Morante, the official Yankees historian, who has
worked at the Stadium since 1958, says that when the 1970s
renovation occurred, there wasn't much resistance from the
public. "I think because the team wasn't doing all that well at
that time. We hadn't been in the World Series for a long time.
There wasn't that much of an outcry." Morante himself felt nos-
talgic about the changes and his own personal "ghosts." "My
father was an usher here before me. So when I walk around
here, I see him everywhere." Morante will have some mixed
emotions when the team moves, but doesn't feel as connected
to the current version of Yankee Stadium as he did the original.
"Once that disappeared, this replacement couldn't match it."

The city owns the site of the current Yankee Stadium and has not
yet said what they will do with it. Many believe the building will
come down, with the baseball field preserved for community use.

For many fans and plenty of players, the real question is
whether or not the ghosts will relocate to the new stadium.

In typical Yankees fashion, the new park is designed to
honor the past. An exterior façade will replicate that of the

1923 ballpark, complete with latticework in the original copper. Monument Park will be more accessible to fans during games. Pennants from all the winning seasons—which could not be flown at the renovated park—will be on display. At least one current shrine won't make the trip: Thurman Munson's empty locker will not be a part of the new clubhouse. Still, there will be many visible signs of the team's glorious history and on-field legends.

Does that mean the ghosts will make their way across the street? Derek Jeter is optimistic.

"We're gonna see. Hopefully that does carry over. Yeah, it's gonna take a little while before people get used to the new stadium. But the tradition doesn't change just because you move venues."

As a person who embodies that tradition, Jeter not only respects Yankee Stadium's ghosts, but also may one day become one, giving the ball a little extra push to start rallies and score runs. "Oh yeah," says Jeter with a smile. "I would help out. No question."

The shortstop has already won four World Series rings, been voted Rookie of the Year, represented the Yankees in seven All-Star games, and been named both an All-Star and World Series MVP. But he knows that being talked about as a ghost of Yankee Stadium is the ultimate Yankee honor.

"I'd love for them to say that I was out there!" he laughs. "That means you've had some kind of an impact."

THE SPIRIT OF THE STADIUM

"There's so many legends that have played the game over there and I think they just still hang out and maybe put their touch in here and there, and get a ball to drop or whatever."

—DAVE DELLUCCI

"I've been involved in some games where everybody thought the game was over, but you're never quite out of it. We get that big hit or that big play. Something weird always happens and before you know it, you have the lead again."

—JASON GIAMBI

"The baseball gods are there. Anything that can happen good or exciting or different always happens in Yankee Stadium. That's where all the stuff goes down."

—DAVID WELLS

"Things would happen that you couldn't explain or justify, whether it be a call from an umpire, or the way a ball bounces. And everybody always just says it's that mystique of Yankee Stadium."

—SHEA HILLENBRAND

"We didn't have a lot of success there and I think people attributed it to guys that have played there in the past. Any ballplayer is going to think about it. It's kind of the fun part of playing in the historic parks."

—DAVID BELL

"You're not only playing against the nine Yankees on the field, but you're playing against all the ex-Yankees and all the legends that are out in centerfield. You gotta beat the Yankees and the ghosts of the past."

—ALEX S. GONZÁLEZ

"I think it's hard not to believe that there are ghosts in Yankee Stadium, just because of the games that are played there and how the Yankees come back. You walk through the interior of the stadium and you see so many photos of the old superstars and you just kind of get a vibe from them. You feel their presence in that stadium. You just feel like that person still might be hanging around."

—JEFF WEAVER

"You can feel the people that died, the people who played at the Stadium. And it feels great."

—KARIM GARCÍA

"I played in the old Yankee Stadium—the original. It's an eerie feeling to go in there knowing the history behind Ruth and Gehrig, DiMaggio and Mantle. It was special."

—BOBBY COX

"I compare Yankee Stadium to St. Patrick's Cathedral and get the same feeling of awe. I can't see the Pope appearing at Ebbets Field or the Polo Grounds, or Shea Stadium. But I can understand and think it appropriate that a pope would say mass at Yankee Stadium."

—BOB SHEPPARD

"I believe there are ghosts in Yankee Stadium. You go around there and walk through those tunnels, you know you're not by yourself. You just have that feeling that there's always someone there. I think [the old-time ballplayers] walk around that place. I truly believe that. It makes me feel like I'm a part of something."

—DAVID ELDER

"It's a friendly thing. The chills are basically of excitement. Thinking, 'Wow—Joe DiMaggio, Lou Gehrig, Mickey Mantle—the greats were actually here.' When you're alone you really feel it. It's like someone taps you on the shoulder and says, '*Hey, remember me.*'"

—MIKE GALLEGO

CHAPTER 4

UNSAFE
AT HOME

Baseball is a battle of home versus visitors, and some ballplayers find that playing out off the field as well. They believe their own homes have been subject to visitors of a supernatural—and most unwelcome—nature.

Johnny Damon was enjoying a lazy afternoon at his house on Lake Butler in Orlando, Florida, when he experienced what he says was an otherworldly encounter. He awoke from a nap in a panic: Lying on his stomach, he was suddenly paralyzed.

"I couldn't move for about fifteen minutes," he says. "It wasn't a dream, because I know that type of dream and this was definitely real. I was awake and I was trying to move and I just couldn't. I passed the time thinking, 'A ghost is holding me down.'

"It was a strange feeling. I looked out and I saw people on the lake Jet Skiing, driving their boats and everything, and I couldn't move."

The episode lasted about twenty minutes, with Damon feeling pinned down by the spirit. "Then I started talking to the ghost. 'Okay—you got me!' And the minute I thought to myself, 'Oh, okay, it's fine,' the ghost got off of me. He released me and went off on his merry way."

Damon has always subscribed to the notion of ghosts. "An old friend of mine told me stories about how he had one that lived in his basement, that picked his dog up and put it on the pool table," he recalls. His own incident confirmed his beliefs. "It was a bit freaky, but I always believed in the paranormal. Fortunately, he was a good ghost and he kind of just came and left."

Ron Davis didn't feel that the ghosts inhabiting his home were quite as friendly. While pitching for the Yankees in the late 1970s, Davis shared a home in Dumont, New Jersey, with catcher Jerry Narron. "We didn't have any money," recalls Davis. "Minimum wage was $19,000." A Realtor friend offered an abandoned house that was going to be torn down at the end of the year. The ballplayers could live in it for free.

The house had been empty for a while and was creepy. "It had no water, no gas. We had Coleman stoves we were cooking on," recalls Davis. "We used a skeleton key to open the door."

Millie Davis—the pitcher's girlfriend at the time, who would eventually become his first wife—never felt comfortable in the house. "I think it was condemned," she says. "It was old and dusty and scary." She tried to brighten the place up, but "no matter what I did to it, it just always looked spooky and creaky and scary as hell. That place gave me the creeps."

The very first night the couple spent there was marked by a ghostly event. They got home late from a game and climbed the stairs to the bedroom. Entering, Millie reached up for a light switch in the middle of the room. "Right as I reached my hand up, the window flew open," she says. On its own, the heavy wooden frame suddenly shot straight up, bringing in a gust of cool air. The couple was stunned. Ron turned and ran down the stairs, and Millie followed him. "You're leaving me here to get killed by the ghost?" she yelled.

"We never slept in that room again. We never went in that room again," she says. After the window incident, "I wouldn't even go upstairs to the bathroom by myself."

Ron tells an even scarier tale. One night, he claims, he, Millie, Narron, and Narron's girlfriend came home and were walking up the stairs when fire instantaneously broke out around them.

"Just flames in the hallway—everywhere in the hall," he says. The ballplayers ran out to the street, abandoning the women ("I said somebody's got to live to tell this story," Ron jokes) and called out for help. In time, the fire and police departments responded, but to everyone's surprise, "the fires went out." As quickly and mysteriously as they'd begun, the flames suddenly extinguished themselves.

"We went in and there was nothing burnt; there was nothing charred," says Davis. "No one could figure out anything."

But eventually Davis did learn more about the house itself, and why it had been abandoned. "There was a family of five that was killed there," he says. "And no one would ever move into it."

Living in a condemned building may be unusual, but temporary lodgings are certainly a part of the baseball player's life. Especially in the minor-league system, where players often move among several different cities in short order.

When infielder Trent Durrington was doing a stint with the Double-A SeaWolves in Erie, Pennsylvania, a long way from his native Australia, he took an apartment with three teammates in an old downtown building. "It was a department store that had been turned into an apartment complex," he recalls. "We were the first tenants in there."

The apartment house was within walking distance of the ball field. The foyer had some new amenities alongside the building's classic architecture. A beautiful grand staircase still stood, but was not in use. About 90 feet away, across the old marble floor, a bank of elevators provided access to upper stories.

It was in this foyer that Durrington had his ghostly vision.

"I came home one night after a game. It was probably about midnight. I walked in the front door and went downstairs in the foyer." Durrington walked by the old staircase and over to the elevators. As he did, he thought he glimpsed something on the stairs. "I looked in [the direction of the staircase] and I saw a lady standing there. An old lady with white hair, dressed in a white gown at the top of the stairs."

The woman was standing on a small landing. It was an off-limits section of the building that no resident or worker ever accessed, much less at midnight. The vision was so startling that Durrington did a double take.

"I'm pressing the button and I'm like, 'What the . . . ? What was that?!' And I looked back and she was gone."

Durrington couldn't believe his eyes. When he got to his room, he related his supernatural experience to his teammates, who razzed him about it. But Durrington insisted he was serious. One of his friends went back to the lobby with him to investigate. "I thought maybe it was shadows or a reflection," he says. "I went up the stairs and yelled out. Nothing."

It was the only incident Durrington ever heard of at the place, but it made an impression. "I'm positive I saw something," the ballplayer insists. "To this day, I still say it was a ghost."

Ballplayers aren't always the ones being visited by ghosts. Sometimes they do the visiting. When Patty Ruppert moved into a home in Ashton, Maryland, that had been built and occupied by Sam Rice, she didn't know the departed Hall of Famer still was inhabiting it. Though she did find Rice Manor off-putting from the start.

"The house and I never got along," she says. "I never felt comfortable in that house." She does admit that the quaint brick manor home—surrounded by beautiful old ash trees, and imbued with a rustic quality—was "picturesque" and "had a lot of character." Strangers driving by would sometimes stop and inquire about the history of the place.

But those people didn't have to live there. "I hated the basement," Ruppert recalls. "There was a little room down there that just totally creeped me out. The washer and dryer were down there and I would never do the laundry unless someone else was in the house." Then there was the time her husband was away and Patty heard a scratching noise. Unnerved, she slept in her car that night.

One afternoon in 1981, the house moved from creepy to haunted. Ruppert still gets goose bumps when she tells the story.

It was the weekend, and her husband was out of town on business. "I was in the house by myself. It was during the day and I was sitting in the living room reading a book. My guitar was leaning against the wall in the living room. All of a sudden there was one strum against the open strings of the guitar—just a single strum."

The noise was loud and the musical nature of it unmistakable. "I looked up and there just didn't seem to be any explanation at all," Ruppert says. "It wasn't a mouse, it wasn't a curtain brushing against it, it hadn't shifted. But it was a very clear single strum on all six strings."

Ruppert wasted no time. "I closed my book, stood up slowly . . . and ran out of the house." She didn't reenter it until someone else was there with her.

Ruppert has no doubt about what she heard on that day, but she does think that some of her unease with the house had to do with what she learned about Sam Rice. "I was really taken by his story," she says. "He just struck me as a man who had been through tragedy."

Rice was certainly a man who had an air of mystery and of sadness about him—though you'd never know it on the field. In a brilliant twenty-year career spent mostly with the Washington Senators, he hit .322 and belted 2,987 hits. He twice led the AL in hits and twice led it in putouts for outfielders. No less than Ty Cobb—a man not known for his generosity—lobbied for Rice's induction into the Hall of Fame.

Fans, friends, and family knew few facts about his life: He was born Edgar Rice in 1890 on an Indiana farm, joined the navy at twenty-three, and didn't start professional ball until he was twenty-five. At thirty-nine, he married Mary Kendall and the couple had a daughter. They lived on the property in Ashton—which would one day be home for the Rupperts—where Rice raised chickens and champion racing pigeons after retiring from baseball.

When Rice was in his mid-70s, he was interviewed by a newspaper reporter, with his wife at his side. The writer unexpectedly made reference to "the tragedy in Indiana." Mary Rice had no idea what the reporter was referring to and was stunned as her husband's sad past suddenly came to light. She learned— among other things—that she was not his first wife.

That title belonged to Beulah Stam, whom Rice had married in 1908 when he was just eighteen years old. They lived in Watseka, Illinois, and had a son (Bernie) and a daughter (Ethel). Rice worked several jobs to support his family, but always dreamed of a life in baseball. In April 1912, he decided to pursue that dream and spend a few days trying out for the minor-league team in nearby Galesburg, Illinois. While he was gone, his wife and children went to stay with Rice's parents and two younger sisters at the family farm in Morocco.

The timing was disastrous. In the early evening of April 21, Rice's parents' house was hit by a tornado. A newspaper account described the scene as "too terrible to relate" but depicted the carnage in frightening detail.

> The house was blown entirely away as were other buildings . . . The timbers of the house and barn were scattered for nearly a quarter of a mile to the southeast. The furniture and contents of the house were twisted into shapes which would seem impossible to accomplish, and when the wreck had passed, every member of the family except Mr. Rice [Sam's father] lay dead either in the yard or adjoining fields . . . The bodies were found as far as 60 rods from the house, nearly stripped of clothing, bruised and broken.

Rice's father, too, died shortly thereafter.

Because Sam Rice was so reticent about the tragedy for decades, it is not known exactly what ran through his mind when he returned to the devastation. If he had not pursued his dream of playing professional baseball, he may well have reasoned, his wife and children would not have died in the tornado.

Rice bore the pain in silence. Having lost his wife, son, daughter, both parents, and two siblings in one horrific swoop, he abandoned his baseball aspirations and spent the next year in a series of itinerant jobs, eventually joining the navy. The ship he was assigned to had a baseball team. Unable to resist the game he loved, he signed up—a move that would turn out to be the first step on a path that led to a Hall of Fame career. If it's true that baseball had ended his previous life, it's equally true that it provided him with a new one, and a happiness he may have once thought impossible.

"His story resonated with me," says Patty Ruppert, who moved into Rice's house after marrying her husband. "I was really taken by the story of Sam Rice losing his whole family. We were newlyweds, and thinking about family, and having kids ourselves."

The Rice story gave perspective to the eeriness of Rice Manor—and made any potential ghosts more sympathetic. In addition to the odd goings-on in the house they ultimately shared, Ruppert found herself haunted by the story of a man who was haunted by his own tragic past.

A PHANTOM CATCH?

If Sam Rice was responsible for the spooky incidents Patty Ruppert experienced at Rice Manor, it was not his first communication from beyond the grave.

In the 1925 World Series, Rice was involved in a controversial play that was talked about for years. His Washington Senators were beating the Pittsburgh Pirates 4–3 late in Game 3 when Pirate Earl Smith lined a bullet to right-centerfield. Rice raced back and made a leaping catch that propelled him over the fence and into the crowd. There were several moments of nervous silence . . . and then Rice stood up triumphantly, brandishing the ball in his glove. The Pirates protested that Rice hadn't held onto the ball, but they lost the argument—and the game. (Though not, ultimately, the Series.)

The controversy over the play did not die down. Even Judge Kenesaw Mountain Landis (who eventually received 1,600 letters from fans both supporting and denouncing the call) summoned Rice to his hotel room the next morning to ask if he caught the ball. Rice responded, "The umpire said I did," to which Landis replied, "Sam, let's leave it that way."

And so he did for decades. But Rice was still asked about the play, especially on annual trips to Cooperstown. In 1965, he told a group of Hall of Famers there that he had written a letter with the full story of the catch, but that it would not be opened until his death.

Sam Rice died on October 13, 1974. Three weeks later, a press conference was held in which Paul Kerr from the Hall of Fame opened and read Rice's letter. In it, he described that "cold and windy day" back in 1925—how he spotted the ball off the bat, ran to catch up with it, "jumped as high as I could," and fell to the ground. He hit his Adam's apple and was knocked out for a few seconds, but teammate Earl McNeely grabbed his shirt and pulled him up. Rice ended the letter by posthumously answering the question he would never answer while alive.

"At no time did I lose possession of the ball."

CHAPTER 5

STOMPIN' AT
THE VINOY

The origins of the Renaissance Vinoy Hotel in St. Petersburg, Florida, trace back to a prank late one evening in 1923 involving legendary professional golfer Walter Hagen, entrepreneur Aymer Vinoy Laughner, and local financier Gene Elliott. On a dare, Hagen had been using Laughner's pocket watch as a golf tee, driving golf balls without breaking the watch. When the trio retrieved the balls from the property of Benjamin Williamson, who lived across the street, Elliott noticed that the estate offered an expansive view of Tampa Bay, and suggested to Laughner that the land would be an ideal location for a world-class luxury resort. The next day Laughner and Elliott approached Williamson with a generous offer. The deed was signed that very afternoon on the bottom of a brown paper bag.

To hear ballplayers tell it, late-night mischief on the site did not end with Hagen's errant golf balls.

Embedded in Washingtonian palms and crowned by an octagonal tower festooned with archways and intricate ornamental plasterwork, the Vinoy is a landmark on the St. Petersburg waterfront. The plush rooms and postcard-perfect vistas have always attracted the rich and famous (Marilyn Monroe, Jimmy Stewart, Calvin Coolidge), but ever since the resort opened it has been a posh home away from home for baseball clientele. George

Sisler and the owners of the St. Louis Browns frequented the Vinoy when the team used training facilities in Tarpon Springs in the late 1920s, and Babe Ruth is known to have lived a lavish existence in the hotel during numerous Spring Trainings. Today the Vinoy is the visiting team hotel for the Tampa Bay Devil Rays.

But movie stars and ballplayers are not the most famous guests at the Vinoy—ghosts are. While some in baseball openly poke fun at the hotel's numerous sightings, for many the fear of uninvited room guests is no laughing matter.

Relief pitcher Scott Williamson had never heard of the Vinoy being haunted when he stayed in an old section of the hotel with the Cincinnati Reds in mid-June 2003. But he ended up with an experience he says he'll never forget. "I turned the lights out and I saw this faint light coming from the pool area. And I got this tingling sensation going through my body like someone was watching me, you know? I was getting a little paranoid.

"Then I roll over to my stomach. And all of a sudden it felt like someone was just pushing down, like this *pressure*, and I was having trouble breathing. So I rolled back over. I thought, 'That's weird.' I did it again, rolled back on my stomach. All of a sudden, it's like I just couldn't breathe. It felt like someone was sitting on me or something."

This time when Williamson rolled onto his back, he opened his eyes. "I looked, and someone was standing right where the curtains were. A guy with a coat. And it looked like he was from the '40s, or '50s, or '30s—somewhere around that era."

Williamson called his wife Lisa, who worked in an emergency room, and asked if there could be a medical reason for the heaviness on his chest. "She went through all the things that could happen, but obviously hadn't happened. She said 'Why?' And I said, 'I tell ya, the weirdest thing just happened to me.' I told her the whole story."

"ESPN caught onto the story the next day," adds Williamson. "And then a buddy of mine went and did research on it. He came back and told me, 'You're not gonna believe this! There's a guy who died in that hotel. His name was Williamson. He actually owned the hotel property before it was a hotel.' He's going through this whole thing about a fire and all this stuff. I'm like, 'What's his last name?' He goes 'Williamson.' I was like, 'You gotta be kidding me!'"

The Reds headed out of town the following day, and the unsuspecting Pittsburgh Pirates checked in to the Vinoy at three in the morning. Tired from the trip, Frank Velasquez, strength and conditioning coach for the Pirates, didn't hang around to wait for his bags from the bus driver. He undressed, lay down, and conked out. At around five in the morning, he opened his eyes and saw a sandy-haired, blue-eyed man standing in front of the window right by the desk. The figure was transparent and had on a white long-sleeved, button-collared shirt and khaki pants. His hairstyle suggested he was from another era. Velasquez looked, closed his eyes, turned toward the window, and looked again. The apparition was still there, and Velasquez remembers feeling very casual about it. So casual, in fact, that he fell back asleep. "We were so travel disoriented and it was so late," says Velasquez. "You can't do anything but just close your eyes."

In the visitors clubhouse at Tropicana Field the following day, Velasquez shared his story with first baseman Craig Wilson, who asked if he'd seen the ESPN *SportsCenter* clip on Williamson's encounter. Velasquez hadn't and was dumbfounded as Wilson described the story that was very similar to his.

"The fact that it lined up with someone's story that I never knew anything about just kind of helps me know that it was real," says Velasquez. "I don't go telling a lot of people about it other than teammates. I think if it happens just once, then the reaction is, 'Ah, you're full of it.' If several ballplayers said they've had similar experiences at that one hotel, then maybe there is something to it."

Indeed, similar experiences at the Vinoy are rampant—including several from other Pirates personnel *that very night*. The team's staff assistant encountered someone who fit the description of Velasquez's visitor. Struggling to unlock his door, he saw a gentleman in an old-fashioned formal suit pass by in the hall.

Figuring it was the concierge, he quickly turned to ask for assistance. But the gentleman had vanished.

Bullpen coach Bruce Tanner looks upon his own incident that night as a bit more questionable. As he rinsed his hair in the shower, he heard something hit the floor of the bathtub. He looked down and discovered a dime at his feet. Tanner wonders if the dime—which was from the 1960s—fell out of thin air, or if he'd bumped the towels and knocked loose the coin accidentally folded inside.

Those accounts were unsettling enough for Jason Kendall and Alvaro Espinoza that they opted to stay at pitcher Scott Sauerbeck's home in Bradenton for the rest of the series. Pirates hitting coach Gerald Perry wished he had joined them. He swears to this day that on the team's third night in the hotel, he awoke to find his room door wide open when he knew he had bolted it shut before retiring to bed. "That was a door that automatically closes itself, so that was weird," says Perry. "I always lock my door at the hotel, so I know it wasn't that I'd just forgotten. If that had happened the night before, I wouldn't have stayed there that night. I'd have slept in the clubhouse."

Former Toronto Blue Jays reliever John Frascatore heard for years that the Vinoy was haunted, and his family's first stay at the hotel vindicated the stories. Having lived in the area since 1991 when he first came up with the St. Louis Cardinals, he and wife Kandria had heard the legends from old-timers and from articles in the *St. Petersburg Times*. In the mid-1990s, the paper ran a story about a painting crew that fled their job site at the Vinoy after returning from a break to discover buckets of paint knocked off their scaffolding and splattered on the walls. Frascatore had also heard stories from his former Cards teammates Todd Zeile and Gregg Jefferies, who reported waking up to find that someone had unlocked their doors during the night.

The Vinoy stories had so bothered Kandria, who had grown up in St. Petersburg, that she refused to stay in the hotel. Instead, Frascatore commuted the ninety minutes to and from his home in Brooksville, Florida, when the Jays played the Devil

Rays. But wanting a little more rest between a Friday night game and a Saturday day game in July 2001, John convinced Kandria that it made more sense to stay closer to Tropicana Field. On Friday morning, Kandria nervously checked in with the kids while John headed for the ballpark.

Midway into the Jays batting practice that afternoon, club-house assistant Kevin Malloy dashed onto the field and told John, "You need to get in the clubhouse and call your wife *now* at the hotel." John's heart raced as he worried that something had happened to the kids. He rushed to the locker room, grabbed his cell phone, and called his wife. She answered in a shrill voice, "You get the travel secretary on the phone! I'm not staying in that room anymore! That room is haunted!"

Kandria explained that they had just finished lunch, and the kids had brushed their teeth. Then five-year-old Gavin reported something strange. "Mom, the water keeps turning back on." Kandria headed into the bathroom to find that indeed, the water was on. She shut it, turning the knob tight. Moments later, water was again flowing from the tap. Again she shut it off. Over the next couple of minutes, the faucet turned on by itself repeatedly and the toilet flushed three or four times. Thoroughly spooked, the family fled without their luggage. When they transferred to a room in the new wing of the hotel, front desk staff told them "that stuff happens all the time" in the old wing.

Prior to the game, John shared his wife's incident with team-mates, some of whom looked for a rational explanation: The old wing has old pipes, they figured, and water pressure could rat-tle the faucet open. John rejected this. "That whole place was gutted and redone recently. New plumbing. New paint. New Sheetrock. New everything."

Pitchers Joey Hamilton and Billy Koch chimed in that they'd been spooked that previous night, when the lights in their rooms kept flickering. Several teammates echoed similar complaints, in-cluding hitting coach Cito Gaston, whose hotel room door, which he'd locked and chained shut, kept opening in the middle of the night and then slamming. Manager Jim Fregosi reported that his door, too, had slammed. Third base coach Terry Bevington said a similar experience happened to him in the old wing of the Vinoy a few years back when he was managing the White Sox.

Given the huge role of travel in professional baseball, it's not surprising that hotels like the Vinoy come to occupy a good deal of ballplayers' imaginations. Life on the road can be as empty and lonely as Wrigley Field in the postseason. Players—many of whom are superstitious about the game to begin with—pass the time by telling each other stories. Skeptics would note that these tales sometimes grow taller with each retelling, as is often the case with folklore. One can hear supersized variations on these stories in clubhouses thousands of miles away: *Did you hear what happened to Bobby?* But that still doesn't explain why so many players claim firsthand experiences at the Vinoy, or why these experiences are often similar, or just plain inexplicable.

Jay Gibbons's encounter there still gives him the chills. In town with the Baltimore Orioles one summer, the rightfielder made a beeline for his room to catch some rest. He set the alarm clock on the bedside table, then washed up and prepared for bed. As he reached for the lamp, he noticed the clock he'd just set was now off. He sat up to reset it and discovered the cord draped over the dresser with the prong resting over the clock. "It kind of freaked me out," says Gibbons, "because the outlet was near the floor. How the hell did the plug get from down there to the top of the dresser and just stay there? Because I didn't even move the clock." It's an incident Gibbons hasn't forgotten. "I haven't turned the lights off since at that hotel!"

Gibbons's teammate, second baseman Brian Roberts, was more amused than spooked by his own experience. He was at the park when some dry cleaning was delivered to his room. His girlfriend hung the clothes in the closet, then headed to the Trop to watch the game. When the pair returned late that night, the clothes were on the bed. Roberts's girlfriend stared in disbelief. She told Brian she distinctly remembered hanging them up. "Maybe the maid put 'em out there," he said. "The maid had already come through," she replied.

"We just thought it was funny," says Roberts. "We couldn't figure out why in the world anyone would take the clothes out of the closet and put them on the bed. I still don't know whether I believe in ghosts."

For Devil Ray pitcher Jon Switzer, who had a startling experience his first night at the Vinoy, there is no doubt. Called up to the majors for the first time in his career, he and his wife Dana were staying on the fifth floor of the hotel when they awoke from a sound sleep to loud scratching on the wall behind the headboard of their bed. It sounded like a rat scratching from within the wall. The noise continued for a few minutes, then stopped suddenly. Fifteen minutes later, the scratching returned, so loudly that they sprung out of bed and turned on the bedside lamps.

It was at that moment Jon and Dana believed they saw the artwork hanging above their bed come to life. The painting depicted a garden scene with a woman in Victorian dress holding a basket with her right hand. According to John, her left hand, which had been by her chin, was now scratching the glass desperately to get out. The couple stared in disbelief for about three seconds, then raced out the door. "It was crazy because I never believed that kind of thing," says Jon, "and then to see something like that firsthand was just strange. I guess that's why they call it the supernatural."

Vinoy stories have become so legendary that it seems every player in the majors has heard them at least second- or third-hand. Infielder Geoff Blum describes ghosts hovering above players' beds and personal belongings moving around in the room. Outfielder Mike Cameron knows of players getting "locked out of their rooms and seeing things that they normally don't see." "Almost every team I go to," says veteran closer Todd Jones, "when they stay at the Vinoy, they say it's haunted. I've heard that the walls breathe in and out."

On the trip to the hotel with the Blue Jays, righthander Cliff Politte recalls, "José Cruz Jr. got on the bus PA system and told everybody, 'Hopefully you guys got sleeping pills because this hotel is haunted!' And I was nervous from that moment on. I was like, 'Great, I'm not going to be able to sleep all night.' "

Former Red Sox second baseman Mark Bellhorn recalls how uneasy he felt after Scott Williamson shared with him his story. "It's not that big a deal," Bellhorn says, "until you're sitting in your room by yourself with the lights off. That's when all the stories seem to happen."

When Scott Williamson was traded to Boston, his Red Sox teammates Kevin Millar and John Burkett razzed him about the story. Then Burkett hopped on the Internet and found information about Benjamin Williamson once owning the property. He came back to Scott's locker white-faced. "You gotta be kidding me," he told the pitcher. Williamson could only smile. "Coincidence or not, it's hard to make up a story like that."

Why would the Vinoy be haunted? Stories abound of tragic fires, mysterious deaths, and lonely-hearts suicides, all alleged to have taken place in the hotel decades ago. Oakland A's star Eric Chávez heard the hotel was "an old hospital back in the war days"; Velasquez heard that too and figures there may be "a lot of lost souls around there that have never left." Gift shop workers (who report frequently finding store items broken or moved when they arrive in the morning) told Kandria Frascatore a Romeo-and-Juliet-type saga of star-crossed young lovers whose romance was forbidden by the adults around them. They killed each other at the hotel and now haunt its hallways and rooms.

But according to hotel historian Elaine Normaille, none of these events actually happened. Nor could she substantiate any record of Benjamin Williamson dying on the property after he sold it, or staying there after he transferred ownership. Although a skeptic herself, Normaille recognizes that the place has become a magnet for paranormal groups who believe that the hotel is full of ghosts.

Just as the visiting team clubhouse at Tropicana Field is full of jumpy, bleary-eyed ballplayers in need of a good night's sleep.

CHAPTER 6

LADIES AND
GENTLEMEN, BOYS AND GIRLS

On the press level at Fenway Park, photos of Ken Coleman, Ned Martin, and Sherm Feller grace the entrances to the radio, TV, and communications control booths, respectively. All broadcasting immortals and Red Sox legends.

The portrait of Sherm Feller holds further meaning for current Fenway PA announcer Carl Beane. Before every home game he raps the picture three times with his right hand and says, "Hi Sherm. Gotta help me out, Sherm. You and me today." He knocks on the photo again and says, "Thank you very much" and heads into the control box to announce the game.

Beane is convinced Feller accompanies him in the booth during games. "I'm sure he is sitting next to me or standing behind me picking my ears," he says. "So if he's going to be with me, the least I can do is say hello to him."

Sherm Feller controlled the ballpark mike from the Impossible Dream year 1967 to 1993, and his full, strong, gravelly voice set the tone at Fenway for generations of Red Sox fans. His minimalism belied his charisma and talents. Considered one of America's first radio talk show hosts, Feller was chummy with legends in show biz, including Frank Sinatra, Nat King Cole, Danny Kaye, and numerous stars on Broadway. He was a prolific songwriter, penning over one thousand melodies, including the 1950s hits "Summertime, Summertime" and "My Baby's Coming Home."

His baseball friends supported his talent. Former Red Sox centerfielder Fred Lynn overheard Feller composing "Ode to JFK," a symphony Feller had been working on for nearly twenty years, and encouraged him to copyright and publish it. When Feller said he didn't have the nearly three thousand dollars it would cost to register his work, Lynn wrote out a check. The orchestral suite would eventually become part of the repertoire of the Boston Pops and the Baltimore Symphony.

Feller was a beloved personality behind the scenes at Fenway, known for his generosity, his compassion, his playful humor, his pregame catnaps, and his side-splitting anecdotes. Players in both clubhouses loved him and would often give him bats, balls, jackets, and caps as gifts.

In a WBZ radio interview following Sherm Feller's passing in 1994, Red Sox GM Lou Gorman recalled how Feller would often stop by the ballpark on off-days and drop off fried chicken and other foods for front office personnel while they worked. "People like Sherm walk on this earth not too often," said Gorman. "Once you met Sherm you didn't forget him and he was your friend right away."

Back in the 1970s, there was a bar in the press dining area at Fenway Park. After games, team personnel and media would stop there for a few wind-it-down drinks. It was not unusual for visiting managers like Billy Martin to come up and swap stories and talk about the ball game that night. More often than not, Sherm stole the show.

Carl Beane fondly recalls one of Feller's more famous vaudeville stories about his teenage years working as a stagehand at the Boston theaters. Feller used to have the job of telling the performers how many minutes remained before curtain. When there were exotic dancers, he would go to their dressing room and say, "Miss, you've got five minutes." Then he'd go back and say, "Miss you've got four and one-half minutes." He'd keep going back for another peep.

Feller delivered such stories in his standard dry, deadpan manner—much the way that Bob Uecker delivers his humor. He would not crack a smile. He would just tell a joke and everyone at the bar would be rolling on the floor.

As a young radio reporter, Beane, who at age twelve declared that he would one day be a Red Sox announcer, loved listening in and picking up wisdom about radio and the industry. "Just listening to him doing a radio show would be an education," says Beane. "He was very good at phrasing questions in such a way to draw very good responses out of people. And while he was entertaining a lot of people, maybe he didn't even know it, but he was also teaching a group of people how to do it.

"He was an old radio guy and dressed like yesterday's news," adds Beane, "and at the same time he was well respected by everyone who ever met him. He was a true professional and he was fascinating."

Beane was most mesmerized with Feller's deep staccato voice and used to make his peers in the press box laugh because he would imitate Feller, substituting different names. "Instead of having Mickey Mantle come up," says Beane, "I would have Charles de Gaulle, just to be funny. What it would be like if Sherm were to introduce Mao Tse-tung as a pinch hitter for Mahatma Ghandi."

One night Beane angered the press corps of the California Angels when Terry Forster came in to pitch. From the back of the press box, Beane muffled his voice and said, "Now pitching for the Angels, number 27, Terry Forster—'Tub of Goo' Forster." David Letterman had referred to Forster as a "fat tub of goo" in 1985 on his *Late Show*. At the time, the 6-foot-3 Forster weighed 270 pounds. Forster played along with Letterman's joke and even made an appearance on the show. He later made a music video for a number entitled, "Fat Is In." But having a PA announcer use the phrase fell well below the lines of decorum at Fenway or any other park in professional baseball.

"And the writers thought it was Sherm," says Beane. "And they started getting all mad. They thought Sherm was doing it.

'Oh, how disrespectful. That guy ought to be fired.' Finally, I said, 'Hey, it was me. Now chill, will you?' "

"His voice fit Fenway," says Beane, who has been coming to Fenway Park since he was a kid. "He had a big deep baritone rumbling voice that rolled around this place and fit just right. He's the voice of this place. I'm just the present occupier of the chair."

For this reason and more, Beane acknowledges the "Voice of Fenway Park" before games. "It's saying hello to a friend," Beane explains. "It's being respectful to what he created here. When I tap his picture and ask him to help me, in my own mind, he's giving me a wink. 'Okay, kid. Go to work. Knock 'em dead. Break a leg.' Show biz terms. I just have a feeling that he's there."

At times, it's more than a hunch. When a switch flips on or off, when the printout of an announcement to be read disappears, when headphones fall from the desk, Beane blames Sherm. "I just take it as, 'Oh, he's here. He's just saying hi,'" says Beane. "Sherm was also a practical joker."

Mike Gaffney works in the booth with Beane, running the electronic scoreboards. He also knew Sherm Feller very well. If something isn't working right with his or Beane's equipment, the two exchange a knowing look. "Sherm, isn't it?" "Yeah, it's Sherm."

Other than the broadcast booth, Carl Beane's favorite place at Fenway is Section 18, where he always sat as a child attending games with his father, Alfred. He remembers routinely taking the Peter Pan bus from Springfield with his dad, and walking two miles through Boston to the ballpark. His first memory was in 1957, the year Ted Williams hit .388. The Splendid Splinter was on deck. His father said to him, "Watch this guy, number 9. This is the best hitter you will ever see."

Years later, when Beane was a veteran radio reporter covering Spring Training, he had a chance to return the favor when his dad got to meet and spend time with Williams. The elder Beane had come down to visit and one day accompanied him to the Winterhaven compound. As Carl and his father were walking toward the cafeteria, they passed by Johnny Pesky, Ted Williams, Bobby Doerr, and retired umpire Hank Soar, who were sitting on chairs near the bullpen fence. Pesky called out, "Hey Carl, how are you?" Having known them for years, Carl brought his father over and they engaged in small talk when Williams in his big voice said, "Now, who is this guy with you?"

"This is my father, Al."

"Al, how are you? Ted Williams." As if he didn't know who he was.

After more small talk, Williams said, "Carl, [your father] is a pretty good guy. You're an ass, but he's a pretty good guy." (Williams was well known for telling other people they were an "ass.") "Why don't you go do what you gotta do and leave him here with me. He's fine."

The younger Beane left and about an hour later, figuring his dad had enough time and might have worn out his welcome, came back and said, "Dad, are you ready to go?" And Williams said, "I thought I told you to get f——-in' lost. He's fine. We'll bring him. Wherever he's staying, we'll get him back there. Go take off. We're having fun with him."

Al Beane spent the afternoon of a lifetime chatting with the legends. He remembered some games that Ted, Johnny, and Bobby had played and some of their heroics. He never forgot that magical day, and neither did Carl.

After his father died in 1990, Carl buried part of his ashes nine paces from the scoreboard (nine representing Ted Williams's uniform number) in front of "AB" (short for "at-bat," but also the elder Beane's initials). Today he sometimes visits Section 18 to talk to his dad. His first day on the job as Fenway public-address announcer, he brought a photo of the elder Beane taken two months before his death, so father and son could be together in the booth.

"My father had deep, abiding love for baseball," he says. "This is a man who did not see very well and had some hearing problems. He couldn't play baseball other than hit grounders to my brothers and me when we were kids. But he instilled that love of the game and the thinking part of the game. I know that part of him is still in the ballpark, because he physically is. It might be his big toe, I don't know."

During the course of eighty-one home games, there may be one where Carl Beane's energy level dips. When he realizes this, he takes a minute and can almost hear Sherm saying to him, "You have a job to do here. You've got some people that have never heard you before and you owe them. Now, let's go." And he becomes reenergized.

Sherm is often on Beane's mind. When he finishes announcing the coaches at the start of the game, he says, "Thank you." Feller used to do it, and Beane considers it a subtle tribute.

"A lot of the things Sherm did, I do," says Beane. "Not because I can't think of anything else to do, but because the way that he did it was correct with Fenway and the fans liked it and responded to it. First thing I say when I turn on my mike is, 'Ladies and gentlemen, boys and girls, welcome to Fenway Park.' That is exactly the same thing that Sherm used to say. When I go to read stuff, I always tell myself to just read it as is, don't overembellish, don't scream and yell, just do it at a nice even pace. Fenway is a place where you don't need to embellish names. You just say it and get out of the way. These people know what to do. They don't need a cheerleader. They don't need anyone to kind of boost them."

In the earlier twentieth century, ballpark announcers played a more visible role. Longtime Yankees announcer Bob Sheppard, once famously referred to as the "Voice of God" by Reggie Jackson, recalls the way his job was handled before public-address systems were installed in the stadiums, mostly in the 1930s. "There was a man who walked around with a megaphone. He would stand on first base facing the crowd and would announce the pitcher and the catcher. Then he would go to third base and do the same thing." At Wrigley Field, Pat Pieper, who would remain the stadium voice of the Cubs for fifty-nine years, would pick up straw hats thrown by fans and shake hands with Cubs players crossing home plate. At Ebbets Field, Tex Rickart would fetch the Old Gold cigarette cartons (Old Gold was the Dodgers broadcast sponsor) that rolled down the screen netting behind home plate after a Dodgers home run and hand them to the bat boy to carry off to the players in the dugout. It was Sherm Feller who made providing background information to fans a minimalist art form at the asymmetrical little bandbox. Carl Beane honors the tradition.

"Beane is a worthy successor to the late, great Sherm Feller," noted award-winning Boston scribe Dan Shaughnessy in his *Boston Globe* sports column. "Sounds just like him sometimes."

"Sounds like Sherm. I swear to God, it's Sherm Feller," said WBZ sports reporter Tom Cuddy in a biographical documentary on Beane.

Suzyn Waldman, Yankees color commentator on WCBS radio and a native Bostonian, added, "He's sitting in his seat and doing a wonderful job. He sounds a little like Sherm with that offbeat, wonderful, mellifluous, melodious voice. It's very Boston."

Beane appreciates the comparisons, but deflects the credit. "Sherm Feller is the original voice of this place. If you heard his voice, in five seconds you thought Red Sox. If I do this long enough, I might sort of be thought of the same way to the younger generation as Sherm was and still is to us."

And Beane knows he will never be alone at the mike. "As long as there will be Fenway, as long as that booth will be there, he'll be there. I don't even question it. He's there."

CHAPTER 7

THE MAGIC FLUTE

When a Toronto Blue Jays security guard informed pitcher Miguel Batista that the Rogers Centre, then known as SkyDome, was built on a Native American burial site, the right-handed Dominican closer's heart started racing. Not because he believed the superstition that harm would come to those who uproot a Native American gravesite, but because of a possible connection to a "freaky" incident that happened the day before.

The pitcher was no stranger to Native American tradition. His passionate interest in the subject stretches far into his childhood, when his great-grandmother, a Carib Indian, told him stories passed down from her ancestors. The stories set his imagination soaring—they even inspired him to spend as much time playing bow and arrow as he did playing *pelota de trapo* with a broom handle, cardboard gloves, and a ball fashioned from tightly bound socks. Years later, in the summer of 2002, when the Boys & Girls Club of Indian Country contacted the Arizona Diamondbacks, requesting a player to visit area Native American communities, Miguel saw an opportunity to rediscover his roots. During the All-Star break, he visited Hualapai Nation, which occupies a large area of the Western Grand Canyon Corridor. He spoke to children, many of whom traveled great distances on foot to meet him. An elderly woman gave him a rosary made of silver and stones, which he wears to this day.

Since then, Miguel has continued to expand his outreach to the Native American community, donating $50,000 to build a Little League field (now named Batista "Spirit of One Man" Stadium) and prompting *The Sporting News* to name him "Good Guy of the Year" in 2003. He became friends with Grammy Award nominated Navajo flautist Aaron White, who presented Miguel with a flute and started teaching him how to play it. Batista quickly mastered the instrument, performing "The Star-Spangled Banner" before a Diamondbacks home game on Native American Recognition Day.

It was with this flute that Miguel believes he may have made contact with those buried underneath the Rogers Centre.

The Native American flute is an end-blown, vertically held single piece of wood with a history that may stretch back 2,500 years. With its dual air chambers and six-hole configuration, this hand-carved instrument produces a simple tone and limited range of notes—traditionally one octave in one key. "Usually, the Navajos used the flute to imitate the sounds of owls," says Miguel. "It's not actual music that you write down and then perform. You can try to represent a song, but you usually just play notes. It's more what they call 'spiritual' music."

Miguel often ponders whether his playing of this soulful instrument may have stirred the spirits of indigenous people, who had prospered on the northern shores of Lake Ontario long before the European settlers arrived. During home stands in his first season with the Blue Jays in 2004, Miguel would slip away from the clubhouse before every game to practice his flute in a solitary area under the third base grandstands "to rest my mind." One muggy, overcast Saturday afternoon, with the visiting Red Sox taking batting practice and the retractable roof of the Rogers Centre closed due to a threat of showers, the sure-handed hurler felt something other than his own hand take control of his flute.

"I removed the flute from the burlap pouch that protects the wood from moisture, when all of a sudden somebody slapped the flute out of my hands and threw it down. I thought someone had swatted it but no one was there besides me."

Although the pipe body of the flute was undamaged, the bird or saddle block, which overlays a flue on top of the flute near the mouthpiece and controls airflow, shattered.

"I don't know what it was," says Miguel, "but it was funny because a day later the guard saw me by the clubhouse and said, 'How come you're not playing the flute today?' I told him what happened. 'It's so strange—I was getting ready to play and the flute just flew out of my hands.' And he started laughing and he told me about the graveyard. And I was like, '*What?!*' "

Margaret Salt, a land researcher for the First Nations Information Project, has no record of the property ever being used as a graveyard. "Of course, there had been thousands of years of settlement in the region," she says, "so surely there could be the remains of indigenous people."

Indeed, Native Americans have settled along the shores of Lake Ontario for over ten thousand years. During excavation for construction of the Rogers Centre in 1989, a public outcry from archaeologists and historical societies occurred when provincial governmental authorities refused to halt digging after workers uncovered fishing weirs originally used by Algonquian Mississauga Mohawks, who inhabited the region in the seventeenth and eighteenth centuries.

Batista has vowed to learn more about the history of the site—not an unusual field of study for one of baseball's true Renaissance men. During road trips, he often visits museums, libraries, and bookstores. An accomplished novelist and poet, he tapes quotes from philosophers such as Gandhi and King Solomon to his locker and cites them often. His quest for truth has led him to embrace the notion of the supernatural.

"I've seen things in my life that shocked the hell out of me and can't be explained as anything other than a ghost," says Miguel, who grew up in San Pedro de Macorís, hometown of hundreds of past and present major leaguers, including Sammy Sosa, George Bell, Alfonso Soriano, and Rico Carty. Riding through the unofficial world capital of baseball in one of the hundreds of dented cabs that travel on preassigned routes, one will inevitably see infinite variations of stickball on street corners and players in cleats and uniforms walking to or from the nearest field. Look farther—down the side streets and alleys, in shops and backrooms—and baseball is everywhere. Just about anyone around town has a family member or friend who has been in organized ball. On doorsteps and at bridge tables set up in front of corner markets, ex-ballplayers talk about their time in the pros, youngsters discuss their training and dreams, and just about everyone follows Major League Baseball and their hometown winter league team, Estrellas.

According to Miguel, anyone who spends time in San Pedro will also hear ghost stories, oft-repeated legends of spirits possessing animals and cadavers mingling with passersby.

Miguel is still haunted by the events that unfolded one afternoon in the forest and fields behind the Los Angeles Angels Training Academy. Miguel and fellow major-league pitcher Armando Benítez had grown up together in Porvenil, a sugar mill neighborhood on the outskirts of San Pedro, and they would often go hunting for land crabs in the tropical forest bordering the shore. Their journey to the coast was three miles on foot, passing the sugar fields just east of San Pedro. Behind the Angels complex, they'd cut through open grassy fields dotted with cows, some with cattle egrets perched on their backs. Then they'd duck into the forest with their machetes and poking sticks to lure crabs from their holes in the soil.

One afternoon, as they headed home with plastic bags filled with the day's catch slung over their shoulders, they spotted a tiny white mutt following them. Three miles from civilization, the presence of a dog struck them as odd, but they didn't dwell on it as they continued through the forest. The mutt kept its distance. Every time Miguel and Armando stopped, the canine stopped. After a short while they turned back and all of a sudden the dog had vanished. A tiny baby cow was following them.

"That was kind of weird," says Miguel. "We'd never seen a baby cow without its mother. They always walk together." Equally weird was the calf's behavior, which mimicked the dog's. "Same thing," says Batista. "We stop, he stops."

As they neared the edge of the field, the dog suddenly reappeared behind them. "That's when we realized that something was going on," says Miguel. "In San Pedro we call it *baca*, a pact practitioners of *vodun* can do with the Devil that allows an evil spirit to transform into animals to hunt down the enemy. So we started running across the fields and the dog started following. If you're not doing anything wrong, the spirit is not supposed to do anything. Still, you can't protect against it because it's supposed to change forms. So this little dog was chasing us across the field. As we ducked under the barbed fence into private property, the dog stopped and turned around to go back. That was freaky!"

Benítez says he doesn't recall the incident, but his good friend remembers it vividly and considers it just another facet of life in the Dominican Republic. In their native San Pedro, where everyone knows everyone, where the air is sweet with sugar, and where love ballads blast from the tiniest shanty huts, romantic ghost stories are the most popular. One that stands out in Miguel's mind happened near Cementerio de los Viejos (Cemetery of the Elderly), which is in the heart of downtown San Pedro. The cemetery wall bordered Miguel's high school, Juan Pablo Duarte, and he used to hop the wall and jump over the graves each afternoon when school let out.

A cabdriver was barreling through downtown one evening, when he stopped for a well-dressed young woman standing outside the cemetery gate. The woman entered the vehicle and instructed the driver to take her to Twentieth Street in Miramar, one of the most famous streets in San Pedro. Although he wondered why a woman wearing her Sunday clothes would want to travel after dark into the city's most festive district, the driver followed her instructions.

When the cab turned onto Twentieth Street, the woman seemed to perk up in recognition of her surroundings. As they approached a bar with four men playing dominoes in front, the woman instructed the driver to slow down. She stared carefully at an elderly man wearing a button-down yellow shirt at the table. After they had passed, the woman asked the driver to take her back downtown to where he'd picked her up. At the cemetery gate, the woman asked the driver for a pen and paper. He furrowed his brow at the request but complied. The woman wrote a long note, folded it, and said, "Go back to that place, to the poor man, and give him that note, and he will pay for the fare."

Although the driver would normally smell a scam, for some reason he believed her. When he arrived at the bar, he told the man in the yellow shirt, "I'm sorry. This might look crazy to you, but I brought this note for you." He explained the situation and handed the man the letter. The man started reading the letter and burst out crying. He said to the driver, "Where did you find that woman? Take me there! Take me to the cemetery!" The driver did as he asked, and the man paid him as he exited the cab into the cemetery.

"What had happened was that woman was this guy's wife," says Miguel. "She died twenty years ago. And every day for those twenty years, he used to go in front of her tomb at the graveyard and talk with her. That day he didn't go. And the note said, 'Every day you came to see me. But today because you didn't come, I came to see you.' And she'd signed it."

"It really was a freaky thing," Miguel adds, with the appreciation of a man who has learned to respect the mystical. "There are some funny things that happen. Funny, funny things."

CHAPTER 8

FRIGHT
NIGHT IN L.A.

They say at Dodger Stadium there's not a bad seat in the house. But that doesn't mean the view is always pretty.

The reason Ramon Verduzco took a job with the L.A. Dodgers was because he could never get tickets on nights Fernando Valenzuela pitched. Like most Southern Californians, Verduzco was under the spell of Fernandomania during the 1980s.

So at age fifteen, Verduzco started walking around selling programs. At most games, he would earn around five dollars, which he would put toward a hot dog and a Coke, then sit down and watch the game. Within three years he manned a souvenir vending stand on the top deck. Then over the years he was promoted to stand captain, managing several employees and stands. He gradually worked his way "down"—to the loge level.

In his first years on the job, he heard ghost stories concerning the incline along the southern edge of the main stadium parking lot. According to urban legend, long before Chávez Ravine was cleared to build Dodger Stadium, a couple on their honeymoon was taking in the breathtaking view of downtown Los Angeles from the hillside. Answering nature's call, the groom stepped into the forest and in the darkness fell off the ridge to his death. His wife went searching for him, and on discovering his body below, leapt to her death. The story handed down from some of the old-time Dodger employees was that every now and then one could see an image of a shrieking woman dressed in white plunging over the cliff.

Verduzco discounted the story as folklore. Like most Mexican-Americans, he had heard many accounts of *la llorona* (sometimes called "the woman in white" or "weeping woman"), a popular Mexican legend of a mother who drowns her children and herself, and then roams the earth in search of her kids. Verduzco had studied Hispanic folklore in college and decided reportings of a woman in white in the Dodger Stadium parking lot were just another variant.

His outlook changed during his tenure on the top deck. Verduzco, who now works as an assistant sheriff for the LAPD, remembers counting inventory late one evening at his stand behind the leftfield seats. The job, which was required twice per month, often took him deep into the night. Shortly after midnight, the stadium lights went off on a timer and Verduzco relied on just the lighting from his stand. Around 1:00 A.M., he took a break, settling in the stands and gazing into the darkness on the field when he saw a "foglike object" originate at the Dodgers' bullpen and work its way across the field. It dissipated midway between the visitors bullpen and first base. "It seemed to just hover or walk," recalls Verduzco. "I got the chills because I remembered the story of *la llorona*, or the woman in white.

"I saw it quite a few times in my twenty years working there," he adds. "One time I actually brought a laser pointer that I used as part of my selling tools in my stand, and I pointed it at it to see what the hell it was, and it didn't disappear. It pretty much hovered around the field."

Verduzco asked Al, the Dodgers' longtime groundskeeper, if the field had a sprinkler system or something else that could produce the likeness of a ghost crossing the field. "He said, 'No.' After a while I stopped asking around—I just thought of it as normal."

Bordering the property of Dodger Stadium, near parking lot 40–41, is the site of the former Hebrew Benevolent Society Cemetery, the first Jewish cemetery in Los Angeles. Between 1902 and 1910, the remains of 360 people interred on the three-acre tract of land were transferred to Home of Peace Cemetery in East Los Angeles. The site is now a California Registered Historical Landmark and contains the remains of a tomb that was on the site until the late-1990s. It was a popular hangout for hundreds of Dodgers employees after the game, who curiously nicknamed the spot "The Alamo."

Many of these stadium workers beamed with pride at being a part of the Dodgers tradition. They spoke with reverence of Koufax and Drysdale, Sutton and Hershiser, Garvey and Gibson, Valenzuela and Nomo. But when they started talking about the inner workings of the stadium, sooner or later their thoughts turned to the stadium's mysteries. At the Alamo, they often swapped ghost stories.

There were tales of the napping night watchman by the centerfield gate who awoke to a phantom slap on his back, reports of lights turning on and off in the press box, a story about a security guard's dog shuddering and refusing to join him on the loge level.

"A lot of people like to talk about ghosts," says George Delgado, a security officer at the stadium for nearly two decades. "Over the years you hear stories from different officers. If they worked here full time and they worked here during the off-season and have done patrols late at night, most of them have a story or two to tell about the ghosts. And it has passed on throughout us. You hear about it."

Some employees found the whole history of the land haunting, given that the ballpark was built atop the remnants of a Mexican-American community. Chávez Ravine had been home to three self-sufficient, close-knit villages that were rousted in the 1940s to make way for a promised public housing project, which never came to fruition.

Before team owner Walter O'Malley decided to ship his Brooklyn Dodgers westward, he had already scouted the hilltop

of Chávez Ravine by helicopter and deemed it to be an ideal location for a ballpark. To make way for the stadium, the home-
owners who remained were forcibly evicted amid angry protest.
The homes were razed, and after O'Malley won battles in the
courts and at the polls, an army of bulldozers leveled, graded,
and pushed up 300 acres to form a bowl so the stadium could
rest atop and not inside the hillside hollow.

O'Malley strove to make the park a baseball showplace. Tapping his fertile imagination, he provided detailed input in every
aspect of construction from sightlines, which to this day are
among the best in baseball, to the width of seats. Influenced by
Disneyland, he designed a colorfully landscaped terraced parking lot and over the years incorporated horticultural treasures
from around the globe.

Forty thousand cubic yards of concrete were used in the
building of the stadium. And after completion, soil was trucked in
from Sherman Oaks in the San Fernando Valley as surface for the
field. The diamond grass was dyed a spinach-colored green because of unseasonable weather just weeks prior to the opening.

An enthused local media followed construction closely and
dubbed the stadium an engineering marvel and the "Taj Mahal
of Los Angeles." But on April 10, 1962, the Cincinnati Reds
spoiled its much-trumpeted debut. Centerfielder Duke Snider
ripped two hits, but the Reds Wally Post launched a three-run
home run off Johnny Podres with two outs in the seventh inning,
helping lift the Reds to a 6–3 victory in front of 52,564 fans. The
following day Sandy Koufax threw a four-hitter, setting the winning ways for a club that would appear in seven Fall Classics
over the next four decades and capture four World Series titles.

In the early years there were no Gardenburgers, sushi, or
frozen yogurt—just plain old hot dogs for a quarter, soda for fifteen cents, and frozen chocolate malts for thirty cents. Bob
Natelborg, who has been managing a souvenir stand in the stadium since 1968, remembers the only clothing items when he
first set up shop were two white shirts (one for men, one for
boys—none for females) and one jacket.

Over the years, the workforce has grown exponentially, and in some instances achieved fame. Most notable are the peanut vendors. Roger "Peanut Man" Owens built a name for himself for the artistry and accuracy of his under-the-leg, behind-the-back, two-bags-at-a-time peanut throws to fans. His skill became legendary. He threw the ceremonial first pitch (a perfect strike) of the 1976 home opener from his stomping ground in the loge seats to Steve Yeager at home plate, appeared on the *Tonight Show* with Johnny Carson, performed at the Smithsonian Institution, and received a plaque from the city council. Hall of Famer Don Sutton and longtime Los Angeles mayor Tom Bradley attended Owens's wedding and threw peanuts over the newlywed couple instead of rice.

Many of his contemporaries became famous for their piercing cries, witty slogans, and big smiles. Charles Cushman was noted for his ear-piercing shouts, "Haaaay Peanuts!" that were routinely audible during radio broadcasts. Warner Wald's trademark was yelling, "Poor Man's Lunch!" on the field level. Late in the game another colleague would cry, "Peanuts, peanuts, peanuts! Cover up your beer breath!"

Then there's the less glamorous, behind-the-scenes workforce. Some work late hours, heading in after the last fans straggle out after the game. Naturally, this makes them more likely candidates to own a firsthand ghost story or two.

"Some guys [on third shift] don't want to be alone on the loge level," says one member of the overnight cleaning crew, who asked not to be identified. "They say they feel something like a cold wind or a tap on the shoulder."

Bobby Jimenez, who works in shipping and receiving, feels similarly about the merchandise warehouse underneath the stadium. "When you're in the warehouse, you hear stuff and feel a cold breeze in the room. When we get that, we're out of there.

"Sometimes when we're in there locking up by ourselves you get this antsy feeling and the lights turn off. And when they shut off, they shut off all over the warehouse."

Jimenez reports that another supernatural hotspot is a vault in the warehouse where they store damaged merchandise.

Whenever he enters, he finds everything strewn all over the place. Jimenez describes another vault where memorabilia such as old Brooklyn Dodgers uniforms are kept. "When you're in there, it's almost like history hits you in the head," says Jimenez. "You can't help but feel it."

Ramon Verduzco refers to these vaults as "dungeons" and says many are entranceways into "spooky" tunnels that were bored into the bedrock when the stadium was built. "Walter O'Malley's trophies were back there," says Verduzco, "when he used to go game hunting for lions and bears and stuff like that years ago—that's where that stuff was hidden back then." The Dodgers' official team historian, Mark Langill, remembers one former employee entered the tunnel unaware of its holdings and "flipped out. She turned on a light and saw a lion looking at her."

Langill is enthralled by the ballpark's hidden passageways and the numerous temperature-controlled, heavy-door vaults where team photos and slides are preserved. Although he has never been spooked while down there, he is not about to pass judgment on those who have. "Your surroundings are what you know," he says. "If you're like me and don't work here late after everyone has gone home, you're not going to get that feeling. But if you work late at night you might have a different perspective."

George Delgado finds it unnerving up above. "It's completely different at night when there's nobody here than during a game," he says. "You could sit on one side of the stadium on one level and hear steps or anything on the other side of the stadium. And on top of everything, it's dark. I've never been afraid, but I've come across a few things and thought, 'That's not normal!'"

Around nine or ten o'clock at night, the officers used to hear the sounds of an unknown visitor walking the top deck of the park. "The only person who would be here late at night would be someone doing payroll and this stadium would be quiet as a ghost town. You would hear this lady with high heels walking up on the top deck and there was nobody here." This would often be after Delgado and his partner—who also heard the footsteps—had walked through the stadium, including the top deck. "I'm like, 'Okay, let me go up there again.' And when I checked it, it was empty."

Ramon Verduzco thought he heard a different pair of feet on the loge level. One night, taking a break from inventory, he passed through the almost pitch-black aisle from his leftfield/third base kiosk to the elevator. His eyes adjusted to the darkness as he walked. All of a sudden he thought he heard what sounded very much like a small child running barefoot behind him. He wondered if a toddler had gotten separated from his parents during the game. He turned, but saw and heard no one. He continued to look behind him as he walked. "I got to the point," says Verduzco, "where I was looking behind pillars to see if somebody was screwing with me—or maybe even an animal, because sometimes we have a possum or a coyote around there."

He still saw no one, and each time he continued onward, he heard the same pitter-patter. "As I'm walking toward the elevator, I'm getting a little freaked out and my arm hair is rising. I remember feeling really odd and funny about it. And all of a sudden [the elevator] just opens up. I never pushed the button. Now that just freaked me out."

Verduzco contacted security and they assured him no one else was in the building. They turned on the stadium lights but didn't find anyone. "Ever since then I've always had that funny feeling that a little kid was following me at the stadium," says Verduzco. "It didn't stop us from doing our work and I wasn't scared or afraid to be there, but it just always felt funny."

According to Hopi Indian legend, the domed living quarters of one of three "lost underground cities" is said to exist farther below the stadium. Hopi chief Little Greenleaf in the 1930s told the *Los Angeles Times* that the network of tunnels was built five thousand years ago by a highly advanced race called the "Lizard People" as shelter from terrifying meteor showers that had occurred in the Southwest. The labyrinth under the City of Angels was thought to be the capital and had been built in the shape of a lizard, with its head underneath Dodger Stadium and its tail under the Los Angeles Public Library. Various hills around the city were said to contain towering caverns just underneath their crest that housed up to one hundred families.

In 1934, geophysicist mining engineer G. Warren Shufelt claimed to have detected four-foot-long gold tablets in those chambers with a "radio X-ray" device he perfected. So persuasive was Shufelt that he was granted a permit from the Los Angeles County Board of Supervisors to dig one thousand feet into the earth on Ft. Moore Hill, overlooking Sunset Boulevard. Shortly after the story broke sensationally on the front pages of the *Times* and other media outlets, the supervisors mysteriously revoked Shufelt's contract and bulldozed the excavation area. The story fell out of the news and Shufelt vanished from public view.

More recently, a seismic fault was discovered to run underneath Chávez Ravine and the stadium underwent renovations to shore up safety.

All this adds to the folklore of the Dodgers, as stadium workers ponder the source of what spooks them. Asked if it's a ballplayer, most say it's not likely, since few L.A. Dodgers legends have passed on. "I've never heard a story or couldn't even direct you to somebody that would say there is a player story there," says Verduzco. "Not even of Walter O'Malley, although his essence and aura are here. If anything, Tommy Lasorda, when he dies, he'd be the one that probably would be the first to haunt the place, because he lives there.

"The stadium itself does hold sound," he adds. "In the '88 World Series, when Kirk Gibson hit that home run, which nearly destroyed that park, I was there watching it and I never heard the stadium that loud. I never heard such energy. Sometimes working there at nights, you can feel that there is an aura about the stadium. And it's not necessarily a bad aura—a lot of good times have happened."

OH, DOCTOR!

Dodger Stadium isn't the only haunted park in Southern California. Bob Waller, who has worked as a security guard for the San Diego Padres since 2004, says employees at Petco Field have their own stories.

"There's a ghost here supposedly. I've heard a lot of people that work here at night talking about ghosts and all that stuff. They claim it's a white being that spooks a lot of women. Workers all talk about 'the ghost.' Yeah, it's supposed to hang out in the Western Metals building. The super old building—the entire stadium was built around it. The grounds around the building are supposed to be sacred because it was a Native American burial ground. I definitely believe it. Why not? If you didn't, [the ghosts] would make sure you did. They'd scare you to death. Down in the basement people have heard doors slam and different stuff like that and it's not windy. I guess it is alleged to spook the cleaning crew, because they had to be escorted. The story has been rampant."

CHAPTER 9

FRIENDLY GHOSTS IN
THE FRIENDLY CONFINES

In 1998 something eerie was going on at Wrigley Field. Something so unfamiliar, so unusual, and so impossible to comprehend, the team's owners had to look to the paranormal for an explanation.

The Cubs were winning.

Late in the season, searching to understand how this could be, the Tribune Company, which owns the club, brought in a team of paranormal researchers to investigate Wrigley Field. "It sounds like a joke, but it's true," says Ursula Bielski. "They only brought us in because the Cubs were doing so well."

Bielski is well known in supernatural circles and has researched and written extensively on ghosts and hauntings in Chicago. She has published five books on local ghost lore and currently heads Chicago Hauntings, Inc., which offers tours of the city's spookier sites. She got a call from some paranormal colleagues and joined them to investigate Wrigley.

Prior to the 1998 season, the Cubs beloved announcer Harry Caray had died, which had some speculating that his guiding spirit was behind the team's winning ways. The Tribune Company specifically mentioned this to the researchers when inviting them to check out the ballpark. "So of course we went first to the announcer's box," says Bielski. The group had some ghost-hunting equipment with them—electromagnetic meters and thermal guns and cameras. "We didn't find anything in the announcer's box at all."

Given free rein of the place, the researchers checked out a variety of spots. "We went in the dugout, we went onto the field, we went to the pitcher's mound. We didn't find anything anywhere in those places." This surprised the group, who initially thought these would be the most likely areas for paranormal activity.

But then they went into the bleachers and, Bielski says, "It was crazy." Meters started registering unusual energy forces and the kind of "cold spots" that accompany haunted sites. "It would be 72 and then go down to 14 or 4 degrees for a couple of seconds, and then go back up," reports Bielski. "It was very interesting."

The investigative crew did not determine who or what was there, but in retrospect realized that the bleachers "were the most logical place in the world to be haunted." Bielski explains that that's because contrary to the popular belief that ghosts are lost souls stuck in the earthly world, many apparitions merely "stay at places they like to be.

"We're talking about impressions that are left behind by people," she says. "But there's no physical entity there—there's not an intelligence. It's because of the energy that was left behind." While this can be caused by tragic or traumatic events, it can also occur in places where "a lot of emotion happened." And what place on earth could have more accumulated emotion than the bleachers at Wrigley Field?

Bielski notes the paranormalist's distinction between *ghosts* and *hauntings*. "Ghosts are believed to be actual entities—intelligent beings that are surviving death. They'll look at you, they'll look into your eyes, they'll try to interact with you. In hauntings, you may see an apparition, but it will be going through the motions." She cites an example of a family who used to see a woman walking their hallway late at night. "She never looked at them, never acknowledged them, but just kept walking back and forth."

So the bleachers, then, could be said to be haunted, without having technical "ghosts" there. But are there also ghosts in Wrigley Field?

Bielski didn't find specific evidence in her 1998 investigation, but says, "I've heard many stories that Steve Goodman is there."

Goodman was a songwriter, best known for penning the Arlo Guthrie hit, "City of New Orleans." He was devoted to the team and wrote several songs for the Cubs, including fan favorite "Go Cubs Go." Another was entitled, "A Dying Cubs Fan's Last Request."

That song, though filled with humorous references to the team's losing ways, envisions a Cubs enthusiast arranging for his funeral at Wrigley, culminating in a pyre at home plate and the deceased's ashes scattering in the Chicago wind. Goodman debuted the song in March 1983; a year and a half later, the songwriter himself succumbed to leukemia, dying just eleven days before the Cubs made their first postseason appearance in nearly forty years.

Since then there have been published reports that Goodman's ashes were buried at home plate, though the Cubs organization has not officially confirmed this. For Bielski, who has talked to people who claim to have seen Goodman sitting in the stands behind home plate, the question is beside the point. "Whether his ashes are there or not, it's very possible that you would still see him because it was such a central part of his life and he was so emotionally involved."

That description also fits Cubs legend Charlie Grimm, who played for the team and managed them several times, leading the club to pennants in 1932, 1935, and 1945. Grimm's ashes are said to be buried in a box in left-centerfield.

What's more, Grimm himself is thought to be present at the park. Marty Moore, a Wrigley security guard for seventeen years, has worked overnight shifts where the bullpen phone— not far from Grimm's interred ashes—rings in the middle of the night. The phone is a direct line from the Cubs' empty dugout; it can't be dialed from any other phone. "The story is that Charlie is calling the bullpen again," says Moore. "It's very eerie when you are here by yourself."

Other guards have heard the bullpen phone ringing too. The first time Floyd Nix experienced it, "it was freaking me out," he says. "I thought this is not real. Somebody is playing a game. But I know for a fact there was nobody else in the building."

Nix believes he also encountered Grimm once in the team's front offices. "I was walking through from the front to the back and I saw a shadow. When I turned the corner thinking someone was back there, no one was there." It was a weekend, sometime between 6:00 P.M. and midnight, and again, Nix was the only one in the building. When he later told another Cubs employee about it, "he said there was a story about the ghost of Charlie Grimm— something happened with him and somebody in the front office, and that's his ghost up there."

Wrigley security guards report other odd experiences. Sue Waitr has almost twenty years with the team and says it's not uncommon to patrol the park on a solo shift in the dead of night and find lights suddenly turned on that were off during the previous walk-through. "Several times I've heard my name being called and I'm the only one in the ballpark," she says. This happens "in the tunnels, in the open part of the stadium—anywhere, any hour, night or day. It's not a whisper and it's not loud. It's just, 'Sue.'" On one such occasion Waitr was with a coworker who also heard Sue's name called. "We both looked and there was no one there."

When these call-outs occur, Waitr simply talks back to the ghosts. "I just say, 'Well, I'm here to protect you, whoever you might be—Charlie Grimm, or whoever. I'm glad to have the company and I'll be back later.'"

The supernatural phenomena don't bother Waitr at all. "I have never taken it as anything harmful," she says. Such ghostly experiences just come with the territory of guarding one of the oldest and most storied parks in baseball.

Wrigley Field began life in 1914 as Weeghman Park, the home of the Chicago Federals, members of baseball's short-lived Federal

League. When the FL folded in 1916, owner Charlie Weeghman and a syndicate of investors bought the National League's Cubs franchise and moved them to their North Side park. One of those investors—chewing-gum magnate William Wrigley—eventually bought out the others. By 1920 the building was renamed Cubs Park; in 1926 it was christened Wrigley Field.

Today Wrigley Field is probably cited as the most beautiful ballpark in baseball more often than any other. It has undergone numerous renovations over the years (in 1914 its seating capacity was 14,000; today it's more than 41,000) while carefully preserving the feel of an intimate, old-style, fan-friendly park.

Much of the credit for this has to go to P. K. Wrigley, who took over the team when his father died in 1932. Though rightly criticized for not fielding a competitive squad for decades, Wrigley believed that there was no way to guarantee fans a winning team every year—but he could guarantee them a great ballpark experience. As a result, he always focused money and effort on Wrigley Field. It was he who instructed Bill Veeck to plant the now-signature ivy along the outfield wall, he who refused to put lights on the field for night games. (Wrigley briefly planned to illuminate the park after the 1941 season, but then donated the materials to the war effort following the Pearl Harbor attack. Lights were eventually installed in 1988.)

Much about Wrigley Field is considered iconic, from the old-fashioned scoreboard with numbers still changed by hand, to the park's legendary Bleacher Bums, to the rooftop spectators on nearby buildings. Its relatively small footprint gives fans the sense of being right near the action, and led Cubs legend Ernie Banks to nickname the field "the Friendly Confines."

Wrigley has certainly hosted its share of memorable baseball moments over the years. There was the 1917 game—one of the best pitching duels ever—in which Jim "Hippo" Vaughn and the Reds' Fred Toney each threw no-hitters for nine full innings. (The Reds finally scored in the tenth.) Babe Ruth's "called shot" in the 1932 World Series, wherein the slugger allegedly gestured toward a spot in the bleachers and then hit the next pitch there for a home run. Pete Rose's record-tying 4,191st career hit in 1985. More recently, Kerry Wood tied the strikeout record, fanning 20 hitters in 1998. That same year, Sammy Sosa hit 66 home runs; he would achieve 60-plus home run seasons again in 1999 and 2001.

But the Cubs have never won a World Series in all their years at Wrigley. (The Chicago Bears, who used the field from 1921 to 1970, fared considerably better there, winning eight NFL championships in that time.) Even that 1998 season ended when the Cubs lost the first round of the playoffs. Some blame the infamous Cubs curse for this long drought (see Chapter 21: Giving Up the Goat). The team has been labeled the "Loveable Losers" and its fans eternal optimists.

Still, fans and players alike consider the park a winner. As Harry Caray once put it, "Win or lose, we're in heaven."

"You go to so many newer ballparks that are so up-to-date, just beautiful, just perfect," says Ron Calloway, who played at Wrigley with Montréal in 2003 and 2004. "But when you go to Wrigley, it has character. It's like an old car with a couple of dings in it."

For Wrigley tour guide and lifelong Cubs fan Brian Bernardoni—like so many of the Cubs' devoted—the park inspires deep personal emotions. "In 1933, my grandmother played at Wrigley Field. She won the city championship in girls softball there. My daughter took her first steps a few feet from where her great-grandmother once played. So I understand the emotion. It's a living being, as far as I'm concerned."

Bernardoni hopes one day to join Goodman and Grimm as a permanent resident of the park. In his will, he's earmarked a good portion of his cremated remains for Wrigley. "A third of my ashes are to be dumped on Opening Day. That way I don't miss Opening Day for at least a year after I die. And then a third of my ashes get dumped at a World Series game at Wrigley."

That's assuming that the Cubs do not host a World Series game prior to his death. This is a classic Cubs fan lament. Bernardoni, who considers the White Sox's 2005 World Series championship "one of the worst days of my life," says that "the hardest thing about watching the White Sox win was that I went to bed that night not knowing if I would ever get to experience that with the Cubs."

If nothing else, his ashes will.

With such tradition and so many great memories, it is perhaps not surprising that the living and the dead are said to commingle at Wrigley Field. Then, too, any historic place is bound to accrue legends over time, including some with eerie undertones.

"I heard one story when I was a kid that my dad and his friends talked about," remembers Ursula Bielski. "There was a little boy who died at a ball game and he is sometimes still seen or heard." Bielski has since tried to track the story down, but can't find anyone to substantiate it. Bernardoni says that a boy did once die at a Cubs game; he was on the roof of the stadium, reached for a home run ball hit off Christy Mathewson, and fell to his death. But this was at the West Side Grounds—the Cubs' home from 1893–1915—not at Wrigley.

A fan did die at Wrigley on July 3, 1955, falling down a stairwell in the rightfield bleachers. In addition, a rumor has gone around that the pitcher's mound is built over what used to be a cemetery. But this is not true. The confusion may be rooted in the fact that Wrigley Field is on land that used to house a *seminary*.

Players too have had the feeling that there is more going on at Wrigley than meets the eye. "There's definitely people running around that place," says pitcher Andy Pratt, who played briefly with the Cubs in 2004. "You're not alone there." Pratt once spent some solitary time in the park at dusk, sitting in the stands and soaking up the atmosphere. "I swear you can hear the crowd, you can hear the at-bat, and you look around," he says.

Terry Adams pitched for the Cubs for five years and thought there was something funny going on in the ivy. "Balls disappear in the vines," he says. Grounds rules state that balls hit into the ivy vines are doubles, if the outfielder chooses not to field them. "Balls go into the vines and days later, no balls," says Adams. "It's weird . . . they just disappear."

If Wrigley Field is so populated by ghosts and spirits, why don't more people see them? Why aren't fans complaining about ghosts sitting in their seats, or obscuring their view of the field? Another lesson in parapsychology from Ursula Bielski:

"Some people are able to perceive things and some people aren't," she says, acknowledging that this is precisely why supernatural studies are "not accepted by science." Bielski herself, surprisingly, says she does not have this gift, but she is a student of how it works.

"You plug yourself into the environment. It really seems like it has as much to do with a person's natural ability as what's actually in the environment." A person has to be open to the possibility.

In other words, you have to believe—sometimes in the absence of concrete physical evidence—that there's something there. You have to ignore the skeptics, the realists, and the naysayers and have faith that there's an energy, a positive force, and that anything is possible.

And what Cubs fan can't relate to that?

CHAPTER 10

RALLYING SPIRITS

In the days and weeks immediately following the September 11, 2001 terrorist attacks, baseball was something of a paradox. On the one hand, the sport—like so much of American popular culture—never seemed more insignificant, dwarfed by the enormity of the tragedy and the life-and-death uncertainty of world events. On the other hand, baseball was a welcome refuge for many weary Americans who were comforted by its traditions and familiarity.

For many fans, baseball played a role in the emotional healing of the country, particularly New York City. Some even felt that the spirits of the people lost in the attacks were present in some inspirational and heartfelt moments that played out both on and off the baseball field in the fall of 2001—moments that gave people some optimism and joy in the midst of terror and heartache.

A Symbol of Survival

From the start, there were overt connections between baseball and the World Trade Center attacks. One former professional ballplayer was among the heroic dead: Michael T. Weinberg, a NYC firefighter who spent two years in the early '90s in the Tigers farm system. Another former player was among the rescue and recovery crews: Frank Tepedino, a twenty-year veteran of the NYC Fire Patrol, who was a major leaguer from 1967 to 1975, a tenure that included stints with the Yankees and the Braves.

There were also symbolic connections. FDNY Battalion Chief Vin Mavaro was working at Ground Zero in late September when he made a discovery that brought him and others a measure of hope. "I was doing an overnight at the Trade Center," he recalls. "It was at the point where we were realistically knowing there was no more rescue—it was a recovery mission." A backhoe lifted debris from the pit and dumped it in another section. "We'd look through it and see if there were any human remains or whatever we could recover," says Mavaro.

The piles he was sorting through that night, however, held nothing discernible. "It was just pulverized down to sand," he remembers. "There was nothing there. Everything was just totally gone."

The work went on for hours, when Mavaro caught a glimpse of something in the pile that he thought was a piece of concrete. "Then I saw a little bit of red stuff on it. So I took it and I started dusting it off. I saw it was round." He continued cleaning the mysterious object, and was shocked as he began to recognize what he had found. "It was a baseball. I said, 'Oh my God—look at this!'"

The captain was stunned by the discovery—amid the hundreds of tons of dust and ashes, the baseball had somehow survived intact. The ball was a promotional item for a bond-trading firm called TradeWeb, which had operated on the fifty-first floor of the north tower. (Mavaro later learned that all eighty TradeWeb employees made it out safely.)

As a lifelong baseball fan who rooted for the Mets, played in an over-thirty league, and coached his sons' baseball teams, the find was especially meaningful for Mavaro. "It became a symbol to me. Baseball has always been the American pastime. And this thing made it through. And even though we got banged up bad—great losses, great tragedy—we're gonna make it through this."

The story of the miraculous baseball made its way to Ted Spencer of the Hall of Fame and Mavaro was asked to lend the ball to a traveling exhibit called *Baseball as America*, which focuses on the significance of baseball as an American cultural force. The Mavaro ball has become one of the most popular pieces in the show.

Mavaro is happy to share the ball and the story with others, especially if it brings them some hope, as it did him. As a New York City fire chief, Mavaro was confronted with the tragedy of 9/11 on a daily basis. His battalion in lower Manhattan lost seven firefighters in the attacks. "That whole year, all we did was either work at the firehouse, work at the Center, or go to funerals," he recalls.

"I was looking for something positive. I've always tried to be a positive person and that's how I tried to look at it—that this symbol of America wasn't destroyed. It was banged up, but it was basically intact. It was good."

A Lingering Eeriness

For baseball players in New York City at the time of the attacks, Manhattan took on an eerie quality that still colors their experiences there. The Chicago White Sox had flown into the city in the wee hours of September 11, for a series against the Yankees. They were staying about two miles from the World Trade Center when the planes hit.

"It was complete mayhem, complete madness," remembers pitcher Jon Garland. "People didn't know whether to stay inside, go outside, where to go, what to do—we really didn't know what was going on or why it was happening."

With all air travel grounded, the team was stranded in New York. Aaron Rowand recalls going out for pizza on the evening of September 11, and being struck by how strange it all seemed. "The streets were empty. There was nobody out, and the people that were out seemed to be like zombies walking around in a daze. It was very eerie."

Paul Konerko recalls the relief of finally leaving the city. "We took three buses from New York to Chicago. A long bus ride. But no one cared. We just wanted to get the hell out of there."

For some players, including Garland and fellow pitcher Mark Buehrle, this was their first trip to New York City. Buehrle says it left a lasting impression that still haunts him when he's in Manhattan. "Even to this day, I don't leave the hotel when we're there, because I just have so many memories." During the tense days stuck at the hotel, Buehrle would walk down the hall or in a stairwell and "I felt like somebody was following me that was going to come do something—blow up the building or something. It's not as bad, but every time we go back there you still have that feeling, because it's the same hotel."

When the Sox returned in early October to make up the games, the mood at Yankee Stadium was also off-putting. "To me there was that eerie feeling because the season was supposed to be over already," remembers Buehrle. "It was a really weird feeling. It didn't feel like we should be there."

Helping to Heal

While many baseball players recognized the role their sport played in helping people escape the grief and horror of those days following the attacks, New York City ballplayers were most acutely aware of it. Members of the Mets and Yankees were confronted with the tragedy—and with the emotional expectations of fans who looked to them for relief—on a daily basis.

"I played for the team that represents the city that was attacked," says Yankees pitcher Mike Mussina. "And it was every day, it was everywhere from the time you got up until the time you went to sleep. I think everybody was trying to find something to grab onto. Somehow we went out there and played baseball and we let them put it aside for a couple of hours."

"As a baseball player and as a person, that means a lot when you're able to do that," says Joe McEwing, an outfielder with the Mets in 2001. "We were able to put smiles on people's faces and take their minds off things."

Kevin Appier, pitching with the Mets that year, appreciated the role baseball played in getting the city back to normal. "It definitely felt that we were playing more than just the game. Baseball was a sign of continuing on and not being crushed by the terrorists."

McEwing says that statement was important. "This game is America's best. For a hundred years it's gotten people through a lot—through the wars, through the Depression, through everything." Coming back after the attacks showed "that something like this could not break the game of baseball and our country."

Even so, playing a game—a pastime—during a time of national crisis, grief, and anxiety was, as Yankee Bernie Williams put it, "bizarre."

"I felt a little bit out of place because it was obviously one of the biggest tragedies in the history of the United States and we were trying to, in my mind, sort of act like nothing had happened for the sake of normalcy. But once I started playing and realizing how important our role was, it made a little more sense to me."

Williams, like other New York players, got involved in relief efforts. There were financial contributions (the entire Mets team and coaching staff donated a game's pay to benefit the survivors of lost public servants), but contributions went beyond the checkbook. In the days and weeks following the attacks, it was not uncommon to see millionaire athletes greeting workers at Ground Zero, visiting firehouses, comforting families, packing boxes, or helping out in any way they could.

"The first time you go down there, you're almost embarrassed, like, 'What am I doing here?'" remembers Paul O'Neill of his first trip to a family support center. "But when you see a smile on a kid's face that just lost his parents, you realize that it was meaningful to some people."

Yankees manager Joe Torre accompanied players on these trips, and found that the experience helped them all realize that baseball was not trivial in the wake of the tragedy. "When we saw the families of the people [killed on September 11], we realized we were playing more than baseball. The 'NY' on our hat represented more than the Yankees."

Mets manager Bobby Valentine was so involved in relief efforts—spending two days organizing supplies for relief workers
out of Shea Stadium's parking lot (which was used as a staging
area, with many players chipping in), helping out two families of
victims, and donating $500,000 to various 9/11 charities—that he
was given the prestigious Branch Rickey Award for exceptional
community service.

When he first made the trip to Ground Zero, he was surprised at the emotional reaction he received. "These workers
came out of the hole covered in grime and dirt. They were ex-
hausted; they were emotionally drained. And yet when they saw
the Mets hat and Mets jacket, there was a little smile, a little
thumbs-up." Valentine went back a few days later with a hand-
ful of players and "people stopped and lined up and slapped us
five, and thanked us for coming down. And told us to get back
on the field."

Victory at Shea
When baseball resumed on September 17, both the Mets and the
Yankees were out of town. The Mets were the first to return, on
September 21, for a game against the Atlanta Braves.

This was not only the first post-9/11 major-league baseball
game to be played in New York; it was the first large public gath-
ering of any kind in the city since the tragedy. Many people worried that such an event would attract a new terrorist attack.
Tensions and security were high.

So were emotions. The evening was full of ceremony honoring those lost and saluting the spirit of the city. Prior to the
game, Diana Ross delivered a stirring rendition of "God Bless
America" and Marc Anthony sang the national anthem. Rescue
workers from the New York police department, fire department, port authority, and EMS were introduced. The Marine
Corps honor guard conducted a twenty-one-gun salute to those
who died, and the NYPD bagpipe band played a mournful
"Amazing Grace."

"It was one of the more emotional moments I've ever experienced, not only on a baseball field, but in life," says Mets pitcher Al Leiter. "It was very touching and very moving."

Bobby Valentine recalls someone mentioning prior to the game that "the bad guys might be watching" on TV, and being very intentional about the attitude he tried to project. "There wasn't fear on my face, there was joy. I was ready to go. We might've been down for a little, but we were back."

Even so, Valentine acknowledges, "It was difficult to get into it." Not only did baseball seem trivial, the emotions associated with it seemed inappropriate. "In the first two innings everyone was really somber and kind of feeling, 'Are we allowed to feel excitement right now?'" recalls pitcher Steve Trachsel. "As the game progressed, people's emotions and feelings changed."

The game turned out to be a closely contested pitcher's duel. The Braves scored first, in the top of the fourth. The Mets tied it up in their half of the inning. There followed three scoreless frames. During the seventh-inning stretch, Liza Minnelli sang "New York, New York." Everyone felt the energy building, as the caution and sadness people had been consumed by gave way to competitive spirit and a desire to win.

But Atlanta went ahead in the top of the eighth. With the Mets down to their last five outs, Mike Piazza came to the plate with a runner on first.

As it was for so, many players, the evening had been a roller coaster for the Mets' biggest superstar. "When they brought the bagpipes out I just started losing it emotionally," Piazza recalls. "I was so drained and dehydrated from crying that whole week." On top of that, the catcher had made a costly error earlier in the game that gave the Braves their first run. But he found an inner reserve of strength that kicked in when he needed it. "Your body is an amazing machine—just the response that happens when you're in that fight-or-flight mentality. Your body kind of goes to a higher level."

Piazza's game went to a higher level. Though he wasn't trying to be the day's hero ("I was just praying to God to do my best"), he launched a 1–0 pitch from Steve Karsay out of the park. The two-run shot gave the Mets the lead and would prove to be the game-winning hit. Shea Stadium exploded in a swell of euphoria and cathartic release. Those present say they'll never forget the moment.

Some went so far as to suggest that the spirits of those who died ten days earlier were present in the stadium, and helping the team out.

Piazza himself thinks so. "Not to get too much into clairvoyant, or mystical, or whatever. But yeah, I think that there was definitely an energy there."

For backup catcher Vance Wilson, it was a feeling that persisted throughout the game. "No question that night you felt like there were 3,000 people behind you saying, 'Hey, let's move on, let's get some normalcy, and we're going to help you do it.' No question. It was strange. The energy you felt . . . I don't think winning the World Series would give you that kind of a feeling."

Valentine says that "when there's passion and commitment, there's always spiritual movements. When Mike rounded the bases, that passion was displayed. I had a feeling of some spiritual movement."

Sitting in the Braves dugout, pitcher Tom Glavine—who, along with his teammates, had visited Ground Zero that morning—didn't necessarily feel the presence of 9/11 spirits, but acknowledges that "there was so much more going on than the baseball game . . . It was a much different feeling. I just remember the emotion that was involved in that game."

For Piazza, the home run was something he'll never forget . . . but also something he doesn't quite recall. "I still don't remember hitting any base," he says of his trip around the diamond. "It's weird."

Piazza heard from many fans afterward, thanking him for giving them a measure of happiness and hope and NYC pride at a time when those qualities seemed most important. "It's very touching to me when people say that," he says, "because it was a very amazing moment that I'll never forget."

An Extra Home Run

A few days after the Piazza hit that had people talking about a spiritual connection between baseball and the 9/11 tragedy, another home run set the stage for a moment of solace and connection between a grieving widow and the husband she wanted to make smile, one last time.

Among those lost on September 11 was firefighter Kenny Marino. A lifelong baseball fan, Marino played local ball, was an avid Strat-O-Matic junkie, and rooted like crazy for the Mets. When he was killed in the World Trade Center attacks, his obituary in the *New York Times* was headlined: KENNY MARINO. A DEVOUT BASEBALL FAN. At the end of a memorial service for him, members of his Rescue 1 fire squad led a mourning procession to the organist's rendition of "Take Me Out to the Ball Game."

"We used to have a running joke," says his wife Katrina Marino. "His list of favorite things. Firefighting, baseball, the kids . . . and then me!"

Though not a baseball fan herself, Katrina didn't really mind sharing her husband with his boyhood passion. "I was pretty easygoing about it, because it's such an innocent, sweet, good sport, you know? I encouraged it."

When it came to his favorite player, there was no contest. Kenny Marino considered himself the world's biggest Ken Griffey Jr. fan. "He followed him since he was a rookie," says Katrina. Marino had Griffey on all his fantasy league teams. The only picture in the couple's bedroom was of Griffey. When their son was born, he was given the middle name "Ken"—not just because it happened to be Marino's first name.

"He wanted it more because of that—because of Junior—than his own namesake," Katrina says with a laugh.

Early in their relationship, Katrina, then a flight attendant, flew Ken out to Seattle for a Mariner's game. Marino got to the park early to see his idol. He didn't speak to Griffey ("He was

kind of quiet," Katrina explains), but he got close enough to pass
the slugger a present he'd brought along for his son Trey: an
FDNY T-shirt.

In the aftermath of the attacks, Katrina Marino "was in a tail-
spin. I didn't know which end was up." On September 24, she
went online using her husband's account. "I just remember feeling like I wanted to connect somehow," she says. She immediately got messages from Kenny's Strat-O-Matic buddies, who
saw the e-mail address and hoped it was their friend.

Perhaps that was what spurred her to send an e-mail to the
Cincinnati Reds.

Ken Griffey Jr. was my husband's favorite baseball player, she
wrote. *If Ken Griffey Jr. could hit an extra home run for Ken, I
know he will be looking down with a big grin.*

"And I kinda just left it at that," she recalls. "I didn't think
anyone would get it. I was just kind of reaching out in general."

Katrina had no great designs on invoking any kind of spirit. "I
don't really believe in the supernatural. Another life. I wasn't sure.
But I thought, 'Well maybe if he sees it, or if he's around . . . ,' you
know?"

The e-mail made its way to Rob Butcher, the team's director of
media relations. He showed it to Junior shortly before the game.

The 2001 season was not one of Ken Griffey Jr.'s best. He sat out
a third of the Reds games with injuries. After averaging nearly
50 home runs in the previous five seasons, he would hit only 22
that year. His RBI percentage drop was even greater.

In the week since baseball resumed, he was batting a mere
.190. That night's game against Philadelphia seemed unlikely to
turn things around: The Phillies were the only team he'd never
homered against in his career. In fact, he'd never gotten a *hit* off
them.

But in the fourth inning, having already singled his first time
up, Junior got hold of a 1–0 pitch and sent it over the rightfield
fence.

He hadn't been thinking of Kenny Marino when he stood at the plate, but says that "around first base, I realized what happened. I was just shocked. Things like that don't normally happen to me." More than anything, Griffey was happy for the family. He had no explanation for what he did, other than a belief that God had him hit one out for the Marinos.

Back in Monroe, New York, Katrina had been too busy dealing with the tragedy to follow the game. That day in particular had been one of the worst. "I went down into the city. We had to bring in DNA stuff [to help identify remains], like his razor, and toothbrush—whatever we could find. So I had been down there all day filling out all this awful paperwork."

"Then I came back and the phone rang. And someone said, 'Do you know that Ken Griffey Jr.'s just hit the home run for your husband?' And I'm like, 'No! We didn't know that!' And it was pretty neat."

It gave Katrina a small ray of happiness in the midst of some very dark days.

"Everything around that time was just so . . . surreal. I think I said something like 'Well, I know Kenny's looking down smiling.' Because he had the biggest grin. Especially for something like that. I had a warm feeling like, *I know that he saw that*. I know that."

Katrina also appreciated the special home run as something her son and daughter—just one and three years old at the time—would always remember: a connection to their father, through the sport that he loved.

"He would throw balls at three-month-old Tyler," she recalls. "He couldn't wait to play ball with them. He wanted to be their coach; he wanted to teach them how to play. And I definitely feel that's one thing I haven't been able to give them," she says. She then adds with a laugh, "He might be a little angry at me!"

The Reds invited Katrina and the kids to attend a game and receive the home-run bat, but the timing was difficult. ("Around that time, I didn't know if Kenny was going to be found, and flying was really hazardous.") Instead, the team sent her the bat. The following year, she met Junior for the first time at a game at Shea. "I have a picture of my kids climbing all over his back. He threw a ball with them. He's just a genuinely nice guy," she says.

Griffey had another surprise for Katrina. He still had the FDNY T-shirt Kenny had given him years earlier.

The Marinos did eventually make a trip to Cincinnati, where Junior again met with them. In 2004, when Griffey hit home run number 500 on Father's Day, he wore two armbands, one blue and one black. He sent the black one to the Hall of Fame. "He gave us the blue one, which is actually Rescue 1's color," says Katrina fondly.

The whole experience has Katrina rethinking her ideas about what lies beyond.

"I don't usually believe in that stuff, but I started kind of believing in certain things," she says. "When I went to the park and met Ken Griffey Jr. that first time, we were on the field and I remember standing out there feeling so lost. And I started tearing up. I don't cry very often. I don't usually go there. And I remember thinking, *This is Kenny's moment.* He knows all these guys. He would appreciate who every single person is. He would appreciate knowing all their scores and stats, and how many hits they had. And I thought, 'I hope he can see this. Because this is his moment.'"

For Griffey, the homer he hit for Kenny Marino will be "in the top five" of all his dingers.

"This situation is bigger than baseball," he says. "There's not a day that I don't think of [the family]. He risked his life for other people. That's a hero. What I do, I just play baseball. I'm not a hero."

When Griffey sent the armband on Father's Day, his mind was on the Marino children. "I was thinking about their father that they lost. I don't want them to ever forget that."

For Katrina, the story is not about her, and not about Griffey. "It was more like giving something to Kenny. *This is for you.* Maybe he could see that, enjoy it, and appreciate it. It was more for him than it was ever for me. Just knowing the satisfaction that if Kenny was watching, he would see it."

CHAPTER 11

AN OTHERWORLDLY
WORLD SERIES

For New Yorkers—and much of the rest of the country—the 2001 World Series was not about baseball. Coming less than two months after the attacks on September 11, it was a symbolic struggle of New York City to overcome odds—to rise from moments of seeming defeat in a show of strength and pride and victory.

And when the Yankees rallied against the Arizona Diamondbacks to stage emotional, unheard-of comebacks in their home games that year, some felt that more than baseball prowess was at work. As Arizona's Dave Dellucci puts it: "It felt like we were not only playing against the 2001 Yankees, but we were playing against the past Yankee players, as well as the people who had lost their lives in 9/11."

This sentiment—that the spirits of those lost in the attacks were present at the games and a factor in their inspirational outcome—is shared by other players on both teams, and by fans at the games. They intend it not as a trivialization of the tragedy, but as a testament to just how strongly the energy of a grieving city rallied around the team, and how baseball contributed to the long healing process.

From the start, the New York Yankees were aware of their role as representatives of a broken city. When the regular season resumed after a week's break following the attacks, Joe Torre met with the team and spelled it out. "I let the players know my feeling that there was more at stake than just baseball, that we had to distract the people who were suffering, and the country that was suffering at the time."

Like the Mets, the Yankees had been very involved in city relief efforts since the attacks. In addition to players making donations, visiting grieving survivors, and dropping by Ground Zero for moral support, Yankee Stadium hosted a large prayer service on September 23. Originally envisioned as an open memorial in Central Park, officials rescheduled the event for Yankee Stadium to keep a tighter control on security. Some 20,000 people attended, along with performers and participants including Oprah Winfrey, Placido Domingo, Bette Midler, and the Boys and Girls Choirs of Harlem.

What became apparent to players, however, was that the best thing they could contribute to the ailing city was the familiar joy of baseball . . . and the pride of winning. On September 11, the team was first in its division and had the second-best record in the majors. They struggled a bit in the next few weeks, going 9–8 in that time. They clinched the AL East, but faced some daunting postseason foes: Oakland, which finished the season with a 29–4 stretch to win the AL wild card; and Seattle, which won a stunning 116 games in the regular season, setting a new AL record.

The playoffs started rough, with the Yankees losing their first two home games to the A's and facing elimination with one more defeat. But it turned around in Game 3, a 1–0 victory forever famous for Derek Jeter's "flip play," in which he retrieved an errant throw from well across the field and flipped it to catcher Jorge Posada in time to tag runner Jeremy Giambi at home. The Yanks won the next two games and marched on to the ALCS, where they trounced the seemingly indomitable Mariners four games to one.

The stage was set for what would become one of the most memorable World Series in baseball history.

In just their fourth year in existence, the Arizona Diamond-backs made it to the Fall Classic more quickly than any other team. The Yankees, by comparison, had won the previous three World Series and twenty-six overall. Facing the dominant pitching of D'backs aces Curt Schilling and Randy Johnson, the Yankees struggled at the plate, losing the first two games in Phoenix and heading home to the Bronx in desperate need of a victory.

In New York, the 9/11 tragedy was still an inescapable fact of life, minute by minute. The rescue mission at Ground Zero had turned into a recovery effort, as hopes of finding survivors amid the tons of rubble were reluctantly abandoned. Armed soldiers walked subway stations and street corners and the city remained on high alert, everyone worried about another attack. Just before Game 3, the FBI issued a new warning, urging all New Yorkers to be as vigilant as possible for potential new terrorism. The World Series was considered a tempting target.

"I was actually scared to go to the Stadium because of terrorism," recalls Gregg Klayman, who had attended every Yankees postseason home game since 1995. David Freeman, who worked games recording PressBox pitch-by-pitch for Stats, Inc., felt it too. "I remember being prepared to die every time I went to Yankee Stadium."

But fans like these came to the games hoping to find relief from the relentless barrage of mourning and depression that gripped the city. In fact, baseball—though seemingly trivial—became a focal point for New York, which looked to the sport for escapism and joy.

"In the face of all that uncertainty, people were looking for something that was going to be very, very certain," says baseball fan Bob Capone, who lost a cousin in the World Trade Center and attended the World Series that year. "What could be more certain than the Yankees winning?"

It was an expectation the Yankee players themselves were conscious of. "We were playing not only to win a ring, but for the people of New York, and what they deserve," recalls Jorge Posada.

"We felt the emotions of what was going on in the city, obviously," says Willie Randolph, third base coach with the team that year. "I think emotion is a very positive thing. If you channel it right, it can work to your benefit. It can raise your level."

Game 3 was held on October 30, exactly seven weeks after 9/11. A tattered flag from atop the World Trade Center that was discovered among the rubble flew over Yankee Stadium. Security was extreme. Fans passed through metal detectors, bomb-sniffing dogs scoured the locker rooms, a Secret Service agent even disguised himself as an umpire to stand on the field as President Bush threw out the first pitch.

Roger Clemens took the mound and hurled seven strong innings, surrendering one run on three hits. The Yankees mustered two runs, which was all they'd need, bringing elation to the city. Fans turned the area around the Stadium into an impromptu street party and celebrated into the early hours. But the truly magical moments would come the next two nights.

Game 4 was played on October 31, 2001—Halloween night. It was another hard-fought pitcher's battle. Curt Schilling, pitching on three days' rest, gave up just three hits in seven innings, striking out nine. But Yankees starter Orlando Hernández matched him. The Yankees took the lead with a solo shot by outfielder Shane Spencer in the third, but the Diamondbacks tied it up the very next inning. The score remained knotted until the eighth inning, when Arizona pulled ahead 3–1.

The Yankees entered the bottom of the ninth down by two. They were facing D'backs closer Byung-Hyun Kim, who had been unhittable all season and who had struck out the side in the eighth inning. By the time Tino Martinez walked to the plate, Paul O'Neill had gotten to first, but two Yankee batters had been retired. Fans in the park and around the city were spellbound, wanting to believe against all odds that the game was not over. Facing the kind of scenario kids dream of—two out in the bottom of the ninth of a World Series game—Martinez connected with a

Kim fastball and belted a two-run shot that tied the game and sent it into extra innings.

"Tino's home run was the single biggest moment of release I'd ever experienced in my life," says Cory Schwartz, who had attended previous World Series games, an All-Star game, a no-hitter, and even a perfect game. "I remember this explosion of energy and pandemonium. People were jumping up and down. It was unbelievable, the excitement."

In the bottom of the tenth—with the clock striking midnight, ushering in All Saints' Day—Derek Jeter dug in. The idea of the Yankees winning, which seemed folly in the ninth inning, now felt inevitable. As if on cue, Jeter hit a game-winning homer to end the emotional and historic match-up.

The win was more than improbable: In World Series history, no team had tied a game with two outs in the bottom of the ninth and gone on to win it. The only thing more amazing than the Yankees' feat was the fact that they did it again the very next night.

In Game 5, the team was again down by two runs with two outs in the bottom of the ninth. Once more facing a game that seemed all but lost, the Yankees tied it up with a dramatic home run, this time from third baseman Scott Brosius. When Alfonso Soriano got the game-winning hit in the twelfth inning, Yankee Stadium exploded in a cathartic release that even longtime observers say they'd never experienced before. "It was like winning the lottery twice," says Schwartz. "People just started collapsing on each other in the bleachers."

"Looking back, it should have been a little scary," realized Klayman. "It was 55,000 people all going crazy, excited over one moment." Strangers hugged each other and the Stadium rocked with celebration long after the winning run scored. "No one wanted to leave."

Klayman also recalls "going home that night and for the first time, not thinking at all of anything bad that had happened."

For some of the Diamondbacks, there was no earthly way to explain the stunning upsets. "You could do nothing but shake your head and wonder what ghosts of the past were there. Maybe some ghosts of the recent past." Ken Kendrick is the managing general partner of the Diamondbacks. "There was something more than just a late-inning comeback going on," he says. "I'm a believer and I think the spirits of a lot of people were around during that time. A lot of people who weren't there in the flesh were there."

"It was an eerie feeling for us to go over there and lose the games the way we did," says outfielder Dave Dellucci. "It was just a feeling like there was nothing we could do to win. 'Cause we had the games in the bag, pretty much. And to lose them the way we did . . . it was almost a spiritual experience."

Many Yankees couldn't dismiss the startling, unprecedented comebacks as mere coincidence either. "[Coming back to win] one night was just heroic—that's the World Series," says Paul O'Neill. "But back-to-back nights? It was something special."

For Derek Jeter, who hit one of the game-winning homers, the spirits of those lost in September were a factor in the games. "They helped out," he says. "Maybe they helped push some of our balls over the fence and got us some of the right hops and the right bounces. But you couldn't help but feel the atmosphere, the electricity, the presence of all the people."

Fans felt it too. "There was definitely a feeling that there were people [killed in the attacks] there," says David Freeman. "It was almost like unfinished business: *We have to sit around, we have to watch them win this World Series, and then we can move on.*"

Roberta Newman attended Game 5 along with her husband, who was evacuated from the twenty-third floor of the World Trade Center on the morning of the attacks. She remembers that when Brosius tied the game "it almost seemed as if the Stadium itself became a living entity. Like the Stadium was trying to do something—or the ghosts, or whoever they were—to make people feel better."

Gregg Klayman is a little more skeptical. "I can probably say I believe something else was involved . . . but I don't know. All I can say is if anything's going to make me believe in it, that's it."

"I don't have any problem in believing a player who says, 'There was someone on my shoulder in that game, or during that series,'" says Schwartz. "It's a little bit self-fulfilling. If people think there are ghosts and spirits and stuff in Yankee Stadium and that helps them play better, then you know what? There are; they're right. If people think it's a bunch of nonsense, then they're right too. It creates its own reality."

For some players, the emotional rush and electric energy of the game was derived less from the dead than from the living— in particular, the families who were grieving the victims. "I felt like the people that were there that had lost [people] were a part of what the Yankees were doing and affected us," says Paul O'Neill.

"There were some pretty heroic things taking place in that city in real-life situations," adds Yankees catcher Todd Greene. "And obviously there were some heroic things happening on the baseball field in Games 3, 4, and 5."

"It was great," agrees Mariano Rivera. "I don't know if you would call it a blessing, or prayers, but there was something special."

Of course, New York in the postseason is well known for the so-called ghosts of Yankee Stadium (see Chapter 3)—the notion that great players from the past "help out" when big games are on the line. D'backs infielder Greg Colbrunn sensed their presence in Games 4 and 5. "You had that eerie feeling, like the ghosts of Yankee baseball past weren't going to let them lose. It was one of those auras."

Even as they were victimized by that aura, some Diamondback players had to admire it. "Those three games in New York—even though we lost—were the best atmosphere that I will ever see at a baseball game," says infielder Craig Counsell. "It was the energy of the crowd, it was everything. It's something you try to recapture and feel again the rest of your life. It was very special."

When the New York games ended, the Diamondbacks were more than eager to head home. "We were ready to get out of there," remembers Dellucci. "Because we knew that we were up against something superhuman."

The exciting, improbable wins in New York, coming in the context of a city resolutely rebounding after the devastating attacks, gave rise to a sense that fate was at work: The Yankees were meant to win the World Series in a symbolic show of strength and American pride. But that sense of destiny was quickly thwarted back in Arizona. The Yankees were routed in Game 6, falling 15–2. The loss tied the Series 3–3 and led to one of the most dramatic and unforgettable Game 7s in World Series history.

The Diamondbacks scored first, a lone run in the sixth inning. The Yankees responded with a run in each of the next two innings, taking the lead. But once again, bottom-of-the-ninth drama would decide the game. Arizona started the inning down 2–1 and facing Mariano Rivera, the most successful closer in postseason history and a former World Series MVP. Rivera had entered the game in the eighth, striking out the side and lowering his postseason ERA to 0.70. Since 1998, he had saved all twenty-three postseason games in which he appeared.

But the inning belonged to the Diamondbacks. First baseman Mark Grace led off with a single. Damian Miller's sacrifice bunt landed him on first when Rivera threw wildly to second, failing to catch Dellucci, who had entered to run for Grace. Rivera successfully fielded the next bunt, throwing out the lead runner at third. But he then surrendered a game-tying double to infielder Tony Womack and hit the next batter to load the bases. With the infield in, Luis González blooped an 0–1 pitch to shallow center, winning the game and the series for Arizona.

"It was just the right place at the right time," González says today of that momentous hit. "It was just a storybook finish."

But for Yankee fans and others who saw the New York club as "America's team" that year, it was the wrong storybook. "It was basically like God or whoever was scripting this thing messed up on the final page or fell asleep and some evil Mets or Red Sox fan came in and wrote the last page," says Klayman.

While fans were heartbroken over the result, many felt that the New York wins had already given the city the boost it needed. Cory Schwartz found a philosophical perspective on the loss. "Maybe it was supposed to be that way so we wouldn't carry the series around with us too long and lean on it," he suggests. "The Diamondbacks win closed the book on it in a way that we had to go back to the reality of life, which was the city was still in ruins, or an important part of the city, and these people are still out there who hate Americans and want to kill Americans."

Interestingly, some odd events in Game 7 had a few Diamondback players wondering if they didn't have their own guardian angels helping out. Ken Kendrick recalls that in the eighth inning "the wind kicked up. It became very cold and it started to drizzle."

Bob Melvin, the Diamondback's bench coach at the time, found it bizarre. "It doesn't rain in Arizona," he says. "Nothing was on the radar, nothing was supposed to come. And all of the sudden there was a little wind twister in the air."

Dave Dellucci describes it as "almost like a tornado. All the trash was picked up from the stands and was blowing on the field in a circular motion. It was really an incredible sight."

Dellucci was standing next to Mark Grace when the odd weather hit. "We said man, we were up against all the supernatural in New York and now we come here and it seems like we've got our own little spirits being churned up. That's what it looked like—it looked like we had a higher being involved in our stadium."

Grace himself started the ninth-inning rally with a leadoff hit. As he reached first base, the digits on the scoreboard clock in Bank One Ballpark read 9:11.

Kendrick says, "It was surreal. You almost think the ghosts of Phoenix, to the degree we have any, appeared."

The Diamondbacks—who would inscribe the phrase "9/11/01 Never Forget" on their World Series rings—were well aware that the sympathy of the nation was with the Yankees, and that some viewed their victory as ruining a story of American resilience and triumph over adversity.

"I didn't feel bad about it, but I think you kind of knew the way that most people wanted the story to end," says Craig Counsell. Randy Johnson, who shared the series MVP award with Curt Schilling, says that viewing the D'backs as spoilsports ignores the fact that the team deserved its victory. "I think it was a real feel-good story to have the Yankees in the World Series after everything that had transpired," the lefty ace says. "But it was our opportunity and everybody on our team worked extremely hard to get to the World Series."

Todd Greene agrees. "To be honest with you, the Diamondbacks outplayed us." Indeed, Arizona outscored New York 37–14 in the seven games—an inequity that further motivates some fans and players to look to the supernatural to explain the Yankee wins.

"It didn't come out the way it was supposed to," says Jorge Posada. "But I think it was one of the best series ever. It was great to try to get that fun part back to New York. It was good to see that."

Joe Torre, who had won four World Series titles with the club in the previous five years, agrees. "I hate to talk about it being the best World Series, since we lost," the Yankee skipper says. "But those three games in New York were by far the most inspirational games I've ever been involved in."

For haggard New Yorkers, still finding their way in the wake of the attacks, what those games gave the city is incalculable. "I was working at a church at the time and we were in the process of burying a lot of people," recalls Freeman, who performed music at the funerals. "I felt as comforted to go to Yankee Stadium as to go to any church or kneel in my house and read the Bible. This was the sanctuary, so to speak."

"It was safe to talk about the game," says Yankee fan Andrew Schall. "If you were talking to somebody, you didn't know what their life was like on September 11, you didn't know if they knew anybody who was lost, you couldn't really talk about anything related to that. But if you say, 'What do you think of the Yankees?' then you have a common denominator."

And what about the idea that the spirits of the departed were behind those spectacular late-inning comebacks? Yankee reliever Mike Stanton pitched in several World Series with the Yankees and says "there was definitely something different going on in [2001]." He tried to keep it all in perspective. "I think what we did more than anything else is we gave the country, and specifically New York, the ability to stop thinking about the world for a couple of hours. And if that helps in healing, great."

A 2001 Postscript: Lose a Series, Save a Life

For fans like Gregg Klayman, the Game 7 defeat undid any faith in destiny or a supernatural touch to the 2001 World Series. Especially since Mariano Rivera was the source of the loss. "He's my God. To me he's the perfect ballplayer, the greatest pressure pitcher ever," says Klayman. "If that ninth inning had been different I'd believe in ghosts and I'd believe in the mystique and I'd believe in everything. But having him lose, it killed a lot of that right away."

Indeed, when the Diamondbacks won—in dramatic fashion, against arguably the most dominant closer in the game—it suddenly seemed this World Series was merely about *baseball* after all.

But was there another potential reason—maybe an otherworldly one—for the Yankees' collapse? Rivera himself thinks a higher power was at work, providing a twist of fate that could only be appreciated in hindsight.

The city of New York had already scheduled a victory parade for the Yankees, were they to win the series. Enrique Wilson, the Yankee utility infielder, had, like his teammates, planned his postseries travel around that date. He was to fly back home to the Dominican Republic some time after the parade, on American Airlines Flight 587, leaving La Guardia Airport at 8:40 A.M. on Monday, November 12.

When the Yanks came up short in the series, the parade, of course, was called off. Wilson changed his travel plans to head home earlier. As a result, he was not on Flight 587 when it crashed into Belle Harbor, New York, three minutes after take-off, killing all 265 people on board.

"If we won that game, I would have taken that flight," says Wilson. "If I had taken that flight, I would have died."

The near tragedy changed Rivera's perspective on what happened in Game 7.

"[The loss] was stunning," says Rivera. "My throwing the ball away, losing the way we did . . . something was wrong." Naturally, Rivera "wasn't feeling good at all" about his performance. But when he learned about Wilson's brush with death, "it was like a relief." Suddenly, the Yankees losing the World Series made cosmic sense.

Today, Rivera and Wilson both view the World Series loss as divine intervention.

"I think that God let things happen," says Wilson. "[Rivera] is the best closer in the game. You don't see him lose very often." Wilson adds that Alfonso Soriano had also planned to be on that flight, though unlike Wilson, he hadn't bought a ticket.

The notion that losing the Series saved Wilson's life was eerie enough. But for Rivera, it added perspective that helped rebut criticism from some teammates for comments he made to them on the night he blew the save.

Prior to Game 7, the Yankees held a team meeting in which Torre stoked the team's already strong passions for a win. He asked Gene Monahan to speak, and the normally reserved trainer "out-Rockne'd Knute Rockne," according to one player. Torre then invited any team member to say something if he wanted. Rivera spoke up quietly. "Just get the ball to me, and we will win," he told his teammates, to their loud approval. The Yankees were juiced to bring a World Series trophy back home to their aching city.

But Rivera went further, talking about his religious sense of fate. The gist of it was: "It's in God's hands. We can only do what he has in store for us." While the closer intended this to be reassuring for his teammates, some found it sucked the energy out of the room. Instead of "let's go get 'em!" the message was more like "que sera, sera."

So when Wilson's life appeared to be saved by the loss, Rivera saw it as confirming evidence that God's hand was at work, and that his own performance was merely a conduit for fate.

"That was the answer I was looking for," Rivera says now. "Yes, we're playing a game. But somebody's life is more important."

CHAPTER 12

"CLEAR
MY NAME"

Dr. David Fletcher doesn't remember the first time he heard the story of disgraced Chicago Black Sox player Buck Weaver (Fletcher was probably seven or eight years old, he figures, and in the throes of a classic boyhood baseball obsession), but he does recall the first time he *encountered* Buck. The occasion was auspicious—and not merely because Weaver had been dead for forty-two years. It was Fletcher's wedding, a ceremony held at the site of Old Comiskey Park. Fletcher, standing at home plate with his bride, looked over his right shoulder and saw the former third baseman standing right where the former third base used to be.

"I saw this flicker of light and it was really weird," Fletcher recalls. "And there was this smiling figure." In a voice as distinct as the officiant's marrying him at the moment, Fletcher heard Weaver utter the phrase that would ultimately launch the doctor on what he now regards as a personal mission, a baseball quest in which he would invest countless hours and hundreds of thousands of dollars in the coming years: *"Clear my name."*

To understand Fletcher's story—a story of baseball redemption—one first needs to understand the circumstances that dropped a man from grace and led him to fight to restore his reputation, which he felt had been unfairly tainted.

The basic elements of the 1919 Black Sox scandal are familiar to most baseball fans: A small group of players on the Chicago White Sox team (including superstar Shoeless Joe Jackson), feeling financially underrewarded by owner Charles Comiskey, conspired with professional gamblers to throw the World Series. Whispers of foul play began immediately, and led the following year to a full-scale investigation and eventual court trial. While the eight players in question were exonerated of legal wrongdoing, they were banned for life from baseball by Judge Kenesaw Mountain Landis, who had become the first commissioner of baseball in order to repair the sport's tarnished reputation in the wake of the scandal.

George "Buck" Weaver, whose nickname originated from his big-toothed smile, was unique among the "eight men out." He refused to throw the games, accepted no money from the gamblers, and—by all accounts—played to win. (He hit .324 in the series and made no errors.) However, he knew of the conspiracy among his teammates and failed to report it. Landis banned him along with the others, declaring, "Men associating with crooks and gamblers could expect no leniency."

Weaver was thirty at the time and, according to Ty Cobb, the best third baseman in the league. He would live another thirty-five years, during which time he petitioned major-league baseball six times for reinstatement, always with the same disappointing results. He stayed in Chicago, playing semipro and even sandlot ball, and working odd jobs as a day painter, racetrack teller, and handyman. While he was still known to family and friends for his distinctive grin, he was also engulfed in a sadness that remained until his death in 1956.

"He died of a broken heart," says Fletcher.

Dr. David J. Fletcher runs medical offices in both Champaign and Decatur, specializing in occupational health. He is an assistant professor at the University of Illinois College of Medicine, and is an active member of a number of medical societies and associations. An industrious and energetic man with a certain amount of charisma, Fletcher is one of those people who seems to fill

every waking hour with some purposeful activity–
cise, reading, and the like. He has a fondness for e
derground rock and bohemian poetry that see
incongruous with his working-class ethic.

Prior to his first encounter with Buck in 1998, Fletcher was
not a man who believed in ghosts. But he has always believed in
baseball. "It has meant to me a generational bond of familial love
that is just transferred down from generations," he says. Indeed,
Fletcher got his own love of the game from his parents, who
were originally from Cleveland and rooted for the Indians. Born
in Peoria, Illinois, in 1954, David grew up devoted to the St. Louis
Cardinals. But when the family moved to Chicago in 1966, he
quickly became a Cubs and White Sox fan—dual allegiances he
maintains to this day, despite the fact that most fans of one team
consider it traitorous to root for the other. His father still holds
season tickets for the White Sox, and the two attend several
games a season together.

Fletcher has shared his love of the game with his own children. He built a ball field by the family's home in rural Illinois,
and set up a batting cage in the barn. They watched baseball
movies together, like *Eight Men Out* and *Field of Dreams*. And he
made sure he shared with them the special thrill of Comiskey
Park before it was razed in 1991.

"I love Old Comiskey," says Fletcher. "It was heartbreaking
to see them tear it down. My daughter was born in '83 and my
son was born in '87 and my two kids did both get a chance to go
to Old Comiskey Park. I always feel great because they had that
opportunity."

Even after the new stadium opened, the Fletcher family kept
the spirit of Comiskey Park alive. "I had this tradition with my
kids that I started every time we went back for a game after they
tore down the old park. We'd always have to go to touch home
plate." The site of the old stadium is now a parking lot across the
street from the current stadium. The original home plate is
marked by a bronze plaque, and is a frequent stop for fans on
their way into U.S. Cellular Field. "It sort of became a ritual."

Eventually, Fletcher was compelled to visit home plate any time he was in Chicago, no matter how far off his path the trip was. "My kids would go, 'Oh, Dad, you're not going to stop again are you?'" Fletcher would run the bases (the foul lines are still outlined on the parking lot) and touch home plate. At around this time, he started developing a fascination with Buck Weaver and incorporated this into the ritual by running the bases in character, sometimes playfully shouting, "I'm Buck Weaver. I played to win!"

"I knew around '91 or '92 that there was something with this thing with Buck Weaver that was going to take over my life," he says, unable to explain it any further. "Just a weird feeling."

In the mid-1990s, Dr. Fletcher's first marriage ended. The divorce hit the family hard. "My kids were obviously devastated with the situation. My daughter was very angry. She was thirteen and had just had major back surgery—the timing was horrible." The doctor's daughter even tore down her White Sox memorabilia to express her anger with her father when he moved out.

Nine months later, Dr. Fletcher met the woman who would become his current wife. On a trip to Chicago to introduce her to his parents, he made his ritual stop at Comiskey's home plate, running the bases as Buck Weaver. When they decided to marry a few years later, it was she who suggested they hold the ceremony at the site, knowing that it was hallowed ground for her husband-to-be. The White Sox liked the idea and the publicity that would accompany it. About thirty people attended the wedding in the parking lot during a Sox doubleheader. Another famous third baseman, Bill Melton (the Sox 1971 AL home run-champ-turned-baseball-analyst) attended. Fletcher wrote the ceremony, skillfully working in references to Buck Weaver, Shoeless Joe, . . . even the infamous Disco Demolition night.

It was in the middle of the wedding when Dr. Fletcher saw Buck down the third baseline, and heard his urgent message. "'Clear my name. Clear my name.' I thought, 'I don't know what this means.'"

It was already a day of many emotions for the doctor. "My kids didn't come to the wedding; they were mad at me. When they heard I got married [at home plate], they were pissed off at me because it was a special place I had brought them to. They thought I sort of desecrated their special bond with me."

Still, the couple enjoyed the day, watching the Sox win from skybox seats. Fletcher made no mention of his otherworldly experience. "I couldn't tell anyone," he says. "They would think I was crazy."

He put the episode aside for four years, until he had another encounter in December of 2002. It was night, and Fletcher was driving down Interstate 72 in southern Illinois, on his way home. A news item came on the radio that baseball commissioner Bud Selig had met secretly with Pete Rose to talk about Rose's possible reinstatement. Since no banned player has ever been reinstated, the meeting was thought to buoy the hopes of the families of Joe Jackson and Buck Weaver, since a new precedent for reinstating athletes could help their causes too.

"I'm listening to this and I'm mesmerized by the story—just like this weird feeling because I knew I had this prior experience at my wedding, and I had this thing for a long time about Buck, how I knew I was going to do something. Suddenly I look at the exit sign and I think I must be hallucinating. It says, RESTORE MY HONOR. I could read it clearly: RESTORE MY HONOR. I couldn't believe it."

When Fletcher stopped his car to examine the sign, the message was gone. "It went back to 'Argenta Exit 150.' But it was really weird. *Restore my honor.* What does this mean? Am I losing it?" The next day he saw a newspaper interview with Weaver's eighty-nine-year-old niece, Marge Follett. "She talked about how before she went to heaven she wanted to see him reinstated. It was very touching and it kind of reiterated the story that I knew: He would never take the money. He played to win."

A little over a month later, Fletcher was in Chicago for a meeting, which meant he had to make his ritual stop at home plate. It was the same day the White Sox announced that they had sold the naming rights to their new stadium, and that

Comiskey Park would now be known as U.S. Cellular Field. Fletcher was right there as the park was being renamed. In that moment, he had another supernatural experience, one that clarified his mission once and for all.

"I was on home plate and they're putting up the sign of U.S. Cellular. Suddenly I was possessed by this spirit and in a trance. And then this whole aura of [the original] Comiskey Park reappeared out of the shadows of the parking lot." Fletcher actually saw and felt the old stadium, circa 1940, rise around him. For about thirty seconds, he was standing not on the cold asphalt of a parking lot, but on the green grass of a baseball field.

"This cosmic thing began with the Comiskey name—that's when I really felt the experience," he says. It was "an epiphanal moment in my life.

"I saw Buck and it was like this ethereal type of thing—just by himself, old Sox uniform, smiling. And he was doomed to stay in these old confines—he can't go to the next place until he gets that closure in his life." Fletcher heard Buck instructing him to take up the cause, contact his family members, and fight to clear his name.

"That's how I got started on the mission."

A BLACK SOX REUNION

If Buck Weaver has been hanging out at the White Sox ballpark, he may be in the company of some old friends. Legend has it that Katherine Wynn Jackson, the wife of Shoeless Joe, visited Comiskey Park after her death, looking for her husband.

Shoeless Joe himself is the subject of a current story. Starting in the mid-2000s, a seagull has been regularly spotted at U.S. Cellular Field. It is said to be the reincarnated spirit of Jackson. "It always sits around the backstop," relates third baseman Joe Crede, "just watching us the whole time. It walks around by the dugout sometimes."

Crede thinks "it's a pretty neat story," but also says, "I'm not some-one who totally believes in it." Teammate Russ Gload thinks it's bunk: "If Shoeless Joe came back as a bird, I'd feel sorry for him. He was a hell of a guy." But when the gull is there, some say, odd things happen: bizarre plays, emotional home runs, manager ejections, game delays. The bird leaves and things return to normal.

Crede heard the tale of the gull from Herm Schneider, the White Sox's head trainer. Did Schneider make it up? Hear the story from some-one else? Notice that the bird had no shoes and draw his own conclu-sion? Asked about the rumor that the great hitter may be prowling the stadium, Schneider isn't spilling the beans.

"I talked to Shoeless Joe," he says with a mischievous smile, "and he said to keep it between the two of us."

David Fletcher is well aware that his story sounds incredible. He knows that people "will probably think I'm a nutcase." A man of science, he understands that what he says he experienced is not compatible with traditional, rational thought. With a large, suc-cessful medical practice, he has much at stake when talking about ghostly visitations and stadiums that arise out of thin air.

"Here I am, a doctor in downstate Illinois, you know? This can't be real. I've seen the *Field of Dreams* story, but this is not an Iowa cornfield. This is the real world."

But he also knows what he was feeling at the time—the real-ity that engulfed him, and his empathy for Buck Weaver. That night he told his wife about his new mission to clear Buck's name, leav-ing out some of the more fantastical details that led him to start the fight. Her reaction: "You're not really going to do this, are you?"

He did. The very next day he contacted Marge Follett. Marge had been passionately campaigning for Buck's reinstatement since before his death. She welcomed Dr. Fletcher to the cause and shared reminiscences about Uncle Buck that gave Fletcher a new appreciation for the Weaver story.

"She talked about the last time he met with Judge Landis. He thought he would be reinstated, and he came home heartbroken. She said he just cried and cried. It was touching. It just became a different story. I had this otherworldly experience, but then it became really real."

Next he met Marge's cousin, Pat Anderson. Buck and his wife never had children of their own, but they took in Pat and her older sister Mary when the children's father died suddenly in 1931. Mary was just four years old, and Buck regarded the girls as his own daughters. "He gave us a home and he was good to us," says Anderson. "He set a good example for us and taught me quite a bit as far as doing right and not being afraid to stick up for yourself."

Pat was impressed with Fletcher. "When you get to know him, you can't help but like him," she says. She also noted some similarities between Fletcher and her uncle. Their love of baseball was one. Their sense of justice was another. "Fletcher will fight for what he knows is right. He believes so much in this cause."

Anderson warned Fletcher that a lot of people had tried to clear Buck's name, and it couldn't be done. He told her he was different. "I'm on a mission." He mentioned an idea he had to stage a protest at the upcoming All-Star game, which was being held that year at U.S. Cellular Field. After leaving her, he developed the plan further: He would fly Marge and Pat to Chicago for the game, paying all their expenses and putting their families up in a hotel. They would use his father's season tickets to get in, which would seat them about fifty feet from baseball's commissioner, Bud Selig. How could Selig refuse to meet with these two elderly ladies who only want to clear their uncle's name?

Fletcher was unsure of how to publicize the event and initially had trouble doing so. But he feels Buck helped out there too. The doctor happened to visit the Field Museum one day, where a traveling baseball exhibit was showing. He was standing at one of the displays, which featured one of Buck Weaver's letters to a previous commissioner, petitioning for reinstatement. In the same display case was the bat Sammy Sosa used in hitting his 500th home run.

While Fletcher stood there, a phalanx of reporters suddenly appeared, along with security guards. Sosa had been found with a corked bat, and now the one in the display case was being taken out to make sure it was legit. "I was having a difficult time getting publicity about the protest and then suddenly this cosmic moment happens—and it has to do with cheating at baseball." Suddenly surrounded by media, Fletcher talked up his plans for the All-Star game with a South Side reporter, who thought it was a great story and wrote about it.

Fletcher then hired a PR firm to help promote the event. They advised changing the description from a *protest* to a *rally*, something more palatable to the public. Three days before the event, they started creating petitions, passing around flyers, painting signs, and starting a Web site, www.clearbuck.com. Fletcher spent $20,000 on giveaway T-shirts with CLEAR BUCK splashed across the front, and also created pins to pass out to the crowd.

The movement to reinstate Buck Weaver was suddenly a legitimate campaign. The group attracted much media attention prior to the game. Marge and Pat came with other family members who, along with Fletcher friends and associates, helped work the crowd outside the ballpark.

"It went very well," reports Fletcher. "We had about 5,000 people." That included Chicago mayor Richard Daley and Illinois governor Rod Blagojevich, both of whom signed the petition to reinstate Buck. So did Tommy Lasorda, and thousands of fans. Fletcher says that at least a thousand attendees wore the Clear Buck T-shirts at the game, and they are visible in just about any shot of the crowd.

One person not taking part in any way, though, was Bud Selig. Though he appeared on camera at the game saying he was "looking into it," he declined to meet with Marge and Pat. "I wanted him to give these old women [Marge was ninety at the time] the same courtesy he gave Pete Rose, but he basically snubbed them," says Fletcher. Selig later wrote the doctor saying he wouldn't meet with them.

"So next I tried guerilla warfare," says Fletcher. "I crashed the baseball meetings." Fletcher traveled to New Orleans in the winter of 2003. In the months since the All-Star game, Marge had died. "It was sad," says Fletcher. "Her whole thing was, 'Before I get to heaven I want to see him reinstated.'" But Marge always saw Fletcher as an opportunity to pass the torch, and now the doctor was running with it.

In New Orleans, he chatted up White Sox owner Jerry Reinsdorf (who said, "It can't be done"), Cubs GM Jim Hendry, and ESPN commentator Peter Gammons, who thought it was a good story and offered support. But Fletcher never got to Selig.

In 2004, the Clear Buck campaign got more publicity—articles were written in the *New York Times*, *USA Today*, the AP wire service, and other outlets. In 2005, another opportunity opened up when the White Sox made it to the World Series. There was much talk of the Curse of the Black Sox, bringing Buck's name and cause back in the news. A couple of days before the Series began, Mike Downey wrote a piece in the *Chicago Tribune* asking Selig to pardon Weaver, saying it was finally time to acknowledge his innocence.

Fletcher planned a big media splash for Game 7. He invited John Cusack, the actor who played Buck in *Eight Men Out*, to be his guest in a skybox. (A move sure to generate heat, since Reinsdorf had publicly denied Cusack a ticket to the Series, saying the Chicago native was really a Cubs fan.) Fletcher also had Pat Anderson ready to fly up. But the White Sox swept the Astros in four straight, and Game 7 never happened. The victory seemed to put the Black Sox story to rest for many fans, and the spotlight on Buck again began to fade.

Since then, Dr. Fletcher has been focusing on the Web site and waiting for the next opportunity. He wants to find the right moment for his next move.

"The timing has to be right," he says. He cites the serendipitous scheduling of the 2003 All-Star game in Chicago and the

Sox's 2005 World Series appearance as examples of "the stars aligning" to make the case for Buck.

Currently, the timing is bad. Baseball's steroid scandal has created an atmosphere in which more fans embrace banishing players for breaking the sport's rules of fair play. (Though Fletcher notes that numerous current players who know of teammates who have cheated by using performance-enhancing drugs are not being punished for failing to report it, whereas Weaver was banned for precisely that: not turning in crooked teammates.)

Although he has not yet discussed reinstatement with Bud Selig, Fletcher did get to meet the commissioner in 2005. The crusading doctor had by then launched another campaign: to create a museum dedicated to Chicago baseball (major leagues, Negro leagues, women's leagues, etc.). But he was advised not to bring up Buck at that meeting. A few months later he was on Selig's agenda to talk about reinstatement, but Hurricane Katrina hit and the meeting was canceled. It was never rescheduled.

While the Clear Buck campaign has yet to reinstate Weaver into baseball, it seems incorrect to say it has not been successful. Pat Anderson is pleased that a new generation of baseball fans have been made aware of her uncle and the drive to clear his name. Fletcher, though frustrated that Buck is still banned from the game, has found that his constant striving to restore his honor has reaped benefits along the way. He has reconnected with his children, who respect the hard work he has put into this effort.

"My daughter came to the All-Star game rally. It kind of helped us reestablish our relationship that had been destroyed because of my second marriage." His bond with his son has also been repaired. The two attended a White Sox game in June 2006, and for the first time since the divorce, Fletcher's son ran the bases with him at the site of Old Comiskey, just as the pair used to do.

It has been a while since Dr. Fletcher saw Buck Weaver. In December 2003, back from baseball's winter meetings, he left a Christmas stocking at Buck's grave, and was hoping to make contact. "I couldn't get any kind of vibe, nothing was there. It was sad." Fletcher had worked hard all year and was debating the next step. "I was like, 'How do I get this done?' And I got no signal."

The doctor's last otherworldly experience came at the All-Star rally. Amid all the excitement and attention, Fletcher had a flash-back moment in which he suddenly felt transported back in time to a fan rally that had been held for Buck outside the park in 1923. The experience only lasted about ten seconds, but was intense.

Between the museum and Clear Buck campaigns, Fletcher has so far invested more than $350,000 of his own money on his baseball obsessions. But he considers it worth it, especially for Buck. "He was a guy who had integrity and you have to relate to that," says Fletcher. "And everyone deserves a second act.

"He never ever gave up his integrity and his desire to restore his good name. That's what I'm doing now. I'm continuing that mission."

BUCK'S BALL

As unique and unusual as Dr. Fletcher's visitations have been, he is not the only person claiming to have communicated with Buck Weaver. In 2004, Linda Williamson began working with Fletcher on his dream of creating a museum dedicated to Chicago baseball. Fletcher found plenty of public enthusiasm for the idea, but encountered political ob-stacles that stalled the effort. Williamson works in state politics and knew the right people to call and proper forms to file to help get the project moving.

The doctor didn't know it at the time, but Williamson also claims a life-long "gift" for seeing and communicating with the dead. "My grandmother had this ability; my mother was very sensitive. I have it. My brother does not," she says. "I have one daughter who has it somewhat and another who doesn't have it at all."

In 2004, Dr. Fletcher hosted a conference at the Chicago Historical Society that looked at the Black Sox scandal eighty-five years after the event. Williamson planned to attend, as did Weaver's niece Pat Anderson. That morning, the three of them, along with a few others, decided to stop by the cemetery where Buck Weaver is buried. The group found the grave . . . and Williamson says she found a lot more.

"I was quite surprised to see Buck Weaver slowly forming at his gravesite," she recalls. "It was almost like a swirl—a very small, slow-motion swirl of dirt, and then it took form."

Weaver was not in uniform this time, but in a suit "that almost looked like it didn't fit him. He looked a little disheveled. He had on a tie. I remember his tie was quite short; it didn't come all the way down to his waist.

"He had his hands in his pockets and he was just standing there and sort of shuffling from foot to foot. He was wondering why he was getting so much attention. *'Why are all these people here?'*"

The experience was not particularly novel for Williamson, who says she routinely encounters "energies" on the street, in her car, at funerals, even in her shower. But she was reluctant to respond to the apparition with the others right there.

"I didn't want to say, 'Excuse me, I'm going to go talk to this ghost now.' So I'm very quietly in the background trying desperately to communicate with Buck Weaver, saying to him, 'This is Dr. Fletcher. And you remember your niece, Pat.' He was still very disheveled and he still kept asking why are all these people here.

"Then he started asking, *'Where's my ball? Who took my ball?'* And I didn't even pay any credence to it because I'm thinking 'ball'—baseball, you know? I was just watching him in amazement and was grateful that he was there. But he kept asking about his ball and I didn't know what he was talking about."

After that, the image started to recede. "It was like he lost his energy, which is often what I see. They lose their energy. He sort of slowly faded away. And that was the end of it."

Later that evening, Williamson, Fletcher, and others went out for coffee after the conference. A young woman from Pennsylvania who had come into town for the event joined them. "She mentioned that earlier in the day she went out to the cemetery, found Buck's grave, and left a baseball. There was no baseball when we were there," says Williamson. A few days later, they contacted the cemetery to ask about it and were told that groundskeepers working that area of the cemetery that day would have removed any items left on graves. "Then it all made sense," says Williamson. "This young girl had put her baseball there and he was asking, *'Where's my ball? Who took my ball?'*"

Williamson says she has encountered Weaver since then. "Buck has contacted me a few times where he's tried to communicate with Dr. Fletcher and he gets very frustrated because Dr. Fletcher has so many balls up in the air and Doc won't concentrate on what Buck is trying to get him to do. Doc is going in so many directions and he's very, very stubborn." Does Williamson relay this message to Fletcher? "There's times when I can tell him and there's times when I just have to leave him to flounder and figure it out himself."

CHAPTER 13

I SEE
DEAD PEOPLE

Baseball has its own cottage industry of pundits and prognosticators trying to predict which team will win a given series, or what kind of season a player will have, usually with mixed results. Foreseeing bigger events—life and death concerns—is another matter altogether. Who could have predicted, for instance, that Roberto Clemente would die young, or that the cause of his death would be something as unexpected as a plane crash?

As it turns out, Clemente himself did.

Roberto Clemente was in many respects a living legend when he died on December 31, 1972. In eighteen years with the Pittsburgh Pirates he had earned twelve Gold Gloves (tied with Willie Mays for the most by an outfielder), one National League MVP award, two World Series rings, one World Series MVP award, and exactly 3,000 hits. He was a twelve-time All-Star with a .317 career average.

Beyond his on-field achievements, Clemente was an inspiration to those who knew and admired him. One of the first Latino stars in the major leagues, he was a conscientious man who spoke out against racism, took seriously his role-model status in his native Puerto Rico, and spent much of his off-season involved in charity work. He died a heroic death when, on a New Year's

Eve mission to bring supplies to earthquake victims in Nicaragua, his plane crashed into the Atlantic Ocean.

Clemente was just thirty-eight years old at the time of his death. Family, friends, and fans couldn't believe that such a strong, vibrant figure could be suddenly gone.

But Clemente himself had predicted it many times. He often told his wife Vera that he would die young. Vera disliked such talk and would chastise her husband for it. But it was a theme he returned to repeatedly.

Clemente not only predicted his early death, but also its means. He was always uneasy about flying and almost never slept while in the air. Clemente biographer David Maraniss recounts that the one time Clemente did doze off on the team plane, he awoke with a start. Teammate José Pagán asked what was wrong, and Clemente replied, "I was dreaming that the plane we were traveling on crashed, and the only one that got killed was me."

In fact, plane crashes were a recurring dream for Clemente. He once told another teammate, pitcher Juan Pizarro, that he was going to die in a plane crash. Longtime pal Woody Huyke remembers that Clemente even expressed a distrust of aged aircraft—just like the one in which he died. "He didn't like airplanes. He tried to always fly planes that are used consistently. 'Those airplanes that are sitting down there, they're no good. It's like a car, if you don't use a car, it's a problem. No, I would never [fly in an old plane].'

"But you know what, that's the plane that he went into when he died. It was an old plane that was sitting there in the airport in Puerto Rico, and he hired it." Huyke figures Clemente was more concerned with his humanitarian mission than his own well-being. "You don't think about it," he says. "You do what you gotta do."

The day that he died, Roberto Clemente was not the only one foreseeing his demise. The morning he was to leave, his oldest son, seven-year-old Roberto Jr., had his own premonition. He entered a room his father was in and started walking toward him. When he got in front of Clemente Sr. he suddenly blurted out, "Don't get on the plane. I think it's going to crash." The boy was as surprised as anyone at the outburst—he didn't even know that Clemente was going to be flying on a plane that night. The words just tumbled out of his mouth.

Later that evening, he repeated his warning to his maternal grandmother (babysitting that night), saying that the plane would crash and Clemente Sr. would not be coming back. He urged her to stop the baseball great from getting on the plane. He was so insistent that the woman thought briefly about calling the airport, but decided not to, given the late hour.

After the crash, others also claimed some precognition of the event. Fellow Puerto Rican superstar Orlando Cepeda said the night felt eerie to him even before learning of the tragedy—despite it being New Year's Eve, the mood was quiet and sad. When Clemente's father, Melchor, was awoken and told his son had died, he said that he too had previously dreamed of Roberto's death in a plane crash.

None of these premonitions prepared Clemente's loved ones for his untimely death. But they may have helped prepare Clemente. A few days before his fatal trip, the Great One spoke with his friend Osvaldo Gil (who nearly took the flight with him), and expressed an uncanny sense of fate—and maybe an acceptance of what was to come. "Nobody dies the day before [his time]," he told Gil. You die when you are meant to die.

At Clemente's funeral service, Pirates pitcher Steve Blass read a modified version of a poem that originated as an ode to Lou Gehrig, another baseball great cut down in his prime. The similarities extend to at least one other trait the men shared: a supernatural foretelling of their own deaths. In Gehrig's case, it was not his own dream but a more cryptic message delivered via a Ouija board.

Gehrig and his wife Eleanor were very close friends with legendary sportswriter Fred Lieb and his wife Mary. The Liebs claimed many baseball legends among their inner circle—Babe Ruth, Grover Cleveland Alexander, Christy Mathewson, Connie Mack, and Eddie Roush, to name a few—as well as owners, umpires, managers, and miscellaneous others.

Lieb was a strong believer in the paranormal and embraced some unorthodox ideas: that Abraham Lincoln was dispatched by the spirit world to end slavery, that mental illness is a form of demonic possession, that Native American war dances summon demons who take possession of the dancers, that Lieb himself was reincarnated and had been a woman in a former life.

His wife was also interested in the unseen world. Early in her life, Mary Lieb developed an interest in reading about world religions and Eastern mysticism. She practiced transcendental meditation long before it became an American fad in the 1960s. And, according to her husband in his book *Baseball As I Have Known It*, she had "an acute sense of the supernatural." Lieb said his wife "had experiences of telepathy and precognition of events."

When entertaining guests in their home, Mary Lieb would read their palms and discern their character by interpreting their signatures. In one instance, Mary inspected the palm of the Dodgers lefty spitballer Clarence Mitchell and accurately determined that he owned racing dogs and that a jealous husband had recently chased after the lothario, brandishing a weapon.

One of Mary Lieb's acolytes was Col. Jacob Ruppert, president and owner of the New York Yankees. Each year in Spring Training, Ruppert had Mary read his palm to see if there was a World Championship lurking in there for his club that year. She predicted the team's 1932 pennant, but warned of a dry spell to follow. (Some years an impatient Ruppert would demand she "look again" after predicting the Yanks would not prevail in the coming season.)

When Ruppert's friend Col. Fred Wattenberg died in 1938, the couple claimed to communicate with him via their Ouija board for months—Wattenberg came through loud and clear, insisting he was still alive, they said. One day he told the Liebs to summon Ruppert to their home, because he had an important message for him. Ruppert agreed to come, but then got sidelined with a bad cold and missed the appointment. The Liebs made contact with Wattenberg anyway, and offered to take a message.

"I wanted to tell him that within a year he would join me over here," Wattenberg spelled out. And indeed, on January 13, 1939, Ruppert died—a little less than a year after Wattenberg's death.

The Lieb family Ouija board was a source of much interesting information. For years the couple used it to communicate with the spirit world and were convinced that their conduit was none other than Roman soldier/orator Mark Antony, former friend of Julius Caesar and one-time lover of Cleopatra. Antony preferred to talk about spiritual matters, but would converse with the Liebs on topics including the stock market (he was bullish on Westinghouse and other stocks that ended up doing well, says Lieb), sports, their daughter's boyfriends, the lost continent of Atlantis, and national politics. He correctly predicted the winner of a Schmeling-Louis prizefight, but got the 1936 presidential election wrong.

Through Antony, the Lieb social circle grew to encompass famous people outside the world of baseball. Antony brought with him guests that included Amelia Earhart (right after her disappearance) and Theodore Roosevelt (who discussed the New Deal and his hatred for Woodrow Wilson). On several occasions, the Liebs claim, Antony brought along Jesus Christ for the conversation, but when one of Lieb's pals asked Jesus to predict the winner of an upcoming horse race, the savior seemed to take offense, leaving the room and never returning.

Of all the big-name players that the Liebs became close to, they were most intimate with Lou and Eleanor Gehrig. (In the Gehrig biopic *The Pride of the Yankees*, the sportswriter played by Walter Brennan—depicted as a virtual member of the family—is based on Lieb.) They socialized frequently and held each other's confidences. Lieb learned of Gehrig's diagnosis of amyotrophic lateral sclerosis days before it was announced, but declined to write or speak about it to anyone, out of respect for his friend.

In 1939, the Gehrigs were visiting Fred and Mary at their home in St. Petersburg. It was just before the start of Spring Training. The Gehrigs had asked the Liebs to find them a house near theirs; they wanted to come down a little early so that Lou could fish and relax before the season began. The disease that would hobble the Iron Horse was not yet apparent; Gehrig had experienced some signs of weakness at the end of the '38 season and was being treated for a "sluggish gallbladder," but no one yet imagined the extent of his physical problems.

Sitting in the Lieb home, one of the Gehrigs recommended pulling out the host's well-worn Ouija board. They made contact with Mark Antony and exchanged a few greetings. Then Antony relayed a message for Eleanor:

"You soon will be called upon to face the most difficult problem of your life."

The group was "startled," said Lieb. Used to arguing with Antony, Fred protested the dark and vague message, saying it wasn't fair to scare her like that and not go further. He urged Antony to "let us in on what this big problem is." But Antony declined.

Eleanor asked if it had to do with adopting a baby. The couple had been married for six years but had no children, and had begun to talk about adoption—something Lou thought his overbearing mother would not approve. Antony responded to Eleanor's question. *"No."*

The foursome never got more information than that. But in the months that followed, Gehrig's condition grew worrisome; he was weak and just couldn't make the plays or get the hits like he used to. He muddled through Spring Training and the first eight games of the season before voluntarily taking himself out of the lineup, ending a seemingly indomitable record of 2,130 consecutive games played (a streak eventually eclipsed by Cal Ripken Jr. in 1995). A few months later he was diagnosed with ALS. In 1941, he succumbed to it.

The onus of the debilitating and degenerative disease did indeed present Eleanor Gehrig with the most difficult problem of her life. But when it was over, she declared, "I would not have traded two minutes of the joy and the grief with that man for two decades of anything with another."

AND THEY WILL CALL HIM GODZILLA

Not all premonitions have to do with those about to die. Some involve those yet to be born.

Japanese superstar Hideki Matsui comes from a religious family. His father, Masao Matsui, is a faith healer in the *Tenso Kokyo* religion, a combination of Christianity, Buddhism, and Shintoism. He came into the religion via his mother-in-law—Hideki's maternal grandmother, Miyo— who was a famous faith healer before him.

Miyo died before Hideki was born. But according to Masao, three years before her grandson's birth, Miyo "predicted there would be a pro baseball player coming from the house of Matsui."

The actual prediction came about in a rather mundane moment. Miyo was sitting at breakfast reading her morning paper when she suddenly declared that the Matsui name would one day be trumpeted in the newspaper—specifically in the baseball section. "She predicted that Hideki would be a great baseball player," says Masao.

However, she did not announce this premonition to her daughter or son-in-law. She said it to one of her deciphels, or students. Not until 2004—more than thirty years after the prediction—did the deciphel relate the story to Masao. "I was very surprised [to learn of the premonition]," says Masao. "Very, very surprised. She really had a sense of the psychic. And she could see in the other world—the spiritual world."

Here she had a pretty clear vision of the physical world as well. Hideki Matsui would become a nine-time All-Star in Japan, winning three MVP awards and three championship series before signing with the New York Yankees in 2003. From Japan to the United States, the Matsui name has indeed been celebrated in newspapers around the world.

CHAPTER 14

SHELF LIFE

For some fans, baseball memorabilia has a personal meaning and sentimental value that cannot be measured in dollars. Writer Andy Mele shared a love of the Dodgers with his father Paul . . . and that connection may have provided a conduit for one last contact on the night Paul died.

Like so many baseball fans, Andy learned his love of the game from his father at an early age. "Baseball was our life. He was a huge Dodgers fan, and so was I." Paul Mele played softball into his forties in the Brooklyn neighborhood where they lived, and took his son to Ebbets Field to watch their beloved team.

Mele says attending a game was different then. "You didn't just sit there and root, you could *talk* about the game. 'Watch Pee Wee; see how he covers second on the bunt,' things like that. We were into the game. Today you've got morons who don't know baseball. They're there to drink beer."

Mele attended his first game around 1946 and started collecting scrapbooks of memorabilia. From then on, he attended from fifteen to twenty games a season until the Dodgers headed west in 1958.

Andy also played baseball all his life. His dad always tried to catch his games. "I played at the Parade Grounds and he was a cop in Precinct 74. I'd be playing a ball game and a radio car would pull up on the grass and it would be my father to watch the game for a couple of innings."

In 1953, when Andy was fifteen and consumed by a teenager's passion for baseball, Paul Mele brought him a special surprise. "My father came home with two tickets for the World Series," he recalls. "It was the third game. We sat in the bleachers in the upper deck."

The pitcher that day was Carl Erskine and he had dynamite stuff. "We were looking over Erskine's shoulder and he had a devastating overhand curveball. The thing just disappeared from view." Erskine struck out Yankee after Yankee—14 altogether, which set a new record for most strikeouts in a World Series game. (A record later broken by Sandy Koufax with 15 K's in 1963, and Bob Gibson who fanned 17 in 1968.)

The dominating pitching performance wasn't the only excitement. "It was a 2–2 game going into the eighth inning," remembers Mele. "Then Campanella hit a home run in the lower deck in left field. The Dodgers won 3–2."

Today, more than fifty years later, Andy excitedly recalls many particulars from that day, which he regards as one of the greatest moments of his childhood. It was the most exciting game the father-son Meles had experienced, and created between them a lasting fondness for Carl Erskine.

Though Andy was a rabid baseball fan, he never collected autographs as a child or young adult. But many years later, in the 1990s, Mele was working as a security guard at the Brooklyn Public Library and came across a reference book that listed current and former ballplayers' addresses, for fans to write with autograph requests. "I got the bug," he says, and he began sending some photos to old Dodgers players, who all signed and returned them.

"Somewhere along the way, I wrote Erskine a letter and I sent him a baseball to autograph. I told him that my dad and I had been at the game and now I'm in my fifties, my father's almost eighty. We still remember it, we still talk about it—that type of thing."

Mele was pleased to get Erskine's response. Erskine not only signed the ball, but also sent two 5 x 7-inch pictures of himself, each individually autographed. On the one for Paul Mele he wrote, "Hi Pop, Thanks for being at Ebbets Field." Andy framed it and gave it to his father.

The elder Mele was at the end of his life, and Andy says that in those final years, during which his father was often ailing, reminiscing about the Erskine game "was one of the highlights of our conversations. 'You remember that game?' he'd ask me. And he'd point to the picture and say, 'Remember how Erskine's ball was breaking that day?'" Suddenly it would be 1953 again, and the father and son were reliving that magical day at Ebbets Field.

In 2000, Paul Mele died. "He was bad at the end and we knew it was a matter of time," says Andy. He got the phone call around 12:30 A.M., spoke with his wife and son, and called his daughter to tell her the news. At around 1:15 A.M., emotional and tired, Andy retired for the night.

"I get in bed and turn out the lights and I hear a noise . . . *boom*. So I get up to see if something fell off a wall. I'm thinking to myself, 'I hope I don't have to pick up broken glass.' I start walking through the house and I can't find anything. Then I just peeked into my room."

"His room" is a small bedroom filled with Andy's memorabilia. "I have my trophies all over the place, I have books. One wall is covered with autographed pictures by the Dodgers. And I had baseballs on the shelves."

When he stepped in the room, Andy found the source of the sudden noise. "A ball had rolled off the shelf. The Erskine ball. That's the one that fell down." It was the only ball that fell off an otherwise unruffled shelf loaded with items. The ball had sat undisturbed on the shelf for years.

Mele couldn't help but note the timing. "I just got the news half an hour before that," he says. "What a coincidence, that *that* baseball should fall off the shelf."

Was it a coincidence, or Paul Mele making one last contact with his son, through the sport and player they both loved? Other family members claimed unusual events that night too. "The next day my sister said that at 1:30, which was around the same time, her phone rang once. She picked it up and it was a dial tone. It turns out my mother got a phone call around the same time, but she didn't pick it up. The phone rang once and that was it. Then people were telling us how when somebody first dies, they're trying to make that last contact."

Was his dad the type to try to reach out one last time? "If he could, he would," says Mele. "I don't know how much of a believer [in ghosts] he was—he was a religious man. I'm not a believer, but when it happens, you kind of get that feeling where the hair stands up on the back of your neck."

In the years since his father's death, Andy Mele has had the opportunity to meet and speak with Carl Erskine. In 2005, Mele edited *A Brooklyn Dodgers Reader*, and Erskine wrote the book's Foreword. "He's a very nice fellow and always came across that way," he reports.

Though Andy himself is reluctant to declare the ball-dropping event ghostly, he did find the moment "kind of comforting." Especially since it involved the sport that bonded him and his father.

"Baseball was a major thing in our lives," he says. "And that World Series game was a fond memory that we never forgot."

CHAPTER 15

COMING
HOME TO REST

Baseball fan Mary Ennis loved the Red Sox and was a staple at Fenway Park for decades. Once, in the 1980s, the team named her Fan of the Year. About the only thing that could keep her out of the ballpark was death—and that, only temporarily. After Ennis died in 1997 at age 103, her family decided an apt memorial for her would be eternal rest in the sight of the Green Monster.

Figuring that the team might not think this was such a good idea, her grandnephews hatched a James-Bond-like plan. On July 5, 2002 (it took the family a while to pick up her remains from the funeral home), they put her ashes in six small plastic bags, went to Fenway, and fanned out across the park. While the stadium crowd was watching a tribute to Ted Williams, who happened to have died that day, Ennis's emissaries quietly deposited her remains onto various parts of the field. They even scattered some ashes in the stands where Aunt Mary used to sit.

Mary Ennis is just one of hundreds of baseball enthusiasts who give new meaning to the phrase "diehard fan." Spending eternity on the ball field of one's favorite club—mingling with the players and never having to worry about parking or ticket prices—is the superfan's dream come true, and perhaps the ultimate expression of team devotion.

The surreptitious ash drop, however, is never appreciated by ball clubs. In fact, it's something security guards are trained to look out for. "You see someone who is looking suspicious—looking left and right, and fidgety—and then they pull out a vial," says Sue Waitr, who has worked security at Wrigley Field since 1988. "They do it on game days and on tours."

The guards try to interrupt the deed before it is done, but that's not always possible. Waitr's coworker Floyd Nix once spotted a man leaning over the outfield wall with an envelope, shaking ashes onto the field. In addition to violating the rules, such actions pose a danger to the playing field. "Ashes kill the ivy," explains Nix. When they catch someone in the act, "we try to make sure it doesn't touch the vines. If it does, we'll water it down right after the game."

The irony, both guards note, is that if fans go through the proper channels, the Cubs will grant requests to spread ashes on the field. It happens on a regular basis. The organization lets families come in prior to games or on off days. Sometimes the event is accompanied by a small religious ceremony.

Nix has worked at Wrigley when these minifunerals take place. "Some of the ceremonies are so touching and unbelievable," he says. "It's a beautiful thing that they let them do that. Some folks have been fans for sixty, seventy years, not missing one game, even during the cold months of the year."

Now they are assured of keeping their attendance record intact.

The Cubs are one of many teams that get requests to spread ashes on the field. (Indeed, the ashes of two men—Charlie Grimm and Steve Goodman—are said to be buried at Wrigley. See Chapter 9: Friendly Ghosts in the Friendly Confines.) Policies vary, but nearly all major-league clubs like to keep such activities under wraps. "We don't advertise it," says one director of guest services, who declines to have her team identified. "But we will accommodate requests if we can."

On Chicago's South Side, the White Sox typically get from three to ten requests to spread fans' ashes each season. They allow families to do so on days when the team is out of town. As is the case at most parks, the ashes are spread on the warning track, to keep them from destroying the grass.

Few stadium workers and virtually no players are aware of it. Asked if he's ever heard of the practice, White Sox outfielder Rob Mackowiak—who plays in a part of the park where the ashes are deposited—says no. What's more, he's a little creeped out by the idea. "I don't [go for that]," he says scrunching his face. "I don't think I want to play with anybody's ashes out there."

Other players feel the same way. Told about a rumor that the ashes of Joker Marchant are buried at home plate in Joker Marchant Stadium, the Tigers Spring Training park in Lakeland, Florida, catcher Iván Rodríguez isn't pleased. "I wouldn't like that," he says. "I wouldn't like that at all." (Good news, Pudge. The rumor turns out to be false.)

But Roger Bassard, the White Sox's longtime groundskeeper, whose father held the position before him, knows how meaningful the gesture can be for fans and their families, and he supports the activity. When the Sox moved to a new stadium in 1991, he got a call from a woman during the very first homestand.

"She said, 'I just want to find out—is it true that you brought the old clay over and you put it in the new stadium?' I said yes and she started crying, which I didn't understand. And she said, 'Years ago, your father allowed us to spread my dad's ashes on the infield. And now I still know where he is.' "

"That meant so much to me," says Bassard. "If that's someone's last wish, so be it. I've done it a number of times and it always hits home with me."

Indeed, for the folks doing the spreading, leaving ashes at a ballpark can be an emotionally meaningful moment. Baseball writer and former minor leaguer George Gmelch shared a love of the game with his father, a semipro player who worshipped the

Giants. When the elder Gmelch died in 2003, George felt that the most fitting tribute he could give his dad was to scatter some of his ashes on the Giants' home field.

"I knew of others who had spread ashes in ballparks," he says. "And I had a vague memory of playing in a stadium where I knew someone's ashes had been spread around first base, which was my position."

Gmelch decided to do it in his own quiet way. Credentialed at the park to talk to players as part of research for one of his books, he tucked some of his dad's ashes in his pocket and looked for an inconspicuous moment to drop them on the field before the game.

"At first I spread a small amount on the field, but the white ashes were too visible against the green grass. Then during BP I stood behind the cage and every so often clutched some of the ashes from my pocket and bent down as if to tie my shoe, and then spread some on the ground." Making the moment sweeter, Felipe Alou—Gmelch Sr.'s favorite player—happened to be standing next to George at the time, though he never noticed what was happening.

It took about half a dozen shoe-tying bends over the course of half an hour to deposit the remains. The small amount of ashes was invisible in the dirt, but for Gmelch, they left an indelible mark.

"It felt great leaving a bit of my father in the dirt behind home plate," he says. "Each time I am at the ballpark or watch a game on TV I am reminded that a part of my dad is down there behind the catcher, with a commanding view of the action. I think he would really have liked knowing that some of his re-mains were to be laid to rest at the home of his favorite team, and in a ballpark that he adored."

Gmelch is typical of most fans who spread ashes: They want to salute their loved one's devotion to the team. But in rare situa-tions, the ballpark may provide a final resting place for those with nowhere else to go.

In 1998, the Rochester Red Wings, Triple-A affiliate for the Minnesota Twins, were asked to scatter the ashes of a man at their home park, Frontier Field. The request was unique in that the deceased was homeless, and had no immediate relatives. He had befriended a local family, who had taken responsibility for his remains, which themselves were somewhat "homeless." With no family crypt or obvious place to repose him, the family thought of Frontier Field. The man had been a baseball fan, and they knew he would like the idea of residing at the park.

Director of Media Relations Chuck Hinkel attended the service, along with a priest and the couple who brought the cremated remains. "All of his ashes were spread here," he says—unusual, since most people scatter a few symbolic remains.

Some time later, another family requested to spread ashes at Frontier Field. This time, says Hinkel, "It was a ceremony of about thirty people."

Hinkel appreciates the dedication of fans who want to make this ultimate commitment to the team, but he has developed rules about that kind of thing. He won't honor requests during the season ("that would be just too freaky") and he prefers to keep the numbers low. "You don't want to turn this into a cemetery."

As it is, Frontier Field has been officially declared haunted by a local Rochester paranormal group who visited late at night and claimed to spot hundreds of swirling spirits. Spreading people's ashes can only contribute to the park's ghosty reputation.

That's what happened in Reading, Pennsylvania, home of the Double-A Reading Phillies. In March 2005, a fan honored his brother's request to scatter his ashes at First Energy Stadium, where the two had long rooted for their favorite team. When the season started shortly afterward, strange things began happening.

Much of it involved electronic bugaboos around the stadium: wavy lines on the park's video screen, problems with the scoreboard lights, malfunctioning valves that control water supply to the stadium's heated swimming pool, switches turning off by themselves. Rob Hackash, the team's PR director, says the snafus extended to the front office as well. "Things would be goofy with the computers. You'd click on one thing and something else would happen."

Charles J. Adams III, who sits on the team's board of directors and wrote a full account of the bizarre incidents in his book
Haunted Berks County, hosted a "Chills at Phils" event following
one ball game. During it, the stadium microphone broke. The
next day, a power surge knocked out four of the six light towers
during the game. Fans sat in darkness for twenty minutes.

Groundskeeper Dan Douglas even suspects he saw what
might be the departed fan's ghost. He was in the storage area in
the rightfield corner of the park when he spied a mysterious
shadow high up on the wall "where critters couldn't get." He
turned on the light and looked around, but couldn't find anything.

Most of the odd occurrences happen pregame and, fortunately, don't seem to impair the team. "Balls aren't taking crazy
hops, or anything like that," says Hackash. But the strange
glitches, coming right after the ashes were spread, has led to
speculation that a ghost is in the machine. "I'm sure there's a
logical explanation for everything bizarre that's going on," reasons Douglas. "But right now I blame [the ashes]. It's easier."

For fans who want a little more glory than a particular team's
ballpark, there's always Cooperstown. Doubleday Field, just
down the road from the Baseball Hall of Fame, has accommodated numerous scatterings—allegedly, ashes have been spread
at all nine field positions. Among the remains known to have
been deposited are those of baseball historian Harold Seymour
and Emmett Ashford, the first African-American umpire in
major-league history. Numerous amateur players also call the
field home for eternity.

Those spreadings were quiet and respectful, but not all fans
have that kind of tact. On August 31, 2005, John Griswold
jumped over the third-base fence at Safeco Field and raced into
the outfield. He was holding a Seattle Mariners souvenir cup,
and quickly poured the contents onto the grass before police
could catch up with him. When they did, he explained that it was
his mother Dianne's birthday. The Mariners were her favorite
team. And that was Dianne in the cup.

But even that was better than the scene at Safeco in May of 2002. An airplane pilot had been hired for what he called a "routine ash drop," in which the cremated remains of a Mariner's fan were to be released over the field. The plan went awry when the container holding the ashes fell out of the plane and smashed against the roof of the stadium. The contents scattered far and wide. Authorities, who saw a white substance being dropped from a plane over south downtown Seattle less than a year after the 9/11 attacks, began cordoning off the area and evacuating people before discovering what had happened.

Fans who wish to avoid such a fate will be happy to know that they have other options. In 2006, Major League Baseball announced a new venture with a company called Eternal Image, in which officially sanctioned caskets bearing the logos of fan favorite teams will be available for sale. One can, for example, rest in the peace of an official Yankees coffin, complete with interlocking "NY" and blue-and-white design. Caskets and urns will also be available for the Red Sox, Tigers, Phillies, Cubs, and Dodgers as of 2007, with hopes to eventually license all thirty teams.

Well before the deal was announced, Eternal Image said it had already received over a thousand requests for such burial receptacles, from fans literally willing to take their baseball devotion to their graves.

A REPOSITORY FOR THE IMMORTALS

Fans aren't the only ones looking for a safe baseball haven to spend eternity. Players need a final resting place too. When Orioles 1965 Rookie of the Year Curt Blefary died in 2001, his wife fulfilled his wish of scattering his ashes at Memorial Stadium, which was in the final stages of demolition at the time.

The Gehrig family had a harder time finding eternal rest. When Lou died in 1941, his body was cremated and his ashes locked in a monument at Kensico Cemetery in Valhalla, New York. But his parents and his widow, Eleanor, didn't like the fact that fans frequently visited the grave, leaving notes and baseballs and other memorabilia behind. On one occasion, Eleanor claimed, vandals tried to steal Lou's ashes, going so far as to break into the crypt. She wanted a more private and respectful resting place for the Iron Horse.

Gehrig's parents may have been the first to suggest moving the ashes to the Baseball Hall of Fame in Cooperstown. Eleanor came to favor the idea too. In 1946, she began discussing the possibility with staff from the Hall, who quickly embraced it. In fact, they envisioned an entire new area of operations for the museum: housing the remains of baseball greats. They would call their mausoleum a "Repository for the Immortals." The museum's architect drafted some designs, one of which would store the ashes of enshrined players directly underneath their Hall of Fame plaques.

The project was kept top secret as numerous details were looked into, such as the legal ramifications of storing human remains on site. As late as 1949, Eleanor Gehrig was still interested in the idea. But she put the plan on indefinite hold after the story was leaked to a New York newspaper, and seemed to abandon it altogether after that. Having lost their big fish, the Hall of Fame did not pursue the notion of storing the remains of the greats any further. Gehrig's ashes are still at Kensico Cemetery, where they were joined by Eleanor's ashes in 1984.

CHAPTER 16

ROOM 231

The saying goes that you "Don't Mess with Texas," but it seems ghosts don't pay that much heed. Players in the Texas Rangers' farm system have been messed with at team hotels for years. Travis Hafner, Michael Young, Scott Podsednik, Craig Monroe, and Carlos Peña all heard the stories coming up through the minors. Some of them even had a few encounters of their own.

The trail of terror started in the late 1990s with the Savannah Sand Gnats, which allegedly had run-ins with the paranormal at the Partridge Inn, visiting hotel for the Augusta Green Jackets. Teammates complained about lights flickering in their rooms and disembodied footsteps in the hallway, but the most oft-mentioned story on the team had to do with Travis Hafner and a bed. Asked about the incident several years later, the hulking Indians slugger neither confirms nor denies that the incident happened, saying he has hardly any recollection of his visits to Augusta. But at least a couple of his teammates vividly recall Hafner telling them that he had woken during the middle of the night to the sensation that someone was forcefully shaking his bed. "He was all freaked out," says left-hander Andy Pratt. "And we were all over him, 'No way! No way!' He's a big guy—who's gonna shake a bed with him on it?"

The Hafner story had made the rounds in the South Atlantic (Sally) League, so frightening veteran Seattle Mariners starter

Horacio Ramírez, then with the Macon Braves, that he feared leaving his hotel room after dark. "Sometimes you go out to the vending machine or to walk around and you feel like somebody is behind you all the time. You just kind of freak."

Sand Gnats catcher Jason Torres had the Hafner incident on his mind and was bracing for the worst on the next visit to the Partridge—and the hotel promptly delivered. Torres was shaving in his room with the water off when he noticed the mirror fog up and felt the room temperature drop suddenly. Then things turned weird. "I started seeing my breath and it was getting freezing cold. The light started flickering and out of the corner of my eye I saw somebody. When I looked, there was an old lady there. It was a large white dress. She had a hat on. She was just staring. I ran down the stairs screaming like a little b——. I mean everybody knew I saw something, because I was sweating and I was pale and my heart was beating fast. And everybody believed me because they knew some s—— was going on. They were like, 'Calm down, calm down, we know, we know.'"

Pratt found the hotel's stately southern charm unnerving. "The place was an old southern mansion and had real old wooden floors," he says, "so everything you did made a noise. You could be lying in bed and you'll hear the floor creak. I remember there were rocking chairs in the middle of the room and you'd always wonder, 'Are you gonna wake up in the middle of the night and see the rocking chairs rocking?'"

In late July, Andy Pratt was called up to the Tulsa Drillers and was paired to room with future MLB All-Star shortstop Michael Young, who had been traded from the Toronto Blue Jays only ten days earlier. According to Pratt, the Drillers were unique; not only were they stacked with future major leaguers—himself, Young, Carlos Peña, Darren Oliver, Matt Miller, Craig Monroe, Jason Grabowski, David Elder, and Scott Podsednik—but there were a "bunch of jokesters" on the roster who kept the team loose. And it was their sense of fun that made some of the more unsettling moments at the Shoney's Inn in Bozier City, Louisiana, a little more bearable, particularly after Pratt and Young were assigned Room 231, better known at that time in the Texas League as the "Haunted Room."

Everyone on the club had heard stories from other players in the league about the infamous room. "I stayed in the room when we went back to Shreveport that next year," says pitcher Dave Elder. "I didn't see nothing, but I can't dismiss it. There are too many things that suggest that they're there."

"Every time I was at that hotel, I had a tough time," says Carlos Peña. "Jason Grabowski stayed there by himself in the room because he was trying to be tough. 'Why are you trying to investigate stuff?' I kept telling him. 'Use my room, dude.' And he said, 'I'll stay in there. I'll show you.' "

Young got wind that a ballplayer had hanged himself in haunted Room 231, although he "was not believing a thing." His roommate had heard a number of stories about the room, including a traumatic night L.A. Dodgers blue-chip prospect Luke Allen spent there earlier in the month.

"I still get goose bumps and the hair on my neck stands up when I tell my teammates," says Allen. "Around two or three o'clock one morning, I woke up and saw a lanky, shadowy figure with its arms waving by its hips as it walked past the bed toward the bathroom. For some curious reason, the bathroom light was on. As the figure turned back toward me, I stood up and called out my roommate Rich Siatta's name and at the moment Rich woke up, the figure vanished, before I could make out its face. I told Rich what had happened and he freaked out. 'Let's get out of here!' he said. So we go down to the front desk and the night clerk looks just like the shadow I'd seen in the room—same build and posture. He was kind of pale-faced, almost looked like a ghost. I sent a security guard to the room. He came back down and says he didn't find anything, then tells me, 'Well, I believe you. Somebody died in that room twenty years [ago tonight].' "

At the game the next day at Shreveport's Fair Grounds Field, Allen was at his position at third base when all of a sudden he started having double vision. He saw Shreveport batter Tony

Zuniga both at the plate and behind the plate. He called time and the trainer and coaching staff came out. The coach pulled him from the game and the trainer drove him to the hospital where he underwent tests. A doctor sporting cowboy boots and a long beard told Allen he'd experienced hypoglycemia and that what Luke had thought he saw in the motel room that previous night was due to the drop in blood sugar. It had been all in his head.

To this day, Allen strongly disagrees. "Maybe that doctor didn't believe that kind of thing," he says. "I'm convinced I saw what I saw. I was awake. I was conscious. I know I saw a moving shadow."

Four days later the highly touted third baseman, ranked that year by *Baseball America* as having the best infield arm in the Texas League, took a groundball to the face, fracturing his right orbit bone and knocking him out for the season.

The Drillers got word of Allen's misfortunes because right-hander David Elder and Allen were close friends and kept in touch during the season. During the nine-hour bus ride from Wichita to Shreveport the following week, the subject of Shreveport ghosts came up several times and players accepted the idea that the Shoney's Inn was indeed haunted. They had heard that their bus driver Jesse had suffered a mild heart attack in his room during his previous stay at the hotel and many players jokingly wondered aloud if supernatural forces were not at work in both his case and Allen's. As the bus drew near Bozier City, Carlos Peña was one of many players with a sinking feeling in the pit of his stomach. "We always knew it was haunted," says the Rangers former first-round draft pick. "Just getting there, the front desk, everything just seemed like out of those horror movies. It was scary, it really was. I always had a hard time sleeping in that hotel. I always thought the worst in my own mind. I didn't like going there, just because of the stories that we heard. Nothing specific—I think it's just the anticipation of something happening that probably gets you more than anything else."

Fortunately, baseball provided a distraction. In a rain-shortened game that evening, Tulsa pitchers Derrick Cook and

J. J. Pearsall shut down Shreveport, allowing only two hits over six innings. Following the game many players headed straight to the nearby Horseshoe Casino because, as Andy Pratt puts it, "We didn't want to spend the night hanging out in that hotel." With sleep a necessity, players eventually did have to face their fear or revel in it. As they retired to the hotel that evening, some players did not want to go anywhere near Room 231, whereas the team clowns gravitated toward it. David Elder recalls Tom Sergio stating over and over that he wanted to stay in the room, while outfielder Scott Podsednik was "freaked out" by it.

Podsednik had a reputation for being squeamish. Two months earlier, Elder had been chopping ice in a cooler at his locker one morning before a day game when his hand slipped and the pick traveled straight through his thumbnail and out the other side. Podsednik was sitting right next to Elder at his locker and watched in horror as Elder sat down and studied his punctured thumb. He'd missed all the nerves, the bone, the blood vessels. Elder pointed out to his neighbor that it didn't hurt and he could see right through the thumb. Podsednik fell off his seat—he'd fainted.

"Yeah, he didn't want anything to do with that room," notes Pratt. "He was one of a group of guys who were born not to deal with it. But a lot of the rest of us wanted to stay in the room or play jokes on those who didn't. Michael and I were among a group of guys who were walking through the hallways pounding on room walls of nervous teammates."

Laughter was ultimately the way Young and Pratt dealt with a night forecasted to play out like a bad dream. The two new roommates barely knew each other and had hardly spoken about how they truly felt about staying in the room, but they got along well and shared the same sense of humor, which put their minds at ease as they dozed later that evening.

One hour into his sleep, Pratt awoke and noticed a shadow in the corner of the room by the door. "It was kind of this thing where you don't know if you saw it or not," he says. "I remember waking up and seeing something, and waking Mike up and saying, 'Did you see that? Did you see that?' "

"I think we might have even put something against the door—like a chair or something," recalls Pratt. "I think that was the point where we started joking around and writing stuff on the walls—anything we could think of. I think it was more of just like a joke or superstition to scare whatever it is off."

Young tells a different tale, in which Pratt was much more agitated. "Andy wakes me up in the middle of the night and says he saw a ghost above him. He started freaking out." Young wasn't having any of it. "I got a big glob of toothpaste and put a big cross on the door and I told him, 'Is this good enough for you? 'Cause I'm going back to sleep.'"

Young says that he didn't witness any ghostly activity that evening and jokes about his roommate's sighting. Pratt claims that Young reacted seriously to a series of events that happened that evening. The discrepancy between the two accounts may have to do with the passage of time and the embarrassment of talking about it.

"We were freakin' out because we had just gotten into town," says Pratt. "And we were thinking about every little thing we heard that night. So we were just doing all kinds of stuff. 'Did you hear that? Did you hear that?' At the time, all of it was real."

CHAPTER 17

IF THE
MONSTER COULD TALK

After the last fans straggle out of Fenway Park following night games and the reporters head upstairs after postgame interviews, the field becomes dark, lit only by the glow of the surrounding city, wall advertisements, and the press box. In the darkness, cleaning crews with blowers pass through every seating aisle in the ballpark, taking cups out of the holders and pushing floor debris into the main aisles, where it's shoveled into carts. The work is tedious and can stretch until six in the morning. The ballpark is silent except for the humming blowers and the sounds of carts being loaded with trash. The field below, which holds memories of Ted Williams's good-bye home run, Carlton Fisk's foul-pole theatrics, and David Ortiz's walk-off magic, is resting. Or so it seems.

José Matos has supervised the overnight cleaning crew for two years and very often late at night he hears what sounds to him like the rhythmic crack of a bat. "When I hear it I always go check it out, and it's dark and always early in the morning. At times it's a person, because we have many personnel. But often I don't see anyone and when I call out no one answers."

The noises aren't confined to the field. On several occasions he has heard an otherworldly cry coming from the Green Monster seats. "I always hear someone screaming," he says. "Like a fan to a player." When he investigates, he finds nothing. His first year he heard it just once and thought maybe someone was horsing around. Then an old friend who used to work at the ballpark mentioned a rumor that the "phantom" of Babe Ruth comes out usually at night. That's when Matos became convinced that something out of the ordinary may be calling Fenway home.

It may even be using the urinals. Matos was cleaning a restroom on the second level when he got the sense he was not alone. "I felt like someone came into the bathroom while I was there. I heard the faucets. So I asked, 'Hey, who is there?' " Nobody answered. Matos investigated and found the restroom empty. He went downstairs and asked his coworkers if they had been up there. They had not.

Fellow cleaning crew supervisor Francisco Cotto hasn't had odd experiences himself, but his granddaughter used to work in the press cafeteria at night by herself and was spooked by it. "One day she told me, 'Grandpa, send somebody else to work with me. Because they are closing and opening the doors on me up here, and I'm not going to be here by myself!' She didn't identify who "they" were, but it was clear she was not talking about flesh-and-blood coworkers.

The strange happenings sometimes have Matos questioning his own senses. "I think, 'Damn, am I going crazy?' " Sometimes he finds earthly answers for the odd noises—a red-tailed hawk on Fisk's pole, a security guard making the rounds, or wind rattling the ballpark gates. But more often than not he searches the park and finds no source. "Sometimes I hear steps coming up behind me," he says, "and I see nobody."

Nevertheless, Matos insists, "I can't say I'm scared." That's because working at Fenway is a treat for this baseball fan, who pitched and played third base in his native Dominican Republic. "I feel a bit happy to have these experiences," he says, "because of the history of this stadium. It's a large satisfaction to be closer to the field where many major leaguers played."

John Cushing, a third-shift security guard on Friday evenings, agrees. He grew up in North Roxbury and used to take the trolley to games. "First few days I was working, I was like, 'I can't believe I actually work here.'"

His love for the Sox makes it a pleasure to handle what oddly enough can often be a social job. The night security guards who sit by Gate B are in many ways overnight spokespersons for the team. Late-night passersby will ask the outcome of the game, or pound their fists and cheer as they walk by and shout "Let's go Red Sox!"

"People driving east on the turnpike may pull off after passing Fenway. They'll park, come up, and say, 'I don't want to go home. I came here all the way from Buffalo and I just want to be around the ballpark.'"

As a diehard Sox fan himself, Cushing understands their motive. "When you walk through here [Fenway] alone at night you definitely feel like someone is here with you. Not so much a ghost—it's not like the ghost of Ted Williams appears. It's just that there's so much history in this building. You really feel it, especially when the Sox are on the road and I'm the only one here. These walls contain history."

CHAPTER 18

LET'S TAKE
THE STAIRS

Perhaps no baseball tradition is more time-honored on the road
than the veteran player teasing the rookie. Unless it's the tradition of ghosts haunting players' rooms.

Ellis Burks learned this the hard way in 2003. The veteran
outfielder has always been a team leader with a statesmanlike
presence in the clubhouse. Players who came up as rookies
under him, including C. C. Sabathia and Coco Crisp, cite him as
one of the players they learned from the most—not only about
the game, but how to handle the pressures of fame and the big
leagues. Burks, they say, is someone they respect completely.

But they both know Burks's impish side too. On team trips to
the Westin St. Francis in San Francisco (the visiting team hotel
when playing the Oakland A's), Burks loved to tell players that
the hotel's famous glass elevators were haunted. He repeated a
story that years ago, the elevator had suddenly dropped, killing
all the passengers inside. The victims now haunt the confined
glass booths that led them to their deaths.

As stories go, this one had bite. The elevators in question are
known for their speed: They move at a thousand feet per minute,
and can travel from the thirty-second floor to the lobby in less
than thirty seconds. Located on the exterior of the building, they
offer a panoramic view of downtown San Francisco and the bay.

Riding in them and looking out the windows, it's easy for passengers to imagine they are in freefall.

What's more, the Westin St. Francis itself is rumored to be haunted. It certainly has an infamous history. Entertainer Al Jolson died there while playing cards in one of the rooms. Sara Jane Moore attempted to assassinate President Ford in front of the hotel. Silent film comedian Fatty Arbuckle hosted a wild party in his suite in 1921, which led to the death of one of his guests, and eventually criminal charges of rape and murder that ended his career. (The suite is still there, and players such as Luis González routinely stay there.)

In short, the Westin St. Francis is the kind of place tailor-made for prankish baseball veterans looking to have some fun with the young and impressionable.

C. C. Sabathia had Burks's voice in his head whenever he rode the elevators. He won't room at the hotel—partly because of the stories and partly because he lives nearby—and stays at home when the team is in town. But like all players, he's still assigned a room there, and ends up spending time at the St. Francis when playing the A's.

In May 2004, he had a memorable experience. Five buddies came to pick him up on the fifteenth floor. The group stepped onto the elevator and pressed the button for the lobby. "We're going down. The elevator stops on the eleventh and opens up." Nobody was in the hall. Instead, "a gust of wind comes past us," Sabathia remembers. "I had chills."

The doors closed and the elevator reversed direction. "We go back up past my floor to the seventeenth—two floors past mine. The elevator door opens up and a gust of wind goes past us."

The spooked player and his friends got off. They took another elevator back to Sabathia's room.

"I was like, 'Man, dude, that was pretty weird, man. That was really weird.' I believe in ghost stuff, and they say when they're by you, it's a chill or a gust of wind or something like that. So I believe [a ghost] got on the elevator and was going to seventeen."

Coco Crisp arrived at the hotel in April 2003. On the Indians char-
ter bus ride, Burks had been telling him and other rookies about
the haunted elevator. Crisp sensed he was being joshed, and
wasn't buying it. "I was like, 'Ah, shut the hell up!'" says Crisp.

As soon as they arrived at the hotel, all the players made a
beeline inside. They wanted to get a few hours' rest that evening
before an afternoon game the following day. The veterans took
the first available elevators, one of the unwritten rules in the
baseball hierarchy.

When the next door opened, the rookies all got in together
and pushed the button for the twenty-first floor. They soon found
something strange happening. "It started doing that flickering
thing," Coco says of the elevator lighting. "It starts off bright.
Then it dims. Then it comes back bright. I'm like, 'Dang!'"

Crisp knew that the light fluctuation was normal for those elevators, but it jarred him enough that he couldn't sleep that
night. "I know [Burks] was joking," says Crisp, "but at that time
I didn't. That whole night I was wide-eyed."

The man responsible for Crisp's unease slept solidly through the
night. But he got his comeuppance in the morning.

Burks rose at 8:30 A.M., fetched a newspaper outside his
hotel room door, and returned to his comfortable bed. As he lay
there reading, he saw someone out of the corner of his eye walking across his room. He looked up and saw "the back end of a
woman with a long blue dress walking past the door" to an ad-
joining bedroom.

Startled, he said, "Excuse me, Ma'am. I don't need room service." There was no response. He assumed the woman hadn't heard
him. "I don't need room service," he repeated. Not even a stir.

He got up and went over to the doorway and didn't see anyone. He looked behind the curtains and in the other bedroom. "I
know I saw that," he thought. "I'm not tripping." He closed the
door to that room, and started to get jittery. Burks called the
Cleveland Indians' traveling secretary and said, "Hey, Mike. Do
you happen to know if any other rooms are available?"

"It's sold out," he was told.

"I just saw a woman walk across my room. And I'm not tripping. I don't drink. I don't smoke. I wasn't imagining it."

But the kicker was yet to come. Burks says he turned on the hotel channel, which runs a video highlighting some of the troubled history of the place. "There was a murder at the hotel two years before, and it was in that room," he says. "Same room!"

The woman-in-the-blue-dress experience may not have happened in the elevator, but Burks is convinced something supernatural was going on. And the lesson left its mark. The next time Burks came through San Francisco, he was with the Red Sox. "I got the same room," he remembers. But not for long.

"I said, 'No! Change that room now!'"

CHAPTER 19

FOWL BALL

When lefthander Bill "Spaceman" Lee says that the late Tom Yawkey is looking down on him from above, he's not referring to the heavens.

According to Lee, the paternalistic team owner of the Red Sox first dropped by to say hello in the players' parking lot the day after his passing. As Lee headed into Fenway Park that afternoon, a pigeon landed right in front of him. Lee stepped to his left and the bird walked in front. He stepped to his right and again the bird blocked him. The shuffling continued until Lee said, "Tom! I gotta get to the ballpark." In deference, the bird flew off.

"Tom keeps coming back," says Lee. "He's like a bad meal."

The friendship between Yawkey and Lee in life—never mind the hereafter—might seem improbable: the conservative owner of the Red Sox and the pseudomystical, free-spirited southpaw. Yawkey would take a limo to the stadium; Lee would jog in from Harvard Square. Yawkey was a private, guarded man who did charity work around the city and never trumpeted it. Lee, who was outspoken, whimsical, and the perennial go-to man for the press, once wore a gas mask during BP to protest air pollution. Yawkey was thought to be racist, signing the Red Sox's first African-American player—Pumpsie Green—long after every

.ther team in the majors had integrated. Lee expressed strong views against racism both on the team and in Boston.

Yawkey was close with team personnel. During the off-season he would often invite players to go quail hunting on his twenty-thousand-acre South Island Plantation in South Carolina. In the early years, he even took BP with the team. In his advancing years, he played pepper with the clubhouse staff while the team was on the road, came into the Red Sox clubhouse to get a rub-down from equipment manager Vince Orlando, then took a whirlpool. He mingled with players and took interest in their personal lives. He kept a locker next to Carl Yastrzemski, so the pair could talk baseball.

Lee shared Yawkey's respect and love for the game. Between the lines, the southpaw was one of baseball's fiercest competitors. In the mid-1970s, he won 17 games three years in a row using a juggernaut of pitches with pinpoint accuracy, before tearing a ligament in his shoulder during a classic brawl with the team he hated and taunted, the New York Yankees. In front of the scribes, he voiced his dissatisfaction with the state of the game—mainly, the various changes over the years (artificial turf, concrete stadiums, designated hitters, treating ballplayers as commodities) that made baseball feel more like a business and less a kid's game.

The two men also held an appreciation for the outdoors. Lee subscribed to *National Geographic*, and when he went for a run, he would often leave the latest issue at his locker. During the course of the 1975 season, when he returned, the magazine would be gone. One afternoon he was meeting with the team's GM Dick O'Connell in his office when Yawkey popped in, handed Lee a brown paper bag full of *National Geographic* magazines, and said, "I think these are yours." Then he sat down with Lee and they started discussing wildlife in South Carolina.

Yawkey mentioned the southern pine beetle, a bark-boring insect that would decimate the saw timber used by his lumber companies, and how he used to spray his forests with DDT.

He recalled how in the 1930s he used to love watching the massive ivory-billed woodpeckers as they flew with swift, arrow like precision through the forest of his property. The birds had brilliant white bills, white patches on the trailing feathers of their enormous wingspan, and prominent scarlet or black crests. He lamented that the birds had become extinct.

Lee told him that by eradicating the soft pine beetle, he in fact had decimated South Carolina's ivory-billed woodpecker population, which were natural predators of the insect's larvae.

Lee remembers that Yawkey's eyes welled up and he acknowledged that he had never made the connection. It was at that point that Lee first introduced the idea of reincarnation. "I think you gotta get it right on this planet. And you gotta tread lightly on the planet."

Just as Yawkey differed from fellow run-of-the-mill owners, Bill Lee was a breed apart from his peers. Having attended USC on an academic scholarship and earned a master's degree in geography after entering professional baseball, he was more well read than the average ballplayer who signed out of high school. His eccentricity and sometimes outrageous statements also detracted from his message, which was often insightful and always consistent.

"[He was] obviously very intelligent, very well read and able to invoke unusual metaphors and personalities and names and literary references," noted *Boston Globe* columnist and author Dan Shaughnessy, in the award-winning documentary *Spaceman: A Baseball Odyssey*.

"His theories on everything were completely different, for they were the opposite way of what you would normally think," added former Red Sox manager Dick Williams. "But a lot of times he'd be proven right in the long run."

Out of the assortment of unusual opinions he shared from day to day in the clubhouse, his spiritual ideas were probably the least confounding to his peers. After all, the locker room is a superstition shopping mall, and players go through a litany of unusual practices to concentrate and tap a vein of fortune. Luis Tiant worshipped Santo Barba and wore white from head to toe outside of Fenway. In the spring of '76, Laurie Cabot, a practicing witch from Salem, "un-hexed" outfielder Bernie Carbo's bat to halt a Sox ten-game losing streak. So the fact that Lee practiced transcendental meditation before he pitched, spouted off wry cosmic ponderings to media, and once theorized that Carl Yastrzemski's longevity in the game was due in part to his uniform number 8 (which, when Yaz lay on his side on the trainers table, represented the symbol for infinity), made few waves among his peers. Particularly because he was intensely loyal to his teammates and one of the harder working players on the team.

No one knows for sure why the largely conservative Tom Yawkey was open to reincarnation-as-a-bird beliefs. During Lee's off-season visits to Fenway to pick up his *National Geographics* from the owner's office, Lee and Yawkey would engage in more talk about the environment. And the men seemed to truly enjoy the conversations, particularly when the discussion turned to stewardship of nature.

Lee narrowed his forecast when he informed Yawkey he would most likely return to earth as a pigeon. It was well known that in the 1940s, Yawkey and Ted Williams would shoot the birds to reduce their population inside the ballpark. Yawkey had stadium workers go up and rattle the rafters. The birds would then fly around in a circle, and Yawkey and Williams picked them off with 20-gauge shotguns. Lee embraced the Hindu notion that wildlife should never be killed unnecessarily.

"Hindus say a prayer every time they get up in the morning," explains Lee, "just for all the things they kill on their lawn mower. I say a prayer for all the animals I kill. You step on them intentionally and you shouldn't. They've got a reason to be out here, too."

Lee's theories on the afterlife took on added meaning the following season when Yawkey was in the late stages of leukemia. "Near the end I used to go visit him a lot," recalls Lee. "I kind of put the idea in his mind, as far as the hereafter and thinking of the future. We had some nice discussions."

Lee felt sure his comments had an impact: "It really relaxed him. I think I have a soothing way and am pretty blunt. I don't dodge questions and I kind of tackle things head on. I think he appreciated that frankness."

Yawkey lost his battle with leukemia at New England Baptist Hospital on July 9, 1976. Lee remembers a thunderhead forming over Fenway, on an otherwise perfectly sunny late afternoon, moments before the team got word. Then it began to sprinkle.

"The next day the pigeon landed in front of me right where you make the turn off of Yawkey Way into the parking lot," says Lee. "And then someone told me that after the last game of the season, a pigeon crashed headfirst into the centerfield bleachers. Kind of committed suicide because he knew he could only live so long as a pigeon and he wanted to evolve up with what the Hindus call these different life lines to kinda get back to perfection."

According to Lee, the upgrade may have been to a blackbird. When the Sox sent Lee packing to the Montreal Expos, the blackbird may have been the player to be named later. As he ran sprints around Montréal's domed Olympic Stadium, he noticed a bird perched on the centerfield fence. In an interview in *Penthouse*, he said, "He watched me do all my running. And I talked to him every time I went around. I knew it was Tom reincarnated. I knew it was because he really liked me."

Now "retired" for twenty-five years, Lee plays amateur ball around the globe, writes books, and still has Yawkey on his mind. "Every time I see a bird, I see Tom," he says. "He keeps coming back on me. Because I have this in my brain about all the DDT and all the animals that he had killed through reckless management of the earth. Being a forester, he should have used different insects to eat other insects and try to keep the birds. I've always been a birder kind of guy, even though I've shot more ducks and pheasants than probably even Tom Yawkey."

Lee has had various fowl encounters that support his convictions: red-tailed hawks following him in the woods; a kite knocking a dove out of the sky, with the dove landing at Lee's feet; a mature bald eagle stealing a mullet from an osprey before Lee's eyes; and a crow that came after him in Medicine Hat.

"[The crow] was on a pole and he just took exception to me and he kept diving on me. I was the only person he was attacking. I was wondering what that was all about—if I had said some disparaging words about the [Red Sox] organization or something. That was a pretty bizarre day, too."

THE CALL OF THE WILD

Longtime baseball manager and coach Tom Trebelhorn shares Lee's belief in reincarnation. When he was managing the Tri-City Posse in Pasco, Washington, in 1995, he formed a relationship with a coyote that came to the park late at night.

"I believe it was a reincarnated former major-league player," says Trebelhorn. "There's no doubt in my mind."

Trebelhorn certainly knows how to spot a major leaguer. As a manager in the minors, he saw the potential of Rickey Henderson and worked with him one-on-one on stealing bases. Henderson never forgot him, and after swiping his 893rd base to move to second on the all-time list, he presented Trebelhorn with the bag.

Over the years numerous players, including Hall of Famers Paul Molitor and Robin Yount, praised Trebelhorn's ability to work with younger players. Perhaps the coyote sensed this as well. The animal stopped by the park nightly and responded to the manager. "Every game he came back and every game he got closer," recalls Trebelhorn. "Most coyotes will take off; they're very skittish. But this one just looked me right in the eye." Trebelhorn started talking to the animal and feeding him hotdogs and chicken, which he would practically eat out of the manager's hand. "We became fast friends."

The ritual lasted the entire season. On nights when there were no games, the park staff told Trebelhorn, the coyote didn't show up.

The perceptive manager sensed an ancient spirit from "the way it looked at me. He had a human look to his eyes, like he knew what was going on. I figured he had to be an old ballplayer reincarnated. If you believe in the Native American spirits, you would believe in that."

Trebelhorn's familiarity with Native American folklore isn't surprising to those who have witnessed his wide-ranging intellect. During managerial stints with the Brewers and Cubs, he was known to circle grammatical errors in fan letters, grade them, and send them back to fans. (This was a habit carried over from his off-season job as a substitute teacher in Portland, Oregon, where the well-rounded Trebelhorn taught history, language, arts, and algebra.) Noted former umpire Steve Palermo once complained that Trebelhorn's vocabulary was so large that he would confound umps when he ran onto the field to protest calls.

The thoughtful manager has never been reticent about sharing philosophical views about baseball and life in general.

"I buy into a lot of [Native American] mysticism, " he says. "I think that in the whole timeline of history, all creatures are interconnected—all of them. I don't see it farfetched for an animal to have human characteristics or humans to have animal characteristics. I think it's a very narrow plank we walk between creature and human, and either can go to either side at any time. And I think we're all equal. We all have a place and we're all interconnected, and whenever either side gets out of balance, it's not good for the entire system."

Trebelhorn believes that he too lived another existence in an earlier time. "I think that I was a warrior minstrel," he says. "In Sherwood. I think I was beyond medieval times, but I don't think I was quite Renaissance."

As for the coyote, it makes sense to Trebelhorn that those unique wild animals occupy a special place in Native American mysticism. "I can see why because they do have a look they give you. Almost like there's something more than an animal brain in there. They give you that look and let you know they know more than you do."

CURSES

CHAPTER 20

THE PLAGUE
OF THE PLAQUE

Think of the players most responsible for the San Francisco Giants on-field record over the past half century, and the list is impressive: Willie Mays, Orlando Cepeda, Willie McCovey, Juan Marichal, Gaylord Perry, Barry Bonds, Eddie Grant . . .

Eddie Grant? Though he's not a household name, a growing number of people feel that Grant has had more influence over the team's record—in particular, its long losing streak—than anyone else. (The Giants haven't won a World Series since 1954, the third longest drought in the majors after the Cubs [1908] and the Indians [1948].) A utility infielder from the Deadball Era, Grant had a reputation as a strong bunter, and his penchant for the sacrifice carried into his off-field life as well. When he was killed in action in World War I, the Giants memorialized him with a commemorative plaque—a plaque that today lies at the heart of a team curse story.

Born in 1883, Grant was a Harvard-educated lawyer who played varsity basketball in college (a summer stint in semipro baseball after his freshman year rendered him ineligible for the collegiate team). He was so eager for a career in baseball that he left school before graduation, eventually finishing his law degree during the off-seasons. Nicknamed "Harvard Eddie" and "Attorney Grant" in his playing days, he routinely gave teammates advice on their contracts in the days before agents. He was something of an aesthete athlete, with a taste for opera and theater.

Just under six feet tall and weighing not quite 170 pounds, Grant was gangly but quick and graceful as an infielder. He had a career year with the Philadelphia Nationals in 1909, when he led the league in games (154), at bats (631), singles (147), and outs (492). His greatest day at the plate came on October 2 of that year, when he went 7 for 7 against future Hall of Famers Rube Marquard and Christy Mathewson, in a game against the Giants.

It was in some ways odd that the Giants chose to honor Grant. Though they were the last team with whom he played, he appeared in far fewer games with them (202) than he did with the Phillies (527) or Reds (259). His fielding was strong, but his batting average in his two-and-a-half seasons as a Giant was .247—respectable for the era, but not exceptional. He retired after the 1915 season to little fanfare. Grant was not particularly a Giants hero.

He was, however, something of a national hero. Grant enlisted for WWI in the spring of 1917, shortly after America entered the fray. He was practicing law in New York City, having spent part of 1916 coaching a Giants farm club in New Jersey. Nearly thirty-four years old, Grant faced no threat of being drafted. He joined the army because he believed in the cause.

"I had determined from the start to be in this war if it came to us," he wrote in a letter at the time. "And if I am not successful as an officer I shall enlist as a private, for I believe there is no greater duty that I owe for being that which I am—an American citizen."

He did become an officer—a captain in what was known as the "Statue of Liberty Division" (which hailed from New York City). His company shipped out to France in April of 1918. In early October, just one month before all fighting would end, they were called to the Argonne Forest to help rescue the 550 members of the so-called Lost Battalion.

The plight of the Lost Battalion was straight out of a Hollywood war picture. Surrounded by the enemy, easy prey for snipers, and desperate for food and arms, soldiers literally wrote farewell messages in their own blood on scraps of clothing and sent them off by carrier pigeons to the American lines. General John Pershing had ordered the Seventy-seventh Division— Grant's division—to conduct a rescue mission, a highly dangerous operation given the German army's foothold in the area. On the morning of October 5, Grant was given command of the battalion and led the infantry deeper into the Argonne. As fighting broke out, he was hit in the abdomen and killed immediately.

Ultimately, 193 members of the Lost Battalion were rescued in the initiative. Grant's bravery in battle and fidelity to his fellow soldiers were lauded by all who knew him.

Two-and-a-half years later, on Memorial Day of 1921, the Giants honored Grant with an on-field ceremony. Fellow soldiers, former teammates, and family members were present. Famed sportswriter Grantland Rice wrote an elegy for Grant, which spoke of "a final box score that is written in glory."

And the Giants unveiled a plaque in Grant's honor, mounted on a five-foot monument in deep centerfield. The inscription read:

IN MEMORY OF

CAPT. EDWARD LESLIE GRANT

307TH INFANTRY—77TH DIVISION

A.E.F.

SOLDIER—SCHOLAR—ATHLETE

KILLED IN ACTION

ARGONNE FOREST

OCTOBER 5, 1918

PHILADELPHIA NATIONALS

1907—1908—1909—1910

CINCINNATI REDS

1911—1912—1913

NEW YORK GIANTS

1913—1914—1915

ERECTED BY FRIENDS IN BASEBALL,

JOURNALISM, AND THE SERVICE

This was before the famed monuments of Yankee Stadium were erected in centerfield—indeed, before Yankee Stadium itself was erected. While the concept of a monument actually sitting on the field of play is unthinkable today, the Grant plaque was set so far back in the cavernous Polo Grounds it was regarded as more of a museum piece than a ballpark obstacle.

But it was sometimes an obstacle—and that could be good luck for the team. On June 15, 1940, Harry Danning hit a ball that sailed 460 feet and lodged itself behind the Grant memorial. Pittsburgh centerfielder Vince DiMaggio could not extricate the ball in time to make a play, and Danning raced all the way home. The Giants won that day and Danning hit for the cycle—the last player of the twentieth century to do so with an inside-the-park homer.

The plaque certainly presided over some great Giants moments during its thirty-seven years in the Polo Grounds, including nine pennant wins and four World Series titles—starting with the very first year the plaque was installed. It was in the outfield when Bobby Thompson's noted "shot heard 'round the world" flew by in 1951, sealing the pennant for the Giants. It is visible in the familiar photo of Mays's famous catch that saved Game 1 for the team in the 1954 World Series.

The plaque was truly Grant's legacy. He had become a widower at twenty-eight, when his wife of nine months died suddenly in his arms due to what doctors later concluded was lingering damage from a childhood bout with typhoid. He never remarried—when he died in battle seven years later, he still carried his wife's picture in his pocket—and had no kids. The Polo Grounds monument was the only thing that kept the spirit and memory of Eddie Grant alive.

In 1957, the Giants announced that they would move to California the following season. Though owner Horace Stoneham himself said at the time that the team would take the Grant plaque with them and give it a home at the new stadium, it was in fact never seen again. Its whereabouts ever since have been a mystery.

According to Mike Murphy, with the club back then as a batboy, and now clubhouse manager at AT&T Park, the plaque was
packed up with other ballpark items and shipped to San Francisco, with the intention of eventually being installed in the new
park. "Somewhere between New York and here, it got lost,"
says Murphy. "It never turned up."

Some say, however, that the plaque disappeared well before
that. After the last Giants game at the Polo Grounds on September 29, 1957, fans stormed onto the field. They began pulling up
bases, ripping seats from the stands, scooping up dirt, and gen-
erally ransacking the place in a mad scramble for memorabilia. A
common story has it that three teenagers stole the Grant plaque,
prying it off its monument with a crowbar. The youths were later
apprehended by police, but the plaque was never recovered.

Or was it? In 2002, the Baseball Reliquary—an offbeat "museum" of sorts for unusual memorabilia (among their artifacts
are the jockstrap worn by midget Eddie Gaedel in his only plate
appearance, and a half-smoked cigar Babe Ruth left in a Philadelphia brothel)—claimed to be in possession of the Grant plaque.
They said it had turned up in the attic of a New Jersey home formerly owned by a police officer who worked the Polo Grounds.
They had "negotiated a price and arranged for its delivery." The
authenticity of the plaque was disputed, and the Reliquary responded by saying, "Why would anyone forge a seventy-five-
pound plaque?"

But it turns out someone did. The Baseball Reliquary now
says that they were misunderstood, that what they have is a fac-
simile of the original plaque.

Another red herring appeared when a story claimed that
three beat reporters took the plaque from the Polo Grounds and
brought it to Toots Shor's, a well-known midtown Manhattan
restaurant frequented by baseball players and entertainers in
the '40s and '50s. (Toots Shor's is known by baseball fans as the
site of a famous Yogi-ism. Introduced to Ernest Hemingway at
the bar one night and told that he was an important writer, Berra
reportedly asked, "What paper you with, Ernie?") Shor then sent

the plaque to American Legion Post Number 75 in Franklin, Massachusetts, Grant's hometown. The story is unsubstantiated and the Legion Post does not have the plaque.

In fact, nobody knows what happened to the bronze memorial. In 2005, *Sports Illustrated* listed the Eddie Grant plaque among its "25 Lost Treasures" and estimated its worth at $20,000.

The whereabouts of Grant's plaque may be unknown, but the fate of the Giants since its disappearance is well documented. The team has won no World Series titles in the fifty-plus years since they lost the plaque. They have been to the Fall Classic three times in that spate, each appearance memorably disastrous.

In 1962, rain that bordered on the biblical delayed Game 6 in San Francisco for four days. Game 7 ended in heartbreak, when Willie McCovey's potential game-winning line drive in the bottom of the ninth screamed right toward second baseman Bobby Richardson's glove. The Giants—who outperformed the Yankees in team batting average, ERA, home runs, triples, and doubles over the course of the Series—lost the championship.

In 1989, Candlestick Park was rocked by an earthquake, just minutes before hosting its first World Series game in twenty-seven years. No one in the stadium was seriously injured, though the building shook and swayed with great force. The game was delayed for ten days and the Giants went on to lose the Series in four straight to their crosstown rivals, the Oakland A's. (As one staff member notes, "We won the pennant that year and weren't even the best team *in town*.")

In 2002, the Giants headed into Game 6 up 3–2 in the series; a victory that night would have clinched it. They led 5–0 heading into the seventh and were eight outs away from glory when the Anaheim Angels rallied for three runs in each of the next two innings to take the game. The Giants went on to lose Game 7 and the Series.

In addition to World Series fiascos, the team has had other postseason problems. From their unexpected 1971 NLCS loss to Pittsburgh to Jose Cruz Jr.'s dropped fly ball in the 2003 Division

Series, the Giants have continually found ways to lose in big games. In 1998 they lost a one-game playoff for the wildcard berth to perennial postseason bystanders the *Chicago Cubs*.

Even the team's high points have had bugaboos associated with them. When superstar Barry Bonds surpassed one of baseball's most cherished records—hitting his 715th home run in May 2006 to pass Babe Ruth for second on the all-time list—a bizarre radio glitch prevented hundreds of thousands of fans from sharing the moment. KNBR's play-by-play announcer Dave Flemming's microphone inexplicably went dead in the broadcast booth just as the ball came off the bat, and listeners heard only silence as the historic homer left the park and Bonds rounded the bases.

Throughout most of the Giants' first five decades in California, nobody seemed to pay much attention to the lost Grant plaque. New York fans were more likely to pin the team's troubles on its move west than its poor stewardship of the missing memorial. But in the early 2000s, interest in the plaque began to grow.

In late 2001, the Great War Society and the U.S. arm of the Western Front Association, eager to see a veteran honored, contacted the Giants and offered to help defray the cost of replacing the plaque. "Frankly, we sort of blew it off," says Pat Gallagher, president of Giants Enterprises. "We get all kinds of requests, and this was something we didn't know much about at the time."

The Great War Society was affronted. They may have been the first to note that the team's decades of frustration coincided with the loss of the plaque. (Though their request was actually the second time the Giants rejected an offer to replace Grant's plaque. In 1994, Joseph Tekulsky, who had written a profile of Grant for *Harvard* magazine, petitioned Giants president Peter Magowan to put a reproduction of the plaque in Candlestick Park. The Giants responded by saying that the plaque was part of New York Giants history, not the San Francisco Giants.)

Public awareness of Grant was also rekindled with a well-researched 2004 *Smithsonian* magazine article on his life and military service. Talk of a curse began to grow. In early 2006, a *Contra Costa Times* piece by Neil Hayes explicitly linked the lost memorial to the Giants' postseason woes. The article was entitled, "The Plague of the Plaque."

At some point in all this, the team got curious. Pat Gallagher began a search for the plaque among old items from the Polo Grounds. "Candlestick Park had a bunch of old storage rooms with all kinds of stuff. We've got the big copper letters that were sitting on top of the Polo Grounds that say G-I-A-N-T-S. There were big bronze plaques for John McGraw, Mel Ott, Carl Hubbell, Christy Mathewson. But we couldn't find the Grant plaque."

When it didn't turn up, Giants owner Peter Magowan himself ordered a replacement plaque be cast. The team used pictures from the era to create an exact duplicate of the original bronze piece. Even that process seemed snakebit. "It took three or four different casts for this thing to take," says Gallagher. "For whatever reason, this project went on for a couple of years."

Finally, during Memorial Day weekend of 2006, the new Grant plaque was unveiled in AT&T Park. Not visible from the field, let alone located *on* the field, like its predecessor ("We put it in a place where people can actually go see it if they want," explains Gallagher), the plaque hangs near the park's elevator and rightfield entrance, known as the Lefty O'Doul gate. A wreath of flowers was placed next to it at the unveiling, but the event was without ceremony—there was no fanfare, no press release, no overt attention paid. A memorial that was missing for so long, and had begun to cause so much fuss, was suddenly a part of the Giants again.

Did the team replace the plaque for the sake of honoring Grant, or to help end the curse? According to Gallagher, it was a little bit of both. "Originally we were not doing it because of any curse or anything, but just because it looked like a promise had been made and if we could do it, fine. Then all of a sudden people start talking about the Curse of Eddie Grant. Baseball fans are so superstitious, and players are too, so you have to take this stuff seriously, to a point. And if by putting up a plaque we can break some sort of curse, who's to say it's not the right thing to do?"

On that day in 1921 when Grant's plaque was unveiled at the Polo Grounds, Judge Kenesaw Mountain Landis, newly appointed commissioner of baseball, praised the slain athlete and declared that his "memory will live as long as our game may last." But his memory really lived only as long as the plaque was displayed—for thirty-seven years, fans and players who filed past the memorial were reminded of the accomplishments of a baseball war hero.

Today, few fans—even gung-ho Giants aficionados—know the name of Eddie Grant, much less his achievements on the field of play or the field of battle. The new plaque in AT&T Park may change that.

The Giants hope it will also change the luck of a team that hasn't won a World Series since Harvard Eddie disappeared more than fifty years ago.

CHAPTER 21

GIVING UP
THE GOAT

Quite possibly no curse in any sport is as infamous as the Chicago Cubs' long-standing Curse of the Billy Goat. The casual baseball observer usually relates it like this: A Cubs fan tried to bring a goat to a game at Wrigley Field back in the 1940s and was denied admission. Indignant, he put a curse on the team that has kept them from winning a World Series—or, for that matter, appearing in one—ever since.

The story sounds apocryphal but is actually true in essence, though the version above gets one important fact wrong (the goat was, in fact, admitted to the park) and omits a second important fact—that the hexer later lifted the curse.

Vasili Sianis, a Greek immigrant nicknamed "Billy Goat" for the goatee he always wore, owned the Billy Goat Tavern in downtown Chicago. He had something of a reputation as a savvy promoter of his business via attention-grabbing media gimmicks. Sianis once requested that the State Department issue him the first restaurant license for the moon. When the Republican National Convention was held in Chicago, he posted a sign in the tavern saying he did not serve Republicans; the place was filled with them the next day.

On Saturday, October 6, 1945, Sianis may or may not have had business promotion on his mind when he headed to Wrigley

Field with two $7.20 box-seat tickets in one hand and a leash tied to a goat in the other. The Cubs were up 2–1 in the World Series against the Tigers, and Game 4 was the first to be played in Chicago. Sianis had outfitted the goat, named Murphy, with a sign that read, WE GOT DETROIT'S GOAT.

Ushers were reluctant to let the goat in the park, but relented at Sianis's insistence that a ticket is a ticket, and nothing said it couldn't be used for an animal. Once inside, the goat—being a goat—seemed to prefer the field to the grandstand. Prior to the game he made his way onto the grass and Wrigley workers responded by taking him into custody. But when newspaper photographers asked for pictures, security let Murphy and his owner return to the field for some poses.

There followed what the *Chicago Tribune* called "a heated argument" between Sianis and Andy Frain, the head of Wrigley's security force, regarding whether or not the goat could be permitted to stay for the game. *Tribune* writer Gene Kessler reported that "while flourishing the ticket, Mr. Goat grabbed for it and Andy Frain remarked: 'If he eats the ticket that would solve everything.'" But the goat didn't eat the ticket, and Sianis's argument again prevailed: If you don't want people to bring barnyard animals to baseball games, you should print that on the ticket. Sianis and his companion were shown to their seats.

But they did not make it through the game. It was raining that day and the goat—being a goat—smelled like a goat. A wet goat. Nearby fans did not enjoy this and the disruptive odor finally provided ushers the reason they needed to eject the ticketholders. Sianis was outraged. Standing outside Wrigley, he cursed the team.

The Cubs lost the game 8–4 and Sianis reportedly sent team owner P. K. Wrigley a telegram asking, "Who smells now?" In his book *Da Curse of the Billy Goat*, author Steve Gatto quotes a different telegram the Sianis family claims Vasili sent to Wrigley, saying, "You are going to lose this World Series and you are never going to go to another World Series again. You are never going to win a World Series again because you insulted my goat."

And they haven't. The Cubs lost in 1945 and have yet to return to the Fall Classic.

All those years of not winning a National League pennant have contributed to the Cubs' reputation as "Lovable Losers." Their fans are among the most devoted in baseball, and some have embraced the notion of the curse as one of the defining elements of the team.

The organization itself has had an uneasy relationship with the Billy Goat curse. "I don't believe much in the curse stuff," says Cubs GM John Hendry today. "Obviously we go about our business not putting much stock in that." But this has certainly not been the case over the years.

In fact, the curse has been officially acknowledged numerous times by the Cubs, and the team has made repeated efforts to lift it. P. K. Wrigley was superstitious (one season he reportedly paid a man $5,000 to sit behind home plate each game and give opposing pitchers the "evil eye") and in September of 1950, at the end of yet another losing season, he wrote a letter to Billy Goat Sianis:

> Will you please extend to Murphy my most sincere
> and abject apologies as well as those of the Chicago
> National League Ball Club for whatever it was that
> happened in the past, and ask him to not only remove
> the "Hex" but to reverse the flow and start pulling
> for us.

Sianis refused (though he claimed to show the letter to Murphy, and said the goat forgave Wrigley) and the losing continued. For twenty years—from 1947 through 1966—the Cubs never finished higher than fifth in the National League.

The team started to improve under legendary manager Leo Durocher and finished third in 1967 and 1968. In 1969, the year before Sianis died, the Cubs got off to a fast start and were first in their division by mid-April. Then came the word everyone had

been waiting for: Sianis was lifting the curse. David Condon reported the news in the *Chicago Tribune* on April 15, saying that
the rift between Wrigley and the tavern owner had "healed" and
that Billy Goat had "[made] the truce official. Yesterday he dispatched Wrigley a letter seeking to reserve four seats for the
Cubs' 1969 world series matches."

In the months following Sianis's de-hexing, the Cubs
seemed indomitable. They were in first place longer and later
in the season than they had been in decades; by mid-August
they held an 8½-game lead in their division. But the team hit a
rough patch and a losing streak began. Curse talk started up
again when, at a game in New York, a black cat—a classic har-
binger of bad luck—ran onto the field, circled Cub favorite Ron
Santo in the on-deck circle, and hissed at Durocher in the
dugout. The Cubs lost that day, and their lead dwindled to half
a game. The next day they gave up the lead for good. They finished the season 8 games behind the Mets, who went on to
win the World Series.

Afterward, fans began mumbling about the Curse of the Billy
Goat exerting itself again, but Sianis himself was indignant.
"Yes, for many years my Billy Goat hex cost the Cubs pennants,"
he told sportswriter Condon. "When the Billy Goat hex is on you,
there is nothing except trouble." But, he added, "I removed the
Billy Goat hex from the Cubs. So that is not why they blew the
pennant." The real reason, he said, was "the New York Mets just
played like hell!"

Nevertheless, talk of the Billy Goat curse only seemed to
grow, and was intensified by a midseason incident in 1973 involving Billy Goat's nephew Sam. Patrons at the tavern he had
taken over since his uncle's death had urged Sam to lift the curse.
The younger Sianis pulled up to Wrigley Field in a limousine accompanied by a goat of his own. The goat wore a sign that read,
ALL IS FORGIVEN. LET ME LEAD YOU TO THE PENNANT. YOUR FRIEND, BILLY
GOAT. The pair were denied entry. The Cubs, in first place by 8½
games, won that day, but lost 16 of their next 20 games and finished the season in fifth place.

In 1984, the Cubs seemed to have learned their lesson. They invited Sam Sianis and goat to attend the Cubs home opener, which happened to fall on a Friday the 13th. The duo complied and the goat nonchalantly roamed Wrigley Field in a pregame ceremony.

For the rest of the season, the Cubs played like a team possessed—or, perhaps, *un-possessed*. They dominated their division and produced the NL's Cy Young Award winner (Rick Sutcliffe) and MVP (Ryne Sandberg) on the way to claiming their first NL East title. Facing the Padres in a best-of-five playoff series, Chicago won the first two games at home and needed only one win in the remaining three games to head to the World Series. But they lost Games 3 and 4. The decisive Game 5 ended in classic cursed-Cubs misery when, after leading for the first half of the game, a routine groundball passed through first-baseman Leon Durham's legs, allowing the tying run to score, and ultimately leading to the go-ahead runs. (The term for a player who makes such a costly miscue is *the goat*—short for "scapegoat"— a coincidence not lost on curse-crazed fans.)

There were other close calls (the team again won the NL East in 1989, but lost the pennant to the San Francisco Giants) but the losing ways continued. In 1994, the Cubs opened their season with a dismal 6–18 record, during which they failed to win a single home game. On April 30, manager Tom Trebelhorn told a reporter that he blamed the goat curse for the rough spell. "I've got to go down to that tavern and talk to that guy about the goat," he said. "We'll let the goat run the bases and water the outfield. We'll let him eat some grass and I'll kiss him. Whatever it takes."

A few days later, with the Wrigley drought now at 12 games and counting, Sam Sianis and goat made the trip to the North Side—escorted into Wrigley by Ernie Banks—and the Cubs won at Wrigley for the first time that season. They went 16–8 over their next 24 games, a stark contrast to the first 24.

Despite that experience, Trebelhorn, who kept a little toy goat in his office when he managed the team ("to honor not the curse, but the tradition") today says he views the curse more as a self-fulfilling prophesy than a literal hex. "I'm a believer in the mental mind-set that comes from repeating things until they have a life spirit of their own. So certainly it exists because so many people talk about it. But it's not factual. If we had better pitching and better run production, none of that would ever have happened, goat or no goat."

As is the case with players on just about any team said to be cursed, most Cubs and former Cubs claim not to buy any of it. But they have sometimes been called upon to take part in rituals designed to end the Billy Goat curse.

Legendary pitcher Lee Smith recalls one of the goat episodes. "In 1981 they brought this goat around the whole outfield. The goat was trying to eat the ivy and everything." The result? "We lost 13 straight. I'm a country boy. I said the best thing we could have done was throw the goat on the grill and barbecue him."

(Lee's memory is a little off, but he's close enough: The Cubs lost their first game in 1981, but won the second. They then dropped the next 12.)

Steve Trachsel was on the 1994 team with the long home losing streak, and on the 1997 team that opened the season by losing 14 in a row. (This, ironically, was after a preseason "curse-removing press conference" held at the Billy Goat Tavern.) Did he ever think the curse was to blame? "No," he says. "Just a bad team."

According to Trachsel, players "think it's just one big joke. I was there six years and I think we did whatever it was we were supposed to do to erase the curse at least a dozen times." Though the methods varied, "it always had to do with a goat," he says.

"We did a goat thing on the Jay Leno show one time. We did a skit with Jay, and then Jay brought out the great uncle's cousin's nephew of the guy that originally brought the goat, or something like that. We burned uniforms and all kinds of things like that."

Trachsel has good reason to resent the goat; he was the winning pitcher on May 4, 1994—the game that ended the home losing streak—but the goat got more credit for the win than he did. Trachsel also took the mound for the critical tie-breaking game against the Giants in 1998. He pitched six and one-third shutout innings for the win, sending the Cubs to the postseason . . . but was again overshadowed by Sianis and his goat, brought in for pregame festivities to give the team good luck.

But Trachsel is hardly the only player to cast aspersions on the goat jinx.

"I don't know anything about curses," says former Cub Juan Pierre. "I just play hard. Whatever happens, happens."

"You hear about the curse of the goat, but I think it's as strong as how you believe in it," says former manager Dusty Baker, who put no stock in it. Sammy Sosa saw it as an excuse. "[The curse] is something to blame somebody, to make it easy for you. I was too busy thinking about winning [to worry about the curse]." Greg Maddux "never got caught up in it," he says. For the future Hall of Famer, the Billy Goat curse was "something to joke about, really. I don't think it's any more than that, as far as the players are concerned."

Former Cub reliever LaTroy Hawkins is more blunt. Asked about the goat curse, he cuts right to the chase, exonerating the team and putting the blame where few people ever seem to: "Who brings a f—ing goat to a ballpark anyway?"

While most players dismiss the Billy Goat curse as something athletes ignore and fans enjoy, the notion that the curse is a fun diversion is debatable.

It would certainly be news to Steve Bartman. A Cubs fan who innocently reached for a foul ball heading into the stands during the 2003 NLCS—inadvertently interrupting a play that might have helped end the game before his team blew the lead and a trip to the World Series—Bartman was so demonized as the curse personified he received death threats for weeks. To this day, his name is an oft-cited synonym for the evilness of the goat curse (see Chapter 22: A Foul Ball).

And why would fans—who presumably root for the team to win—simultaneously believe in a curse that says winning is impossible?

"I think it's kind of a fun thing for them to hold onto since they don't have a World Series," Derrek Lee says. "They can talk about the goat instead. But I think they understand that there is no curse."

Lee thinks that the desire for a World Series is so strong, it creates its own kind of curse. "Every year that goes by, the fans want it so bad. As players, we want it bad too. So sometimes we try a little too hard." He says everyone needs to stop obsessing over the championship drought and "take it day by day. Let things happen instead of always seeming to focus on 'We need a World Series! We need a World Series!' That's not the way it works."

Jim Lefebvre knows how badly Cubs fans and players want a championship, and tried to keep a sense of humor about it during the two years he managed the team. "Fans would say to me, 'I'm not gonna die until the Cubs win the pennant!' And I'd say, 'That's a lot of pressure on me. Because if I win and you die, then I'm up for murder!'"

Indeed, the fact that many Cubs fans have lived and died without celebrating a championship is never far from the minds of the faithful.

"Your parents have never seen [a World Series win], their parents have never seen it . . . hopefully you could relive it for them some day," says one ever-optimistic fan.

Another argues that previous attempts to lift the curse were misguided. Once put in place, it's not as easy as bringing in a goat. "You can only get rid of a curse with an exorcism," says one Cubs supporter. "I think they need to bring in a Greek priest. It can be done in a low-key way."

Others argue that more than anything, the Cubs have been cursed by bad management and bad trades. From 1961 to 1965, for example, the team experimented with a "College of Coaches" concept that essentially replaced the manager position with a rotating uniformed committee. In 1964, the team traded future Hall of Famer Lou Brock for underperforming pitcher Ernie Broglio.

But nothing has held the imagination of baseball fans like the goat curse. In the absence of victory, it gives the team something unique. As one supporter puts it, "Anybody can win the World Series, but it really takes a special team to lose one hundred years in a row."

The curse has become so well known and is considered so potent that it is presumed to doom other ball clubs as well. Fans have claimed that teams with high concentrations of former Cubs players are also cursed. Shortly before the twentieth anniversary of Bill Buckner's famous World Series error that led to the Red Sox losing the 1986 World Series, sharp-eyed fans spotted something suspicious under Buckner's first baseman's mitt in a photo from the game: Buckner was wearing a Cubs batting glove. Is it any wonder he blew the play?

But at least one major leaguer considers Wrigley's famous winds to provide a home field advantage that casts a kind of spell on the Cubs opponents. "I think there's a curse to the *visiting* team," says Atlanta Braves outfielder Jeff Francoeur. "It feels like the wind's always blowing in and you're hitting uphill. It's a tough place to hit until you've got experience."

Search the Internet or the stores around Wrigleyville today and you can find a "Reverse the Curse" hat (featuring the "officially licensed Billy Goat logo") as well as T-shirts, wall clocks, bobblehead dolls, and other memorabilia decorated in goat images and Cubs logos. The Curse of the Billy Goat is big business.

Possibly the biggest financial beneficiary of the curse is the Sianis family, who have franchised the now-famous Billy Goat Tavern name into eight locations, including one in Washington, D.C.

The oldest Billy Goat Tavern is not the baseball mecca many tourists expect. An underground bar located near the Chicago

Tribune (which bought the Cubs from the Wrigley family in 1981), it more closely resembles a beat reporter's hangout, with famous *Tribune* bylines decorating the wood-paneled walls. In addition to its Cubs reputation, the Billy Goat gained fame as the inspiration for *Saturday Night Live*'s famous "Cheezborger! Cheezborger!" sketches in the 1970s, and this image is preserved by showy, impatient fry cooks with Greek accents who bark at patrons.

But there is a goat head mounted on the wall, Cubs games are always on the TV, and Sam Sianis himself is often around, willing to talk goats with curse-thirsty patrons.

Sianis takes seriously his role as keeper of the curse. He cites plenty of instances where dissing the goat led to the team's demise. In the 1984 playoffs, he says, the team did well at home because he was there. "They went to San Diego and left me behind . . . and they lost." In 1989, "they didn't invite me to the playoffs and they lost." Sianis even says he was outside the park on the night of the infamous Bartman play in the 2003 ALCS.

"They lost because they didn't let me in that day. I didn't understand why. Everybody was screaming, 'Let the goat in! Let the goat in!' But they didn't and look what happened."

(For those wondering, Sianis does not keep a stable of goats standing by for the trip to Wrigley. "I have a friend who has a farm in Indiana. That's where I keep the goats. Every time I need a goat, I go over there.")

Given the fact that Sianis and goat have been admitted on a number of occasions to "lift" the curse, how does he explain its lingering effects? He says the Cubs' previous indulgences have been one-time stunts, not sincere attempts at reconciliation. "To lift the curse they have to apologize. Open the doors with their hearts open. 'Billy Goat, let us win the pennant.' Something like that."

In the meantime, Sianis is content to let the curse continue. When he's gone, his son may pick up the mantle. He's a Cubs fan, Sianis says, who attends games all the time. In the great family tradition, he once tried to bring a goat in, but was denied at the gate.

THE CURSE OF FRED MERKLE

The Curse of the Billy Goat, which started in 1945, can't explain the full length of the Cubs championship shortfalls; the team hasn't won a World Series since 1908. To account for the 1909–44 dry spell (during which the team did appear in six World Series), some fans have turned to the alleged Curse of Fred Merkle, named for the nineteen-year-old Giants rookie many feel was victimized by a Cubs dirty trick that gave the Chicago club the 1908 pennant under dubious circumstances.

The Cubs and Giants were in a tight pennant race that year. In their September 23 match-up, the score was tied with two outs in the bottom of the ninth at the Polo Grounds. Merkle was on first with another Giants runner on third, when Al Bridwell hit the apparent game-winning single. The lead runner crossed home plate. Merkle took some steps toward second, but then headed toward the dugout as fans stormed the field and teammates celebrated the winning run. Though technically a violation of the rules, Merkle's actions were common for a player in that situation.

But Cubs second baseman Johnny Evers saw an opportunity. He procured another ball (an outfielder had tossed the game ball into the stands), ran to second to tag the base, and then showed the ball to the ump, claiming that Merkle was forced out and the run nullified. The ump agreed, over rigorous protests from the Giants. The game was declared still tied, and with thousands of fans on the field, it could not be continued. The two teams ended up with identical records for the season, and were forced to play a tie-breaker. The Cubs won and advanced to the World Series.

Fred Merkle, forever labeled a "bonehead" for not tagging second, may be pleased to know the club hasn't won a championship since.

CHAPTER 22

A FOUL BALL

Frustrated Cubs fans would love nothing more than to destroy the Curse of the Billy Goat, which they feel has haunted the team for decades. A few years back, they got a literal chance to do exactly that.

In 2003, the Cubs were on the verge of winning the pennant. They had already defeated the Atlanta Braves in the NLDC (the team's first postseason series win since 1908) and were one win away from an NLCS title that would send them to the World Series. They led Game 6 by three runs with one out in the bottom of the eighth when the Marlins Luis Castillo hit a ball that headed for the leftfield stands. Outfielder Moises Alou raced to the wall to reach for it, but a fan sitting in Aisle 4, Row 8, Seat 113—a guy named Steve Bartman—grabbed it first.

No one can say whether Alou would have caught the ball or not; if he had, the Cubs would still have needed another out to end the inning. But the game unwound from there. The Marlins rallied to score eight runs in the inning, winning the game 8–3. The Cubs went on to lose Game 7. Bartman became the most vilified man in Chicago since Al Capone, and the butt of jokes across the country.

And the ball he reached for became the most hated symbol of the Billy Goat curse.

Later that year, the fan who actually ended up with the ball (not Bartman, who was so jeered by the Wrigley crowd he had to be escorted from the park by security) put it up for auction. Grant DePorter, president and managing partner of Harry Caray's Restaurant, thought about bidding on it. "I kept asking myself, 'What would Harry do?'" says DePorter. He decided that the legendary Cubs broadcaster "would just want to buy it for fans and get rid of it."

The bidding started at $5,000 and DePorter thought he'd go as high as $30,000 if necessary. But once the bidding began, "I just went nuts. I was up until five in the morning and I just kept on bidding." DePorter imagined himself to be bidding against Marlin fans, which spurred his competitive edge. "This time the Cubs are going to win, whatever it takes," he thought.

DePorter also had a feeling he was not alone. "I kind of felt like [Harry] was omnipresent . . . I felt like maybe he was there."

In the end, DePorter (and Caray) did get the ball. The final price tag: $113,824.16.

DePorter says it was worth it, not only for the great publicity it brought the bar, but for the joy it brought Cubs Nation. "I ended up getting twenty thousand thank you letters from Cubs fans," he says. "They also wrote their ideas of how to destroy it. I wanted it to be a cathartic thing for all fans to be a part of the process."

One of the letters was from Michael Lantieri, an Academy Award–winning special-effects artist who offered several destructive options. He and DePorter first tried to "kill it like the Terminator," freezing it with liquid nitrogen. But, DePorter says, "A baseball is designed to take impact, so when we froze it, it didn't work."

The next idea was grander. "[Lantieri] had this machine that was going to shoot, like, a million lightning bolts through Harry's glasses and invoke Harry's spirit and just blow it up." Southwest Airlines offered to transport the machine to Chicago, but "it was too big to get into the cargo hold." Another idea scrapped.

Finally, they went for simplicity. A six-year-old boy in Florida had suggested they drill a hole in the ball, fill it with explosives, and blow it up. This would be, DePorter says, "a symbol to ward off future curses, an example of what will happen to you if you mess with the Cubs destiny." A ceremony was set for February as part of a worldwide tribute to Caray.

The ball was given the royal treatment in its final day. It was taken to Wrigley for one last visit, then spent the night in a lush $300-plus hotel room, where it received a steak and lobster dinner and a massage. In the much-publicized hoopla leading up to the explosion, Chicago mayor Richard Daley declared he would not pardon the ball or issue any stays of execution.

The event itself was broadcast around the country and packed the streets around Harry Caray's with the Cubs' faithful.

"Everyone said we should have a ghostbuster there, so Harold Ramis came," says DePorter. "Billy Corgan [of the Chicago-based and appropriately named Smashing Pumpkins] wrote some original songs as part of it. Everything was to break the curse."

With a space-shuttle-launch countdown, the ball was blown to bits and the remnants were put on display in the restaurant. Nevertheless, the Cubs only finished third in the NL Central that year.

So DePorter decided to try again. In 2005, he went back to the list of proposed ideas and found one that would be "more participatory for Cubs fans." Namely, grinding the ball up and putting it in spaghetti sauce that would then be fed to fans, the notion being that a day or two after ingesting it, the curse would be, ahem, "eliminated."

"I got a call from a guy that specialized in breaking curses, a company called Curse Breaking Laboratories or something like that," recalls DePorter. "He broke down the remnants of the busted ball and isolated the DNA." DePorter also turned to chemists from Northwestern University, who "turned the restaurant's kitchen into what looked like Dr. Frankenstein's laboratory." A food safety specialist and a registered dietician were also on hand to make sure all of this was safe (the outer hide and the superball center were not used in the sauce). Over the course of a few days, 700 fans came in to eat the ball.

"They all said it had a smoky flavor," says DePorter with a smile.

Again, the results were not impressive: The 2005 Cubs did worse than the previous year's team.

But even though the Cubs did not seem to break their curse, DePorter says the ceremonies may have had an impact.

The restaurateur invited Red Sox and White Sox fans to the 2004 detonation and gave them a prominent place for the ceremony. Their teams had the next-longest-running World Series droughts after the Cubs. "I said don't worry guys, we'll take care of your curse too."

The Red Sox won that very season, ending eighty-six years of World Series futility. The White Sox won the following year, erasing their eighty-eight-year dry spell.

DePorter sees this as merely setting the stage for the most dramatic championship of all. "I think it's part of trying to get the world ready," he says. "Like the Red Sox had a curse, so let's wipe that out and let people see what that's like. The White Sox had waited a million years, so let's let Chicago see what that looks like." Blowing up the ball did start clearing the way, then, for the biggest curse in baseball to finally end. "You gotta build up to it."

CHAPTER 23

THE PITCHER BEWITCHER

Baseball is well known as a game of streaks and slumps. Batters go on a tear, and then are hitless for weeks. Baserunners experience months where they always beat the tag, and then get caught stealing on every attempt.

But when pitcher José Lima followed a stellar 21-win season with the Houston Astros in 1999 with 13 losses in a row the following year, it felt like something more than your typical baseball cycle.

"It felt like somebody put a spell on me," says Lima.

That sinking feeling that he might be cursed—literally—quickly became a strong conviction. For Lima, the notion of people casting evil spells on others was not a big leap. Though he's never put a curse on someone himself ("I don't have to, I've been blessed with a great family," he says), he believes such things can happen.

"I believe in that. Where I come from [the Dominican Republic], we are very big believers. I'm superstitious, big time."

There were certainly no signs of a curse for Lima in 1999. His 21 wins were the second most in the NL. His stats for walks per nine innings pitched (1.61), number of innings (246.3), and strikeouts per walk ratio (4.25) were each third best in the league. Lima received votes in the Cy Young race that year and was chosen for the All-Star team. Astros fans coined the term "Lima Time" to trumpet his dominance on the mound.

But a year later he finished the season 7–16 with a 6.65 ERA. His 145 earned runs and 48 homers allowed were the most surrendered in either league. Like any pitcher, Lima had been through cold spells before. This was different. He was healthy and his arm felt fine. "I lost 13 games in a row, pitching well," he remembers.

"Pitching well" may be a stretch—Lima's ERA from April 10 through July 4, during which he lost 13 games, with 3 no decisions, was 7.90. Even in the second half of the season, when his record was 6–3, with 7 no decisions, his ERA was a larded 5.75.

But there were a number of games that could have gone his way, including 6 over which Lima's ERA was 2.27. He pitched at least seven innings in each of these outings, giving up just 4 walks while striking out 26. His record in these half-dozen games? 0–4.

In his final start of 2000, Lima lasted eight innings and gave up just 1 earned run, with 1 walk and 6 strikeouts. He got no decision in the game, which Houston eventually lost.

"I was getting killed. It was the weirdest thing ever. It was like everything was going *not* our way."

What's more, the losing had eerie undertones. Lima always wore a crucifix on a chain, a present from his mother. In the middle of one game, the chain suddenly and inexplicably broke, and the cross fell from his neck.

As the bad breaks and strange twists accumulated, the idea of being cursed solidified in Lima's mind. When he shared his concern with his mother back home in the Dominican Republic, she mentioned a local spiritual leader she knew who could diagnose the case, a woman who ran a Christian church called The House of God. When the season ended, Lima wasted no time.

"I went to the Dominican and the first thing when I was there, I went to church." His suspicions were immediately confirmed. "The lady told me there was a spell. She said, 'Oh my god. I can feel your negativity on you.'"

Who would have put such a curse on Lima? An opposing pitcher? A disgruntled hitter? A fan of some rival team, looking for an edge?

According to the spiritual advisor, it was a Santiago resident whom Lima had somehow wronged. "She didn't mention a particular name, but it seems like I promised something to somebody and I didn't follow through. She said it was a lady too. Age thirty–forty. Maybe I promised it, who knows? I don't remember. I do so many favors in my country. You forget stuff."

Lima made every attempt to learn the identity of his hexer to put the situation right. He even took the extraordinary step of appearing on national television in the Dominican Republic (a TV producer friend arranged it) in a public appeal for the woman to identify herself. "I said if there's somebody out there that I promised something to, please come forward." But no luck.

"Nobody came forward. I know somebody out there did it. I want to know who it is."

Fortunately for Lima, addressing the curse at its source was not necessary for overcoming it. The spiritual advisor prescribed a cure somewhat similar to Catholic penance. "You're supposed to say this prayer, say that prayer. I had to go to nine masses in a row. I went with my mom. Two hours, standing the whole time. One hour with the lady, and mass one hour straight."

Lima started to feel the difference after just the first few masses. "Different air . . . I can breathe better. It's just like . . . I didn't feel the heavy body any more."

As for baseball, "Things turned around," says Lima.

"I started believing in myself and then I started winning again."

To keep future curses at bay—as well as bad luck or any other baseball misfortune—Lima has kept to a steady regimen of devotion "to make sure that all the bad karma is out of there." Whenever he's home in Santiago, you can find him at The House of God.

"I go there every week, Monday through Friday. At 6:00 in the afternoon we go there for an hour. I see the lady, say hi, and then I go to mass for an hour." He finds it calms the craziness that can easily slip into a major-league pitcher's mental game. "You feel peace when you go to church."

In the years since his curse, Lima has had other disappointing seasons, including one (2005) in which his stats were worse than 2000. But he can feel the difference between a curse and a slump.

"Sometimes when things are not going your way, that's the way baseball is. I wish I could win 20 games a year, but it's not going to happen. At least we compete. [In 2005] I was pitching well. One bad inning every time. But I was all right."

And though he never discovered the identity of the mysterious Dominican woman in her thirties who put a curse on him for not following through on some promise, he feels confident that the hex is behind him, and that his spiritual advisor found the cure.

"I got my career back. I'm a good believer in Jesus and I think that's probably why I surpassed all the bad stuff. Most people don't believe. I'm a great believer. Now everything is on track."

DIVINE INTERVENTION

While Lima attributes his bad pitching stretch to his personal curse, many players pin the ups and downs of on-field performance on a cleat-wearing higher power: the "baseball gods."

The notion of baseball gods is commonplace throughout clubhouses and dugouts. The term dates back to the early twentieth century, when it began life as a colorful synonym for fate. In more recent years, ballplayers have taken the expression to heart and imbued it with a variety of mystical meanings.

So who are the baseball gods and how do they work?

"They're the old theoretical powers that be that govern or watch over baseball," suggests Tom Glavine. "They're some designees by the higher God, appointed to watch over the game."

Not only do they watch over the game, they mete out justice based on what they see. "There's a saying—Don't shame the field or it's going to shame you," says Padres pitcher Clay Hensley. "An example might be somebody not running a ground ball out. The baseball gods get them back for not hustling." On the other hand, the gods are known to reward those who play the game right. "If you get some bloopers that fall in," says Mets third baseman David Wright, "you say the baseball gods are treating you well."

According to Diamondbacks first baseman Conor Jackson, that's usually payback for hard work. "If you line out four times, but you hit the ball hard, then you'll get a blooper. You know it's the baseball gods looking out for you."

Most players believe that the baseball gods like humility. The gods insist you "don't take anything for granted," says superstar Alex Rodriguez. "The minute you get this game figured out—and start *acting* like it—I think the baseball gods come calling and kind of humble you." For San Diego outfielder Mike Cameron, that extends off the field. "It's okay to be confident, but I think if you are blowing people off because of your stature, it will come back to haunt you. I've seen a lot of players do that and some of the [bad] things that are happening to them now are related."

Diamondbacks third baseman Chad Tracy says the gods respect those who respect the past. "Don't talk about how Babe Ruth didn't face as good a pitching as we do today. Because the baseball gods will bite you, man."

More than anything, the notion of the baseball gods seems to be tied to the idea of karma: Work hard and good things happen; slack off or get cocky, and you pay a price. Even players like Atlanta's catcher Brian McCann, who reject the supernatural terminology ("There are no baseball gods," he says), express that same sentiment in a "secular" way. "I believe if you go out there and you work hard, it's going to pay off."

That idea—championed by every Little League coach in the country—is as old as baseball itself. The legendary Willie Mays, a different kind of "baseball god," says he never heard the term *baseball gods* in his playing days. But the Say Hey Kid is all about the notion that what goes around comes around. "I think you have to play hard. And then you'll excel. I played with a group of guys who all did that. That's why a lot of them are in the Hall of Fame."

CHAPTER 24

THE SUPERFAN
WITH SUPERPOWERS

Superstitious sports fans have long believed that quirks in their routines can control the fate of their favorite teams and players. Wearing a "lucky shirt," sitting in a certain chair for the big game, eating some ritualistic meal—fans have developed all kinds of routines to ensure their team's success.

But in Des Moines, home of the Triple-A Iowa Cubs, the situation is reversed. There, it's the players themselves who are convinced that the actions of a particular fan not only influence the outcome of a game, but the ultimate success or failure of their entire careers.

In many ways, Becky Cornelius fits the profile of a living good luck charm. Born in 1982 with both physical and mental handicaps, her very existence is a story of improbable survival. She was delivered prematurely, and with her hips out of socket. She learned to crawl as a ten-pound baby wearing a two-pound cast, which developed unusual upper body strength for her size.

At age seven, Becky was hit by a car. The damage was extensive. Five ribs were broken, a lung collapsed, and her jaw was shattered. Doctors said a normal kid her size would have been killed, but Becky's extraordinary strength saved her. Nevertheless, she required a series of operations—twenty-seven altogether—over many months. And there were complications. A respirator was left in too long; as a result, her vocal cords do not work. Her voice is a throaty rasp that often startles those unfamiliar with it.

Her many challenges led to a lot of exclusion growing up. "She never spent much time around other kids," says her father, Tom Cornelius. "They used to tease her a lot." The school district "basically wrote her off," declaring that her learning disabilities consigned her to a fourth grade intelligence.

The one place where young Becky found acceptance was at Sec Taylor Stadium, now Principal Park. The family started coming to I-Cubs games when Becky was just a baby. Even then she showed an affinity for the players.

"Her first favorite was Pat Tabler," says Tom. "She always perked up when he came to the plate." By age six she was yelling to batters from her seat and forming friendships with the players. Outfielder Dwight Smith and infielder Brian Guinn would greet her at each game, lifting her over the fence for a hug and kiss. The two players visited her in the hospital after her car accident.

Over the years, she came to know all the players. The Cornelius family became season ticket holders. Even though they live in Bagley, a small town about fifty miles west of Des Moines, they have made the trip for nearly every home game for almost two decades. Becky held her high school graduation party at the ballpark and about fifteen players attended—appropriate, since her dad says that "most of her friends have been baseball players." Now in her mid-twenties and a sturdy four-foot-six, Becky is still a staple at Principal Park. She sits along the leftfield foul line, right behind the home team bullpen, where she constantly calls out to the pitchers.

"I've known them through the years," she says. "We're one big happy family."

At six, Becky began sending little gifts to the players, a practice she continues to this day. It started with chewing gum she would pilfer from her father's sports collectibles store. "She'd say something like 'grape gum is good for two hits, cherry is a home run,' or whatever," recalls Tom. "And amazingly, it happened that way quite a bit. She would holler out for somebody to get two hits and oftentimes they would."

Eventually she was sending pencils, crosses, notebooks, pictures, and other small items to players. She began writing letters and cards to them, wishing them luck, and thanking them for being her friend. In 1991, the Corneliuses created Becky's own baseball card, which depicts her on the front with five I-Cubs players. Becky still gives the cards out to favorite players, many of whom (including Mark Prior) are said to carry them in their wallets or lockers for good luck.

Somewhere along the way, a clubhouse superstition developed, one that persists to this day. "The old saying goes that if you don't keep everything that she gives you, then you're hexed or cursed," says pitcher Phil Norton.

Cursed? "You get hurt or you play bad if you throw them out," explains catcher Josh Paul. "Or you get sent down, or miss a chance to get called up."

For some players, avoiding such a fate can mean holding on to dozens of items. Becky is apt to send letters and trinkets to favorite players several times a week. A number of lockers in the I-Cubs clubhouse are virtual Becky museums, with cards, pins, homemade crafts, and other memorabilia overflowing from the corners.

Pat Listach, who coached in Iowa, said he got letters once a week, wishing him luck. Pitchers Bobby Brownlie and Jermaine Van Buren—two of Becky's favorites on the 2005 squad—got gifts and cards at least as often. "I save everything," says Van Buren. "It's not going anywhere. I'm going to keep it forever." And why is that? "Becky's special."

Van Buren—like all the I-Cubs—has heard clubhouse tales of players who didn't hold on to Becky's gifts, or spoke coarsely to her. The moral of these stories is always the same: Becky has mystical powers, and you don't want to cross her.

Norton heard the story of a pitcher who got into an argument with Becky. "Then he went on a road trip and blew all but one save on the road. He came back and made up with her, and then didn't blow a save for the next couple of weeks."

Former I-Cub hurler Bryan Corey tells of a player who left for the season without saying good-bye to Becky. He got in a car accident on the way home.

Listach heard one about a player who was a MVP. "He came here, yelled at Becky, and tore up her letter. And he never hit over .200 again. He's out of the game now."

So is Pat Cline, the much-touted 1990s Cubs prospect. According to an I-Cubs clubbie, "He'd throw the letters away, kinda scoff at her. I believe a couple of times he even said bad words to her." The result? "His baseball career ended."

On a Triple-A club—where players are scrambling to get to the big leagues, and looking for any advantage possible—no one wants to take a chance on following in such footsteps. So players try to stay on Becky's good side, even if they are occasionally uncomfortable with her attention. The letters and cards, for example, sometimes go beyond mere good wishes. They are dotted with religious references (players are referred to as her "Christian brothers") and may be accompanied by handmade crosses or religious stickers. They often assume more than an athlete-fan acquaintanceship, and imply a close personal bond with the player.

> Dear Bobby Brownlie. Hi. How are you doing? I am okay. I need to talk to you about something. I need to know that you will always be here for me? I have some great news to tell you. When will I see you again? My Christian brother back home said that you were the right friend for me. He wants me to be happy. Good luck on the road.

> Dear Todd Wellmeyer [sic]. Hi! How are you doing? I am ok. I could have used a friend today. I do trust you. Tell the guys I said hello. From your friend Becky C.

Even players who have felt that Becky crossed a line—and she has occasionally called players at their hotels, or even at their homes, and waited for them in the parking lot after a game—are often unwilling to say so.

"That's the rule," says outfielder Jason DuBois. "You don't talk bad about her. She loves the ball club. She's a great fan. We want to keep her happy, for keeping us going every day."

Even the front office doesn't want to tempt fate. Becky sends cards to Jim Nahas, the I-Cubs assistant GM. Knowing the curse theory that surrounds such gestures, Nahas keeps them. "I can't say if I believe in it or don't believe in it," he says, "but I respect it. So I'm not going to cross the line. I treat [the card] with respect. I read it; I keep it."

After all, Nahas has business to think about. "Ticket sales have been good. We're ahead of the pace of last year. The weather has been good. Just throw one [Becky letter] away and all of the sudden it starts raining and our ticket system goes down, our scanners don't work, we can't get people in the ballpark."

Surprisingly, the Cornelius family says they are unaware that the entire "Becky curse" legend has developed among players. "We've never heard of it," says Tom. "We wondered why some of these guys that are big-profile people carried her stuff." But Tom has a theory about why his daughter's gifts and comments—why courting her favor—has taken on such power with athletes.

"When she got hit [by a car], anybody her size should have been dead. And I guess they figured, 'Okay, the Lord's smiling down on her. If she gives me something, I want to keep it.'"

For the record, Becky claims never to put curses or hexes on people, even when they let her down. "I usually try and talk things out," she says. "Even the other team. If they do something dumb, I just try and talk things out without hurting them."

But players insist that in heated moments, Becky tries to work a little voodoo. An usher in her section says, "I've had to counsel her on her language. She'll swear. She'll start putting hexes on the players."

Former I-Cub Brendan Harris claims that one day a left-handed pitcher ignored her. "The next day there was another left-handed pitcher warming up and he threw out his hamstring. And she said, 'Oh sorry, that was supposed to be for so-and-so.'"

Letters to visiting players sometimes declare that they have disappointed her, or that they are not her Christian brothers. Clubbies wary of upsetting players don't always deliver every missive.

Even her most beloved players aren't safe if they run afoul of her. Brownlie always greets and jokes with Becky; he even sat with her to watch fireworks after a game once, at Becky's request. (The noise scares her.) She describes him as "a real good kid. I look up to him for everything. He's the sort of kid I'd want to have on my pitching staff." But when she perceived a slight from him, she told the pitcher he would "burn in the underworld." Then she said she was just kidding.

"If she says something like that and you ask her why later on, she'll say, 'Oh, I didn't say that,'" reports one player who, like several others, does not want to be quoted by name on the subject of Becky's powers for fear of the consequences. "It's hard to know how much she's aware of what she says and does."

We need two outs here! C'mon!
I said throw to the catcher, not throw to the batter!
You're in charge! You're in charge, Rich, okay?
You're in charge!

For Becky, an I-Cubs game is a participatory event. Throughout the nine innings, she lets loose a steady stream of commentary, criticism, and encouragement.

When she calls a player's name—especially as he's walking on or off the field—she wants acknowledgment, and usually gets it: a quick hello, or a nod of the head, or a wave in her direction. Giving Becky her props is as much a part of some players' routines as batting practice or warm-ups.

"She's been coming to the games for years," says outfielder Corey Patterson. "We try to make sure we stop and say hello to her before our game starts, day in and day out."

Players often joke with her. Recently, pitchers in the bullpen started tossing sunflower seeds at her, a good-natured form of ribbing that Becky enjoyed so much, her father started supplying the seeds. When the I-Cubs won the division title in 2001, players doused Becky with beer. Chad Myers declared her the "tenth player" on the team. The camaraderie is often genuine, even if—as former I-Cubs radio broadcaster Dave Raymond puts it—"they're scared to death of her."

There's no question that the I-Cubs are an important part of Becky's life—in fact, it's quite possible that Becky's love for the I-Cubs saved her life. Immediately after her car accident, the seven-year-old had to be airlifted to a hospital in Des Moines. Medical professionals told her parents it was imperative that Becky stay conscious during the flight; otherwise, she might die. The Corneliuses had an I-Cubs team directory in the car, with bios of each player. They gave it to the nurse on the life-flight to read to Becky, who stayed alert and enthralled throughout the recitation.

It's that kind of inexplicable connection to the team—the sense that this physically and mentally disadvantaged young woman has always been somehow supernaturally plugged into the I-Cubs, and fated to be a part of them—that creates the mystique of Becky.

"She's a part of this ballpark," says Assistant GM Nahas. "She's the type of person that makes this place unique."

Becky appreciates the affection she gets from the team. "A lot of guys that I talk to just love me to death. They don't want anything to happen to me. They tell me if I need anything, just let them know. They look out for me."

And in so doing, they also look out for themselves.

CHAPTER 25

WHEN IS A
CURSE NOT A CURSE

When the 2004 Red Sox made it to the World Series, the media asked if this team could end the dreaded Curse of the Bambino. Boston fans responded with enthusiasm, wearing "Reverse the Curse" T-shirts and bringing pictures of the Babe to Fenway Park to exorcise the ghost they felt had long haunted them. When the 2005 Chicago White Sox reached the World Series, the media asked if this team could end the Curse of the Black Sox. Chicago fans responded with . . . "What curse?"

The result was a philosophical conundrum akin to the unobserved tree falling in a forest: If a team is said to be cursed, but nobody much believes in the curse, does the curse actually exist?

The 1919 Black Sox scandal would certainly seem to have all the makings of a good hexing. Eight Chicago players, including superstar Shoeless Joe Jackson, knew about or participated in a conspiracy to throw the World Series; the following year they were banned from baseball for life. The curse logic follows easily: "We threw that World Series, so we can't win another one," or "We can't win again until Shoeless Joe gets in the Hall of Fame" (a cause close to the hearts of many White Sox fans).

In addition, the legacy of losing that followed the 1919 season would seem ample evidence: For the next eighty-six years, the White Sox didn't win a World Series. In fact, the team only appeared in one Fall Classic during that stretch.

Lay out the case for the curse to White Sox fans prior to the 2005 postseason, though, and it seems nobody is buying it.

"I've never heard of that," says one patron at U.S. Cellular Field, the Sox home park.

"I grew up a White Sox fan and followed them every year for thirty years," adds another, "and I've never heard or read anything about a Black Sox curse."

Fan after fan, as well as White Sox workers with the organization for decades, agree: There was no Black Sox curse. "That's garbage," says an indignant man in full White Sox regalia (jersey, hat, face paint). "You're thinking of that *other* team."

Herein lies what may be a key reason White Sox fans reject the Black Sox curse: It sounds a little too "North Side." The White Sox have long been regarded as the Second City's "second team," and anything that smacks of the crosstown rival Cubs is to be rejected. The Curse of the Billy Goat (see Chapter 21: Giving Up the Goat) is a long-established part of the Cubs' core identity.

Beyond that, many people say that White Sox fans are simply too no-nonsense to indulge in such frivolities. Known as the blue-collar alternative to the yuppie-loved Cubs, White Sox fans repeatedly dismiss curse talk as a lame excuse for a team's poor performance. Chat up patrons at neighborhood bars around the stadium—local institutions like Jimbo's, or First Base—and the dismissal is unanimous: Curses are for suckers.

Most White Sox players, too, claim that the Black Sox curse was simply never mentioned prior to 2005. Greg Norton, a first baseman with the team from 1996 to 2000, says, "I never heard anything. Everybody was always talking about the curse of the Cubs."

Numerous members of the 2005 World Championship team—including Paul Konerko, Aaron Rowand, and Cliff Politte—say the same. It's all a media invention. Prior to the postseason hype, they never heard of a Black Sox curse.

An exception is catcher Chris Widger. "Oh yeah, I heard about and read about it before," he says. "Because the Cubs and Boston are so much more out there in the media, you hear about those curses more. But when you're around baseball, you hear about that kind of stuff. It makes for good reading and good coffee talk."

Widger adds quickly that neither he nor his teammates subscribed to the idea. "I can't remember one conversation where that was brought up, except for when the media would leave [the locker room] and we'd say, 'I can't believe we had to talk about that again.'" He's grateful that in his time with the White Sox "it wasn't like Boston where they have to hear about it every day. Then if you lose a game or something bad happens, all of a sudden it wasn't because you made a mistake, it was because the curse got you."

"Some people really believe that," says Ozzie Guillen, the Sox outspoken manager. "They really believe something is going on there to make them lose." Though he was born and raised in superstitious Venezuela ("a country where a lot of people believe in this stuff," he says), Guillen—who wears uniform number 13—thinks curses are a cop-out.

"When you lose for years, people always blame it on somebody. I think you don't win because somebody's got a better team than you. I think you're not winning because you got a horses—t team."

For Rowand, it simply doesn't make sense that the teams of the past would somehow prevent the teams of the present from winning. "I believe in ghosts and all that, but not curses," he says. "It's about the team you have that year, not about the team you had fifty years before."

Pitcher Jon Garland agrees. "It's hard to think of a team as cursed if you're not winning," he says. "It's almost like you're making an excuse. 'It's just bad luck.'"

"You create luck," says Guillen. "[In 2005] everything we did was right. It wasn't magic, or somebody looking out for us, or just luck."

The White Sox's long-standing lack of luck is precisely what made people look for supernatural explanations. But what many modern-day fans don't realize is that the team's string of misfortunes predate the 1919 scandal. And so too does talk of a White Sox curse.

In fact, in the earlier days of the club—before the Black Sox scandal and before Vasili Sianis tried to bring his billy goat to Wrigley Field—White Sox observers spoke of a "Comiskey Curse." Named for the team's original owner, the curse referred to the bad breaks that seemed to plague the team since early in its existence. While evidence can be cited from the club's first decade (for example, losing the AL pennant on the last day of the season in both 1905 and 1908), the curse was said to have begun with the opening of Comiskey Park in 1910.

Ironically, on March 17 of that year—St. Patrick's Day— Charles Comiskey scheduled a groundbreaking ceremony during which a special brick, painted green to invoke the luck of the Irish, was laid as the cornerstone of the new park. The would-be good-luck charm was visible at the park until 1959, when new owner Bill Veeck had the building's exterior painted white.

Despite the gesture, things started going wrong right away. Construction was delayed for five weeks when local steel workers went on strike. A day before the park was to open, worker Frank McDermott fell off the roof to his death. The Sox lost their first game in their new home (when the somewhat superstitious Comiskey realized that opening day for the stadium would fall on a Friday, he tried unsuccessfully to get the schedule changed) and three players were injured in the first three days at the park.

The coming years held some great moments too, culminating in the team's 1917 World Series victory over the mighty New York Giants. It was the team's second championship, following their defeat of the Cubs in the 1906 Series. They had a losing season in 1918, but came back strong in 1919, winning the pennant and heading into the World Series as heavy favorites over the Cincinnati Reds. Then came the Black Sox scandal.

The game-fixing episode itself can be viewed as a manifestation of the Comiskey Curse. The players who threw the Series were said to be motivated in large part by Charles Comiskey's notorious tightfistedness. He was generous with younger players, regularly giving bonuses to motivate them, and he also invited baseball patrons and beat writers to lavish dinners and hunting parties, effectively courting their professional favor. But with older players and loyal veterans, he broke promises, refused even paltry financial incentives, and released people (including Sox stalwarts like Eddie Collins and Billy Sullivan) unceremoniously.

Even the nickname "Black Sox" is said to have derived not from the disgrace of the gambling fix, but from Comiskey's decision earlier in 1919 to make players pay for their own laundry. The team protested by not washing their uniforms at all, eventually earning the sobriquet.

After the scandal, the Comiskey Curse kicked into high gear. For the next fifteen years, the team finished no better than fifth in the league—in six of those seasons, they were seventh or eighth. Certainly some of this can be pinned on the devastating loss of key players following the banishments. But the losing continued for three decades. From 1921 to 1950, the White Sox had a total of just six winning seasons. In 1932, the team's record was 49–102, as they finished an astonishing 56½ games back in the AL.

Losing was only part of the story, though. Players themselves seemed ill-fated.

- Pitcher Dickie Kerr, angry that Comiskey refused him a meager $500 raise after winning 19 games in 1921, played a sandlot game against several banned Black Sox players. As a result, Kerr himself was banned from major-league baseball for four years.

- Centerfielder Johnny Mostil had an affair with the wife of teammate Red Farber and attempted suicide during Spring Training in 1927, slashing his wrists, neck, and chest with a razor.

- In 1928, the Sox spent a then-record $123,000 on infielder Bill Cissell, only to watch his stats fizzle and a drinking problem grow. Cissell was traded away in 1932, reportedly returning to the club years later . . . as a stadium laborer. He died of alcohol-related malnutrition at age forty-five. (For a while, some fans even spoke of a "Cissell Curse" haunting the team.)

- In 1938, All-Star pitcher Monty Stratton lost a leg when he accidentally shot himself in a hunting accident.

- In 1940, a cinder blew into the eye of star second baseman Jackie Hayes during a Spring Training game against the Cubs. The eye became infected and within a few months, he lost sight in it, ending his career. Three years later Hayes lost sight in his other eye too.

Charles Comiskey himself died in 1931 (of a broken heart, some said, regarding his shamed team) and was succeeded by his son, whose own biography seemed cursed. Lou Comiskey—who could be gruff like his father, but was fairer and had a compassionate side (at the height of the Depression, he had the club pass out the previous day's unsold sandwiches to the homeless)—contracted scarlet fever at twenty-seven and was burdened with its consequences until the disease led him to an early grave at fifty-four.

Family squabbles and court battles over ownership dominated the late 1950s—rebuilding years for the team—and Bill Veeck gained control of the club in 1959. Adding fuel to the talk of a Comiskey Curse, the team's first year under different ownership was also the first year they returned to the World Series since the Black Sox scandal forty years earlier.

The 1959 "Go-Go Sox" were not big hitters—the team batting average was .250, good enough only for sixth in the American League that year, and their 97 homers were the least in the AL. But they were strong on pitching and defense, qualities that proved insufficient to win the Series. They lost to the L.A. Dodgers, four games to two.

The team fared better in the early 1960s, but the snakebit quality never quite went away and they failed to win another pennant. However, the era of new ownership was unmistakable in Chicago. Veeck was surely baseball's most colorful showman, known for introducing exploding scoreboards and gimmicky promotions to lure fans to the stadium. His stunts included cow-milking contests, belly dancers, beer-case-stacking competitions, breakfast games (followed by a "shower" in centerfield), and much more.

Veeck saw some value in exploiting people's interest in the supernatural. Prior to a game in 1959, he staged a "Martian invasion" at Comiskey, in which four midgets dressed as aliens and carrying "ray guns" were deposited by helicopter onto the field and tried to abduct players Nellie Fox and Luis Aparicio. One of the aliens was Eddie Gaedel, whom Veeck had famously used in St. Louis as a pinch hitter, to guarantee a walk. (Veeck unabashedly loved little people, and once deployed a battalion of them as Comiskey Park beer vendors after fans complained that concessionaires walking through the stands obscured their view of the field.)

On May 14, 1977—in his second stint as owner of the White Sox, and following a disastrous last-place finish the previous year— Veeck held Anti-Superstition Night at Comiskey Park, an attempt to flaunt and thereby expunge the bad luck that seemed to plague the team for so long. People deliberately walked under ladders and broke mirrors, witches were brought in to cast spells, etc.

The trick seemed to work. The following day the White Sox beat the Cleveland Indians 18–2. More winning followed and by July 2, the team found itself in the highly unfamiliar position of first place in the American League. By the end of the month, they held a 5½-game lead in their division. But the excitement didn't last long. Just three weeks later, they surrendered first place for good, finishing the season in third with a 90–72 record.

It was one more instance of frustration in a decade of futility and bad luck. The 1970 club lost 106 games. In 1973, the White Sox experienced a remarkable string of injuries, eventually landing thirty-eight players on the DL by season's end. In 1979, Comiskey Park hosted the embarrassing Disco Demolition Night (another Veeck concoction), during which marauding fans so destroyed the playing field that the evening's game had to be postponed.

The team fared much better in the early '80s and early '90s, winning their division in 1983 and 1993. But in both years, the Sox were eliminated in the first round of playoffs, and in both years, they failed to win a single postseason game at home. Their promising 1994 season—fueled by a career year from eventual MVP Frank Thomas—was thwarted by the unprecedented player's strike that ended the season early.

The commanding victories of the 2005 squad—which racked up an 11–1 record through the playoffs and World Series—has done much to erase those bad memories and all talk of curses, be they Comiskey or Black Sox. That makes it easier for players to enjoy what these curses mean to fans.

"It's pretty neat to talk about now that it's over," says Widger. "It's fun to listen to the old-timers that come around the field—'Thank you so much for lifting the curse! We had to wait this long and now it's over, and now we can move on too.'"

CHAPTER 26

CURSE BUSTERS, INC.

Lee Gavin wants to know where his 2004 World Series ring is. Granted, he didn't actually play for the Boston Red Sox that year—at sixteen, he was hardly eligible—but the way he sees it, he's as responsible as anyone for their historic victory that October. In fact, he clinched the title for them on August 31—months before the team's stunning postseason victories over the New York Yankees and St. Louis Cardinals.

That was the day Gavin was in the rightfield stands at Fenway Park with a bunch of friends. In the fourth inning, Lee's favorite player, Manny Ramírez, hit a long foul ball toward his section. The teenager raced into the aisle to try to catch it. The ball flew through his hands and hit his face, knocking out his two front teeth.

And, Gavin believes, knocking out the Curse of the Bambino, the long losing streak that had plagued the Red Sox since they sold Babe Ruth to the Yankees in 1920.

At first, Gavin didn't believe his cut lip, missing teeth, and lacerated tongue could have any bearing on the dreaded curse. "But then I thought about all the other coincidences and it all started coming together for me," he says.

The other coincidences are these:

- Gavin lives in the Sudbury farmhouse that Babe Ruth himself lived in. (Ruth's daughter Dorothy once visited, accompanied by the son of Smokey Joe Wood.) The Gavin family bought the home in 1986—the last time the Red Sox were in the World Series.

• Gavin was at the park celebrating the birthday of his best friend Jarrett Lowe. Also in the party was Jarrett's younger brother Derek Lowe, who shares a name with the famous pitcher, then playing for the Red Sox.

• Gavin's father had season tickets on the leftfield side of the stadium. This was the first time Lee ever sat in rightfield— just the spot where the ball was hit.

• The Red Sox won that day, while the Yankees, playing in New York, suffered their most lopsided defeat ever, losing 22–0 to the Cleveland Indians.(Gavin also says there was a full moon that night; astronomers say not quite.)

The *Boston Globe* got hold of the story and Lee Gavin became a national celebrity, even appearing on *The Tonight Show*. When the Sox won the World Championship that fall—ending eighty-six years of futility—young Lee Gavin had a lot to brag about.

But he has many competitors for the title of Ultimate Curse Breaker. In 2004, as in many previous years, there was no shortage of Red Sox fans doing their darnedest to end the Ruth hex.

In July, a group of Boston schoolteachers, who make a trip each summer to catch a Red Sox road game, traveled to Baltimore. They visited the home where Babe Ruth was born, now a museum, and "walked in a circle three times in reverse in his bedroom," one reported. They then went to Camden Yards and had their picture taken by a Yankee fan ("It had to be a Yankee fan," they say) in front of Ruth's statue.

That September, singer Jimmy Buffett played a concert at Fenway Park, in which he and two band members, one dressed as Ruth and the other dressed as a witch doctor, enacted a curse-breaking ceremony. In interviews, Buffett has suggested that his ceremony helped break the curse. (The following year Buffett played the first-ever concerts at Wrigley Field, with less-momentous results.)

It seems just about every Red Sox fan tried some desperate measure, and attempts to break the curse could be creative and far reaching. In 2001, Paul Giorgio brought a Sox cap and Yankees cap on a climbing expedition to Mount Everest, and asked a Buddhist lama how he might use them to break the curse. The spiritual advisor instructed Giorgio to first place the Sox cap at the *chorten*—a stone altar where climbers burn offerings to the gods—and then to plant it at the summit when he reached it. Giorgio did as told. Two days later he burned the Yankees cap at base camp, for good measure.

Fans have paraded around Fenway's field dressed as Ruth's ghost—some even proposed painting a picture of Ruth on the Green Monster. In one of the oddest curse-lifting efforts, scuba divers attempted to recover from a Sudbury pond a piano that Ruth is said to have thrown into the water, believing that salvaging the instrument would somehow salvage the team.

The basic premise of the "Curse of the Bambino" is simple: In the first fifteen years of World Series play (1903–18), Boston won five championships, more than any other team in baseball. In 1920, they sold the contract of Babe Ruth, their hot young pitcher-turned-outfielder, to the New York Yankees, a somewhat lackluster team with no championships to its name. After that, the Yankees went on to win numerous pennants and World Series titles throughout the century (thirty-nine pennants and twenty-six titles, to be exact), while the Red Sox went decade after decade (after decade after decade after decade after decade after decade after decade, to be exact) without a World Series title.

Though the legacy of losing stretches back to the Deadball Era, the notion of the curse is much more recent. Certainly Ruth himself never heard the phrase in his lifetime. In fact, it may surprise many contemporary baseball fans to know that throughout the eras of Jimmie Foxx, Ted Williams, and Carl Yastrzemski, no one spoke of a Curse of the Bambino or any Boston curse. Even after the team's notorious 1978 dive—in which the Sox squandered a 14½-game midsummer lead in the AL East to eventually lose the pennant to the Yankees on Bucky Dent's infamous walk-off home run—fans of neither team considered the Red Sox's misfortunes to be supernaturally derived.

One of the first references to a curse appeared in 1986, when sportswriter Frederick Waterman wrote that when Ruth left for New York, "he carried away with him the good luck and winning touch of the Red Sox." During the team's ill-fated World Series appearance that year, writer George Vecsey wrote about "Babe Ruth's curse" afflicting the Sox as they lost the last two games of the Series. (Game 6, in which the Sox were literally one strike away from winning the Series, ended when a routine grounder bounced through first baseman Bill Buckner's legs, an error that ultimately cost them the game and the championship, and a watershed moment in the curse legend.) Then in 1990, *Boston Globe* writer Dan Shaughnessy penned a history of the team, viewed through the lens of its heartbreaking losses. The book was entitled *The Curse of the Bambino*, and the phrase immediately entered the national sports lexicon.

If the curse itself didn't haunt the team, talk of the curse certainly did. Almost as sweet as winning the 2004 World Series was simply putting to rest years of media pestering and questions. The Red Sox finally got the last laugh.

"I always heard everybody talking about the curse," says Big Papi David Ortiz, adding with a smile, "but I don't think there's one any more."

Catcher Jason Varitek says that the BoSox "had always just gotten outplayed at the right times. That was the biggest issue." Former star Dwight Evans, who patrolled rightfield at Fenway for the better part of two decades, agrees. "All the things that happened to us would probably make you think that [we were cursed], but not really," he says. "You make your own breaks."

Still, Boston legend Johnny Pesky says that living with the curse "wasn't easy. We got blamed for a lot of things." Even though no curse was said to have existed when he played, Pesky was retroactively cited as an example of its power, allegedly holding a relay throw too long, thus allowing the go-ahead run to score in Game 7 of the 1946 World Series. When the team won in 2004, Pesky was gleeful. "I was signing balls, *'The curse is over!'*" he says.

But most players who have passed through Boston claim never to have taken seriously the notion that the team was doomed.

"I don't think a player would ever think like that," says Lou Merloni, who played more than five "cursed" seasons with the team. "It's more fun for the media and the fans."

Closer Keith Foulke says that if the curse was discussed at all in 2004, "we talked about how stupid it was." Teammate Kevin Millar agrees. "We did a great job of keeping our doors closed to the baloney that goes on—whatever negative energy was outside the doors."

Millar says that such negative energy can creep into your game "if you're weak mentally." It's important to leave previous hardships in the past. "We weren't around for eighty-six years," he says. "We weren't a part of all the negative stuff."

Bill Mueller, third basemen on the winning squad and the 2004 batting champ, echoes that sentiment. The curse "never really affected me, because I'm competing against a pitcher for the other team, not all the other stuff." As pitcher Derek Lowe put it, "Billy Buckner missing a ground ball [in 1986]—I don't know how that was going to affect me throwing a pitch in 2004."

But other Red Sox players admit the curse crossed their minds in those moments when things seemed to go disastrously wrong for the team.

Pitcher John Wasdin, with the Sox from 1997 to 2000, remembers the controversial "phantom tag" in the 1999 ALCS (the Yankees' Chuck Knoblauch missed tagging José Offerman by a wide margin, but Offerman was called out, for allegedly stepping outside the baseline). "At that point we were like, 'Will we ever get a chance? Does it ever fall for the Red Sox?' That was probably the one time we started to reflect on it."

When the 2003 team got close—up 4–0 against New York midway through Game 7 of the ALCS—it looked like the curse was taking a beating . . . until the Yankees tied the game in the eighth inning, and won it in the eleventh. "Oh, we definitely believed in it after the Yankees came back," recalls Johnny Damon. "The ghost is going to stay here forever!"

Reliever Todd Jones remembers that prior to that game, players were joking that they "didn't want to be Bill Buckner." It was all in jest, but Jones notes that "if you're joking about it, you're thinking about it."

Thinking about it could be hard to avoid. While Derek Lowe says he never believed in the curse, he allows that "you could easily buy into it because every August they start talking about when the Red Sox traditionally slide. You get asked about it nonstop."

One danger, says Lowe, is that it becomes easy for a player to "use it as an excuse. 'Oh, the curse got us!' When we're up 5–2 against New York in Game 7, Babe Ruth didn't make us lose that game."

While the team itself never officially endorsed the curse concept, they marketed it in certain ways, hiring exorcists to cleanse Fenway Park, for example, or inviting Ruth's daughter to throw out the first pitch of a 1999 postseason game. In 2003, the Portland Sea Dogs, Double-A affiliate for the Red Sox, hosted "Reverse the Curse" night, complete with skits that had the Babe back in a Boston uniform.

Even Kevin Millar, who says players "don't believe any of it," became a radio spokesperson for "Reverse the Curse" ice cream, a locally made treat that has since changed its name to "Curse Reversed!"

When Boston won, the joy that swept Red Sox Nation after eighty-six years of frustration was profound. Throughout New England, fans took to the streets to celebrate. An estimated 3.2

million people lined city streets and the banks of the Charles to watch the Red Sox victory parade. Many of the faithful couldn't help thinking of those who spent their entire lives rooting for the team, without living to see the day of glory. Droves of fans planted BoSox pennants on graves of loved ones. Walking through a New England cemetery in early November, it looked like Memorial Day for the Red Sox Nation.

For Rebecca Hancock, the graveyard was an appropriate place to celebrate the victory, since she believes it was there that she became the one to break the curse. Her story is a reminder that while most curse-breaking attempts were done in fun, others had a much more personal meaning.

Hancock lost her seventeen-year-old daughter, Amy Gilbert, in a car accident in May 2003. That fall, Rebecca says, Amy's high school field hockey team had "many strange winning games in the playoff season." Friends and teammates felt that Amy was helping them, and would visit the cemetery after games, leaving the game ball on her grave.

In 2004, Hancock wanted Amy's Red Sox–loving schoolmates to experience a World Series win. When Boston lost the first three games of the ALCS to the Yankees and faced a sweep, Rebecca "went through the cemetery holding a N.Y. Yankee Beanie Baby by its neck, and complained big time that it would be nice if the Red Sox could win at least one game," she says. "And that night they won."

The Sox continued winning, trouncing the Yankees in four straight (the first team to win a league championship series after losing the first three games) and then steamrolling over the Cardinals in the World Series. Hancock has no doubt that Amy and her fifteen-year-old cousin Kristin Wagner, also killed in the crash, were responsible for the victories. "Blonde babes is what got the Babe in the end," she claims.

But she also warns that "the Curse of the Bambino was lifted for that one year only." Hancock—a Yankee fan herself—has since sought to reinstate it, praying to Amy, walking the cemetery in a Yankees cap, playing her trumpet at the grave. She has developed theories about the role angels can play in helping sports teams. "Angels can cause injuries to occur," she cites as an example. "They can also alter the weather if it is going to benefit their team."

For Rebecca, petitioning Amy to curse the Red Sox helps maintain a connection with her daughter. "She was my life," says the single mother. "I lost my world when Amy went to heaven. I have had to learn how to live again." Baseball has become a conduit for dealing with her grief.

Sitting in a bedroom in Babe Ruth's former home, safely under glass, is the baseball Lee Gavin caught (almost) on August 31, 2004. "It has a blood mark from my hands, and a bat mark from Manny's bat, and a little scratch from where it hit the ground," he describes. It also bears the autograph of Ramírez—in the wake of all the hoopla, Gavin got to meet his Red Sox hero.

The Gavin house (which still bears a burn mark on the floor where the Babe tapped out his pipe ashes) is filled with other memorabilia too; as fans heard about the story, they dropped all manner of Sox souvenirs at their front steps: notes, cigars, bottles of champagne, even a large portrait of Ruth pitching in a Red Sox uniform, mounted on plywood. Some fans left mass cards for Ruth saying, "Thank you so much. Rest in peace."

For Lee Gavin, taking one for the team made the 2004 World Series extra thrilling. "I watched every single game to the end," he says. "I was so excited. Knowing that maybe it was true that I could have broken the curse."

He pauses a moment, then adds, "But then again, I can't take all the credit for it. The team had to do their own work too."

CHAPTER 27

BEDEVILED

What's in a name? When a new major-league franchise was announced for Tampa Bay, Florida, fans had many suggestions for a moniker. Fruit Blossoms, Pterodactyls, Bigfeet, Backcrackers, Snowbirds, and Toads were among the more than 7,000 suggestions that poured in. Based on percentages, the list was whittled down to two fish-based choices: the Manta Rays and the Devil Rays. The public was invited to vote by phone, and more than 70,000 people called in.

A few religious folks objected to the winner, feeling that the word *devil* was somehow courting favor with the occult. A decade into the team's existence, many fans feel the Devil Rays short history has indeed been hellish. Some have even wondered aloud if the team is cursed.

The stats alone tell a pretty dismal story. Even allowing for the sluggish start-up that most expansion teams experience, the Devil Rays have been unusually slow out of the gate. In their first nine years of existence, they have yet to compete seriously in their division, having finished last in all but one of those seasons (and second to last in the other). They have not had a single winning season, their best record coming in 2004 when they finished 70–91. In 2006, they set an American League record by losing 60 games in which they had the lead.

The Rays are regularly last in many offensive and pitching categories, and often vie for the worst record in the majors. It doesn't help that baseball's other 1998 expansion team, the Arizona Diamondbacks, made the playoffs in three of its first nine seasons, winning the World Series in just its fourth year.

Some losing teams can be said to be less than the sum of their parts, but the Devil Rays players haven't performed much better individually. The team has developed a reputation as a place where good players go to perform poorly, and budding stars die on the vine. A few examples:

The Rays invested over $10 million in pitcher Matt White, expecting him to be a big part of their starting rotation. Nearly ten years after he was signed, he had yet to make it to the majors, and spent much of that time with back and shoulder injuries.

Lefty Tony Saunders, the team's first pick in the expansion draft (who went 6–15 in the club's first year), broke his pitching arm in 1999, and broke it again the following year.

Paul Wilder, the team's first-round pick in the 1996 draft, was nettled by injuries, stalled in Class-A ball, and was eventually released by the team six years later.

Indeed, being labeled a Devil Rays "hot prospect" can be hazardous to your health. Star-in-waiting Josh Hamilton was sidelined by injuries and drug problems, the latter of which incurred a long suspension from major-league baseball. Nick Bierbrodt, another promising newcomer, was shot in the arm and chest while waiting at a fast-food restaurant's drive-through. Five-tool phenom Greg "Toe" Nash—hailed as the next coming of Babe Ruth—was convicted of statutory rape and did time; later arrests for drug possession, robbery, and other crimes resulted in his release from the Rays and subsequent teams.

Then there are the overpriced, underproducing stars. The Rays signed pitcher Juan Guzman to a two-year deal for $12.5 million. For this, they got exactly 5 outs: Guzman made it through one-and-two-thirds innings of the Rays 2000 home opener, surrendering 8 runs . . . and then never pitched in the majors again due to shoulder tendonitis. (That's $2.5 million per out.)

Wilson Alvarez landed the biggest contract in the team's history—five years, $35 million—to become their first pitcher. After several stints on the DL his first two years, he missed the next two seasons entirely following shoulder surgery. In 2002, he finished his lackluster tenure with a five-year, 17–26 record and 4.62 ERA.

Power-hitting Greg Vaughn was a home run machine in the late 1990s, hitting 50 in 1998 and 45 in 1999. The Rays signed him for four years and $34 million. His subsequent annual HR production?: 28 (2000), 24 (2001), and 8 (2002—a year in which he only played in 69 games and hit .163). Having seen enough, the club released him in early 2003.

But Vaughn was an MVP compared to Vinny Castilla, who came to the Devil Rays having averaged .301, 40 home runs, and 118 RBI in his previous four seasons with Colorado. In Tampa Bay he lasted one-and-one-quarter seasons, hitting .219 with 8 homers and 51 RBI, and missing 85 games with injuries. The price tag for such production: $13 million.

But all of that speaks to the *effects* of a possible curse. What about a *cause*?

When Aubrey Huff, one of the few bright spots for the team in the mid-2000s, joined the DL just two weeks into the 2006 season (in true Devil Rays fashion, four of his teammates from the Opening Day roster were already out with injuries), he quipped that maybe Tropicana Field was built over an ancient Indian burial ground, and that the spot—and the team—were therefore cursed.

Actually, he wasn't far off.

Tropicana Field began its life as the Florida Suncoast Dome in 1990. Though the city did not have a major-league baseball franchise then, developers hoped that the stadium might attract a team, something the area had long coveted. In the meantime, the Dome hosted hockey, football, tennis, basketball, and concerts.

Prior to the Dome, the site was part of a larger low-income housing project.

Prior to that, it was a cemetery.

In fact, three cemeteries (Oaklawn, Moffet, and Evergreen) used to occupy the land on which Tropicana Field and its parking lot now reside. They were part of what was once a substantial African-American community in that area, stretching back to the early 1900s. *St. Petersburg Times* reporter Jon Wilson recounts that the neighborhood, bounded by First Avenue South to Fifth Avenue South between Martin Luther King Street and 16th Street, had its own local character.

"The area was known as the 'Gas Plant' for the two big natural gas storage cylinders that sat in the middle of the neighborhood," he says. "There were churches, a school, grocery stores, bars, and other small businesses, but mostly streets and little courts where people lived, sometimes in what most outsiders would consider 'slum' housing, but what were homes— sweet homes, to many."

The Gas Plant had the vibrancy of an active community. Charlie Williams, who ran numbers in St. Pete's for years, lived over by the railroad tracks. There was an affluent section called Sugar Hill, where more well-heeled blacks tended to congregate.

Like any segregated community in early-twentieth-century America, racism was always a fact of life. Wilson tells that in 1914 "a mob of white St. Petersburg residents lynched a black man and shot apart his dangling corpse."

The three adjacent cemeteries occupied the area in and around what is now Tropicana Field. They included the remains of city founders and Civil War veterans. As this land was developed in the mid-twentieth century, the graves were supposed to be moved to other interment sites. In 1958, about 150 coffins from Moffet Cemetery and 225 from Evergreen were relocated to nearby Lincoln Cemetery, to make way for an apartment building that has since been torn down.

Less clear is what happened to the graves in Oaklawn Cemetery. In 1949, construction began at the site for Laurel Park, a low-income apartment complex that was razed in 1990 to build the stadium's parking lot. While all the coffins should have been

moved, construction projects in the area since then have un-
earthed some unpleasant surprises.

In February 1976, road crews building I-275 found old leg
bones, arm bones, and vertebrae on the site. A few months later,
construction workers came upon a human skull. Officials said
they were from the old cemeteries. Gravestones and coffins have
also been discovered.

When construction began in 1990 on what is now the Tropicana Field parking lot, several longtime residents believed
more remains were still at the site, possibly from all three cemeteries. Some graves were unmarked, they said, and efforts to relocate the dead were not always painstaking. Asked about it by
St. Petersburg Times reporter Alicia Caldwell, then–city official
Rick Mussett said he hadn't known the site housed a cemetery,
but that it shouldn't matter, since they didn't plan to dig deep
for the parking lot. "We're just going to pave it over," Mussett
said.

So Tropicana Field is built on a site that used to house three
graveyards, and may or may not still contain forgotten coffins
and remains. Does this mean the team is cursed?

A local medium named Reverend Dakota visited the site in
1999—just a year into its troubled history—and told reporter
Terry Tomalin that it was a place that "needs to be healed." She
sensed that "nobody respects what was here before."

Jon Wilson notes that cemeteries or no, there may be bad
vibes from the fact that Laurel Park residents were evicted to
make way for a stadium parking lot. "Lots of people resented the
way the city and Major League Baseball took over a neighborhood and moved folks out," he recalls. "It's not much of a jump
for people to mutter darkly, 'cursing' the development."

Stroll the Devil Rays clubhouse today, and few if any players have heard of the potential curse or its origins. But the
topic of the stadium's history has been discussed in the past.
"Somebody said something ridiculous like it was built on a

burial ground," remembers outfielder Randy Winn, who played for the Devil Rays in its first five years and dismissed such gossip as bunk. "That was the rumor that was going around when I was there."

Of course, it's possible that the team's losing ways have a more natural origin. Maybe it's just been bad front-office decisions, bad management, and bad play. And bad sportsmanship: In his controversial 2005 memoir, former Devil Ray Jose Canseco claimed that the injuries of Alvarez and Saunders were steroid-related.

New ownership took over the team in 2005 and has been putting in motion an ambitious plan to turn the club around. Better community relations and a more attractive stadium are a big part of the plans.

Ownership is also contemplating officially changing the name. They will likely rechristen the club "The Rays," hoping that if they de-Devil the bedeviled team, good luck will follow.

LUCKY 13

Tampa Bay outfielder Carl Crawford is one of relatively few players in the major leagues willing to wear uniform number 13. "That's the day my son was born," he says. "So it can't be bad luck for me."

Like Crawford, others who wear number 13 usually do so to salute someone dear to them.

Ozzie Guillen: "I wear it to honor [fellow Venezuelan player] Dave Concepción. He was my hero."

Omar Vizquel: "My idol [Dave Concepción] wore number 13. It has been great for me. I love it."

John Valentin: "When I started to really follow baseball, the Big Red Machine was playing very well in Cincinnati and Concepción was the shortstop, and I was a shortstop growing up. Also I have an older brother and 13 is his favorite number."

Rodrigo Lopez: "My brother liked to wear the number 13 when we played Little League. The number keeps me close to him."

Alex Rodriguez: "I wear it for Dan Marino. I don't care about [the superstition] at all."

Vance Wilson: "I just liked [the number]. And Lance Parrish wore it for years. It's kind of an honor to wear it, as a fellow catcher."

CHAPTER 28

LESSER-KNOWN CURSES

When the Red Sox won the World Series in 2004, everyone hailed the end of the Curse of the Bambino. When the White Sox won the following year, the victory was said to put to rest the lesser-known Curse of the Black Sox.

Many don't realize that when the St. Louis Cardinals won in 2006, they continued the tradition of curse-shattering World Series wins. What spell did they unwind? "The Curse of Keith."

As in Keith Hernandez, the Mets first baseman and broadcaster. The Cardinals won the 1982 World Series with Hernandez on the team, but then traded the superstar shortly thereafter for Neil Allen and Rick Ownbey—a trade that would seem to be punishment enough in itself. According to some fans, the Cards thereby incurred a curse that would prevent them from winning the World Series for years. More romantic versions of the story claim that the disgruntled Hernandez practiced Wicca at the time and literally put a hex on the team as he exited.

From 1983 to 2005, the Cardinals made it to the playoffs eight times, advancing to the World Series in three of those seasons, but always coming up short. In many of those years, key players (including Terry Pendleton, Mark McGwire, Scott Rolen, and Chris Carpenter) were sidelined with injuries and unable to take the field in the postseason, seriously handicapping the team.

These injuries could be bizarre. In 1985, Rookie of the Year Vince Coleman got "run over" by an automatic tarp machine in Busch Stadium, injuring his foot and missing the entire World Series. In 1987, Jack Clark's otherwise MVP season ended in September when he injured his ankle sliding into first base. Shortly before the 2000 playoffs, catcher Mike Matheny sliced his hand on a hunting knife his wife had just given him as a birthday present.

Other Cardinal bad breaks included umpire Don Denkinger's infamous blown call in Game 6 of the 1985 World Series (in which he declared Jorge Orta to be safe at first, when replays showed he was out by a full step), which may well have cost the team the championship.

Amid all these woes, Keith Hernandez helped the Mets to a World Series win in 1986.

As the Curse of Keith shows, not all curses are created equal. While the Red Sox and Cubs curses get most of the ink in the baseball press, there are other, lesser-known curses talked about by fans.

The Curse of the Rock

Rocky Colavito may be the most popular player ever to don the Indians uniform, and certainly one of the most successful. He first came up with the team in 1955, blossomed in 1956 and 1957, and exploded in 1958. That year he knocked out 41 home runs and drove in 113 RBI (second in the league in both categories), while hitting .303. The following year cemented his status as a slugging superstar; winning the home-run title with 42 dingers. In one game in July that year, Colavito hit home runs in four consecutive at-bats, becoming only the third player ever to do so (Bobby Lowe and Lou Gehrig preceded him).

The Cleveland Indians were perennial contenders in those days. Between 1948 and 1959, the team won two pennants and one World Series, and finished second in the league six times. Colavito was a young, energetic player who brought charisma and power to the team. His Italian heritage also helped make him a hero in the immigrant and working-class neighborhoods of Cleveland.

So fans were stunned when GM Frank Lane traded Colavito in 1960, sending him to Detroit for AL batting champ Harvey Kuenn, who would play just one season for the Indians. Longtime Cleveland fans still chafe at the memory.

It would be thirty-five years before the Indians would seriously vie for a pennant again, a long stretch in which numerous ill fortunes befell the team. Terry Pluto, whose book *The Curse of Rocky Colavito: A Loving Look at a 33-Year Slump* provided most of the curse's notoriety, documented some of the more vexed moments, including:

- Bad trades: In 1964, the Indians dealt Jim "Mudcat" Grant to the Minnesota Twins. The following year, Grant won 21 games and the Twins won their first pennant. Grant would win a total of 78 games after leaving Cleveland. In 1984, the Indians sent pitcher Rick Sutcliffe to the Cubs; there he won the NL Cy Young Award that year, helping the Cubs win their division. In 1989, he won the Cy Young again. (It should be noted that the Sutcliffe trade involved other players, and brought to the Indians Mel Hall and Joe Carter, the latter of whom contributed much at the plate.)

- Personal problems: Pitcher Sam McDowell's alcoholism sank his promising career and ended it entirely at age thirty-two. Slugger Tony Horton was undone by the mental stress of the game and had to leave the team midseason in 1970. Just twenty-five years old at the time, Horton eventually recovered but never played baseball again.

- Tragedy: In 1993, a boating accident on a Spring Training off-day killed relief pitchers Steve Olin and Tim Crews, and seriously injured starting pitcher Bobby Ojeda.

While away, Colavito racked up another 173 home runs in five seasons, an average of 35 a year. In 1961, he had a career year with Detroit (.290, 45 HR, 140 RBI). He made the All-Star team in 1961, 1962, and 1964.

In 1965, the Indians reacquired Colavito from the Kansas City Athletics. But this trade too was costly: They surrendered pitcher Tommy John (who would go on to win 286 more games in his Hall of Fame career) and outfielder Tommie Agee (destined to become Rookie of the Year in 1966 and contribute mightily to the Mets 1969 World Championship team).

Colavito quickly gave fans what they had missed: In his first year back, he led the league in RBI (108) and walks (93), clubbed 26 home runs, and set a new major-league record with 162 consecutive errorless games. He made the All-Star team and ranked fifth in that year's MVP voting.

However, Colavito fell out with management again in 1967 and was traded to the White Sox in July. He then had short stints with the Dodgers and Yankees before retiring after the 1968 season.

Pluto's book appeared in 1994. As he noted, from 1960 through 1993, the Indians not only didn't win, they didn't come within 11 games of first place. But they were just one game behind the White Sox when the 1994 season-ending strike hit, and went on to win the AL pennant in 1995, losing the World Series to the Atlanta Braves that year. With the team on the upswing, Pluto penned a sequel entitled *Burying the Curse: How the Indians Became the Best Team in Baseball.*

But the Tribe continued to falter in big games. They made it to the World Series again in 1997, losing this time to the upstart Florida Marlins despite leading Game 7 in the bottom of the ninth with one out. They made the postseason in 1996, 1998, 1999, and 2001, but lost either the ALDS or ALCS every time. Pluto recanted his reassessment of the team, and in 1999 published *Our Tribe*, in which he asserted that the curse was alive and well.

The Indians have dueling curse stories to explain their losses. At least one year, the team may have suffered from the notorious *Sports Illustrated* curse, which says that it's bad luck to appear on the magazine's cover. In 1987, the Indians fronted

SI's baseball preview issue with a headline that declared: BELIEVE IT! CLEVELAND IS THE BEST TEAM IN THE AMERICAN LEAGUE! The Indians lost 101 games that year, and finished last in the majors.

Prior to the Colavito trade, Indians fans spoke of another curse, claiming that when manager Bobby Bragan was fired in 1958, the indignant skipper walked out to the pitcher's mound and hexed the team, declaring they would not win another pennant. Bragan says it never happened.

Rocky Colavito also says he never cursed the team, though most versions of the story don't have the slugger deliberately invoking a spell; the curse is a consequence of the team's bad move. (The Rock does admit to still resenting Frank Lane, and won't say the former GM's name in public.)

Whatever the reason, the Indians are still waiting for their next World Series title. Only the Cubs have been waiting longer.

The Curse of William Penn

Some curses are too big for one sport. The Curse of William Penn is said to haunt not only the Philadelphia Phillies, but also all other Philadelphia sports teams.

Penn, of course, founded the city, as well as the state of Pennsylvania, in the early 1680s. He died in 1718 but has continued to preside over the city in the form of a statue perched atop Philadelphia City Hall. At 548 feet, it was the highest structure in the city since it was erected in 1901.

Until 1987. That year saw the completion of a new skyscraper, One Liberty Place, which towered 945 feet over the city. Some years later, Two Liberty Place was constructed, rising 848 feet. The buildings are just a few blocks from City Hall.

These taller towers offended Mr. Penn, legend has it. The result is that no Philadelphia-based pro team (the Phillies, the Eagles, the 76ers, or the Flyers) has won a championship since 1987.

In the years prior to the curse, Philadelphia teams were on a roll. The Flyers won the Stanley Cup in 1974 and 1975. The Phillies won the World Series in 1980. The 76ers won the NBA title in 1983.

Since 1987, it's been a different story. The Flyers lost the Stanley Cup finals in 1987 and 1997, and lost conference finals in 1989, 1995, 2000, and 2004. The 76ers came up short in the NBA finals in 2001. The Eagles lost the NFC Championship Game three straight years (2002–04), finally winning it in 2005 . . . only to lose the Super Bowl by three points.

Some claim the curse might extend to college teams, minorleague teams . . . even Philly-based racehorse Barbaro, who broke its leg in the 2006 Preakness Stakes, ending its chances at the Triple Crown and ultimately requiring the thoroughbred be euthanized.

For their part, the Phillies made it to the World Series in 1993, losing in six games to the Toronto Blue Jays. But is the curse to blame?

Losing is a Phillies tradition that predates the tall skyscrapers in Philadelphia. One of the oldest teams in baseball, the Phillies started life as the Philadelphia Quakers in 1883. When the 1980 club won the championship, they put to end ninety-seven years of futility; it was their first World Series win. That made them the last of the sixteen original MLB teams to take the title.

The Phillies have also experienced some pretty harsh losing streaks. From 1918 to 1948, they had just one winning season (1932) and amassed a record of 1,752–2,939, for a rather bleak .373 winning percentage. And all this while William Penn sat proud and alone as the tallest edifice in Philadelphia.

Since the construction of the Liberty Place buildings, more skyscrapers taller than the Penn statue have been built in Philadelphia. The Comcast Center, scheduled for completion in 2007, will set a new height record for the city. If the Phillies and their fellow sports franchises are to have a chance, Mr. Penn will have to get over his Napoleon complex.

CHAPTER 29

ANGELS IN THE OUTPATIENT CLINIC

Folks who claim that the Tampa Bay Devil Rays are cursed because of their "satanic" moniker may have a hard time explaining the troubled history of the Los Angeles Angels of Anaheim. From the team's inception right up until it won its first World Series title, the Angels were plagued by a string of injuries that had players talking about their own clubhouse curse.

"For a long time we thought something was up because we had a lot of people get hurt in crucial situations," recalls catcher Todd Greene, with the club from 1996–99. "We had a bunch of freaky things happen and they all happened at home."

Injuries are an expected part of professional baseball. Every team has them, and they never come at opportune times. But the Angels injuries were sometimes bizarre. In 1997, Greene remembers, "We were one game in back of Seattle and Chuck Finley was backing up home and he gets his spike caught in his shoestring and falls down and breaks his wrist. The next day I take a foul ball on my arm and break my wrist, and I was done for the season. We lost our number one pitcher and our starting catcher in two days." The team wound up six games behind the Mariners in the final standings.

And there were more unusual injuries. The following year, Greene says, "Justin Baughman, our second baseman, took a line drive right in his face."

"My brain bled the year I was there," says Kent Mercker. It was May of 2000 and the lefty pitcher had been hearing stories of strange injuries to players at Edison Field. "Troy Percival was telling me that they were convinced that place was cursed," he recalls. "Then all of a sudden my brain bled."

Mercker was pitching against the Texas Rangers and had just struck out Ruben Mateo in the second inning when he felt a shooting pain from the back of his neck to his forehead. He stayed in the game, but just four pitches later it was too much to bear. Mercker dropped to one knee on the mound. Team officials rushed out, looked him over, and sent him to the hospital where he was diagnosed with a cerebral hemorrhage.

Though the injury sidelined his career for the rest of the season and the next, Mercker considers himself lucky: Such bleeding is usually caused by an aneurysm and is often fatal. His had to do with spasms in his brain's blood vessels and didn't require surgery. But he certainly came to understand why some players were "convinced there's something going on in Anaheim."

Like the 1999 incident in which George Hendrick, then a coach with the team, accidentally hit shortstop Gary DiSarcina with a fungo bat on the first day of Spring Training. The bat broke the infielder's arm, and he missed the first half of the season.

As the injured Angels piled up, a potential reason for the curse started to emerge in the clubhouse. "They said that they built the stadium on old Indian burial grounds," says Troy Glaus. "That's why a lot of bad things happened to that organization."

By "bad things" players refer to more than just the injuries. From its start in 1961 until 2002, the team never won a World Series. They suffered a postseason meltdown in 1982, becoming the first team to blow a 2–0 lead in a five-game series when they lost the ALCS to Milwaukee. Four years later they were literally one strike away from their first trip to the Fall Classic when the Red Sox homered to take the lead . . . and then won the next two games to send the Angels packing.

In 1995 the team blew an 11-game August lead in the AL West—due in large part to injuries to key players.

Off the field, there had been unusual tragedies as well. In 1978, outfielder Lyman Bostock was murdered in the last week of the season. Bostock was riding in the back of his uncle's car, seated next to a woman he barely knew, when her estranged husband pulled up and fired a shot at her, missing the woman but striking Bostock in the head.

Donnie Moore, forever branded the goat for surrendering the lead in the 1986 ALCS, never fully recovered from the loss. A few years later, released from the team the previous season and suffering from depression and drug addiction, Moore shot at his wife in their home before ending his own life.

Not all of these events have been blamed on Edison Field, but the idea that the park was built on sacred Native American ground had some people talking about "the Curse of the Cowboy." The theory was that because the team was owned by Gene Autry—Hollywood's "Singing Cowboy"—this was some kind of continuation of the classic cowboys versus Indians duel that had been going on in the West for ages.

"Tim Mead [the team's PR director] dug up all kinds of stuff on the stadium," says pitcher Kevin Appier. "He showed it to us and said it wasn't built on Indian burial ground. So we felt better."

Mead's office researched the rumor through historical records and the city of Anaheim. They discovered evidence of various Indian tribes traveling through the area covered by the stadium, but nothing to indicate a burial ground. While this is not the kind of subject most team media relations directors deal with, Mead says he was glad to look into it.

"Kevin was part of a group that was inquiring because they had heard about it. Until we won the World Series, every new group of guys who came in here, all they heard about was *The Curse! The Curse!* We just did some research to alleviate their concerns."

The concerns of some players were also alleviated by two shamanistic women who visited the players with gifts. "We had a couple of weird ladies come into our clubhouse one time and give us these little figurines that were supposed to keep us well," says Scott Schoeneweis. "They were small little animals."

Kent Mercker describes the gifts as "tribal things." They were given to some players. "They said, 'Keep this in your locker for good luck.'"

Troy Percival was one recipient. "I don't know what they were called, but they were some kind of Indian burial ground ritual things," he says. "I threw it right in the trash."

While the notion of Indian cemeteries seemed to arise with the '90s squads, the idea of an injury curse goes back to the team's earliest days. In 1962, outfielder Ken Hunt broke his collarbone while swinging a bat in the on-deck circle. In 1964, rookie phenom Rick Reichardt (whom the Angels had signed that year with a then-record $200,000 bonus) came down with a kidney infection and had to have the organ removed midseason. In 1972, infielder Chico Ruiz died in an off-season car crash, as did shortstop Mike Miley five years later. Bobby Valentine ended his 1973 season—and much of his playing career potential—when he severely broke his leg chasing down a fly ball in centerfield.

Pitchers seem to have had it especially tough. In 1961, the team's first year in existence, Johnny James broke his arm delivering a curveball, ending his career. In 1963, All-Star Kent McBride—then 13–2 on the season—got whiplash in a car accident; he then went 4–28 for the rest of his career. That same year Art Fowler took a BP ball to the head and went blind in his left eye. In 1965, rookie Dick Wantz died of a brain tumor in May, having pitched exactly one inning for the team. (But that's more than Bruce Heinbechner, who was set to debut with the Angels in 1974 but died in a Spring Training car crash.)

Indeed, auto accidents have been particularly calamitous for the Angels—in 1968, that's how Minnie Rojas severed his spine and ended up paralyzed for life. The accident killed his wife and three children. On May 22, 1992, one of the team buses was in an accident on the New Jersey Turnpike when the driver fell asleep at the wheel. Twelve players were injured (none seriously), and manager Buck Rodgers suffered internal injuries that caused him to miss more than half the season.

In 1977, what was supposed to be a promising season for the Angels had again disintegrated with injuries and bad luck. The team had acquired outfielders Don Baylor, Joe Rudi, and infielder Bobby Grich that year—the latter two of whom spent the second half of the season on the DL. (Grich had herniated a disc while lifting an air conditioner.) At a loss for solutions, the Angels turned to a local witch to turn things around.

Dick Miller, a writer with the *Los Angeles Herald-Examiner*, had the idea to call in Louise Huebner, who had once been dubbed "the official witch of Los Angeles County" by a city official. Huebner was an attractive woman whose policies on witchcraft often centered around the libido: She advocated practices to increase "romantic vitality" and had theories on what to eat, drink, or worship "before each sexual union." When she visited the Angels in August, she gave Gene Autry and GM Harry Dalton medals to rub each night (at 9:00 P.M., when the moon is fullest), promising that they would be "drawing on a reservoir of psychic and spiritual energy"—and that they'd also see "an improvement in sexual activity."

Players also received medals and Huebner started corralling energy for the team. At this point in the season (August 3), the Angels were 48–54, and faced the Yankees, Orioles, and Royals in the coming week. Over the next six games, they won every outing, sweeping the first-place Orioles along the way. It was

the team's longest winning streak in three years. Equally important, players stayed healthy. They started talking about getting
back in contention.

But Huebner soon said she wasn't thrilled with the team's
attitude toward her. Some embraced her "intervention" as fun;
others, like Bobby Bonds, derided it as black magic and evil. She
said she grew tired of this and publicly withdrew her support of
the team (though she did not announce this until after the team
started losing again). After their Huebner-blessed winning
streak, the team went 20–34 the rest of the season.

The plague of injuries seems to have petered out over time. Players who have come to the club more recently haven't experienced the curse firsthand. "I heard something about it," says
catcher Benji Gil, who joined the team in 2000. "But I didn't
come across any Indian ghosts or anything like that."

There was certainly no talk of a curse when the Angels finally won the World Series in 2002. As often happens in the
wake of a victory, many players now downplay the idea of a
curse altogether.

"I don't know if players actually believed it or not," muses
pitcher Scott Schoeneweis. "I know there were some strange injuries that would happen."

Tim Salmon feels that curse talk violates his more serious beliefs. "I'm a Christian, so I always refuted that one by saying,
'My God is greater than any curse or God they may think up.'"
He does acknowledge that "the coincidences were there. To a
nonspiritual person, I could see that being an easy belief."

"I didn't really believe that too much," adds Jim Edmonds,
who feels there are always many reasons that a team can struggle. "It's hard to win in this game. I wouldn't say it was a curse.
Only one team gets the winning share, and that's really tough
to do."

Mike Scioscia, managing the Angels since 1999, certainly felt
the consequences of so many injured players, but credits the
team for not getting distracted by it. "I don't think that affected

us at all," he says now. "These guys got hit with some odd injuries, but they never paid a lot of attention to it."

That's important, says Troy Glaus, since curses are as valid as people's faith in them. "If you believe it to be true, then it is."

"Things start happening and you start wondering," he says. "At the end of the day it's one of those things that gives you an excuse or a reason—not necessarily that it's true, but it helps explain why bad things happen."

ACKNOWLEDGMENTS

Our thanks first and foremost to the dozens of baseball players, managers, coaches, stadium workers, fans, and others who shared their stories with us. Their willingness to entrust strangers with stories that are sometimes personal or in need of just the right telling was a responsibility we aspired to live up to as we wrote the book.

At last count we have interviewed well over 800 professional ballplayers—many in locker rooms and dugouts, where our question ("Do you know any baseball ghost stories, curses, legends?") is always the oddest one they've heard all day. We thank them for their comments and interest in the topic.

Thanks also to the numerous team media and PR departments, who provided us access to players and helped track down facts and stats where we needed them.

A number of people helped facilitate our research by providing resources or connections to players and other interviewees. This list includes Charles J. Adams III, Franchesca Arias, Evelyn Begley, Jeff Belanger, Loren Coleman, Glen Creason, Neil Ghiem, Andrew Gordon, June Gordon, Bruce Markusen, Bill Murphy, Rod Nelson, Craig Nesbit, Mark Niles, Shoko Ogata, Mark Peel, Oren Renick, Carl Ruppert, J. D. Schlueter, Carl Turin, Veronica Vaughn, Allison White, Joan Turin, Veronica Vaughn, Allison White, and Robert Whiting.

Our families have been helpful, understanding, curious, patient, and in every way supportive as we threw ourselves into this project.

Certain people must be singled out for extra thanks.

Stephanie Cain voluntarily turned a chance meeting with the authors at the Cooperstown Hall of Fame into a ton of legwork on the history of Tropicana Field. The chapter on the Devil Rays curse would not have been possible without her assistance.

S.F. Giants tour guide Linda Vessa went the extra mile—being a marathoner, she ran it—in providing background and resources on the team and its ballpark.

Brian Bernardoni generously shared his unpublished manuscript on Wrigley Field, a "Tour Narrative and Scrapbook" we look forward to seeing in print.

Jim McDonald provided boundless logistical support in the research stage, made introductions to major-league players, and chimed in helpfully on the written text.

Tim Wiles at the Hall of Fame library offered wisdom, strategies, and advice, as well as the library's voluminous files.

Roger Gans, Gary Joseph, and Bob Kohm provided invaluable feedback on the manuscript in its final stages.

Our agent, Rob Wilson, found our book a home. His sage advice and steady support have been indispensable.

Rob Kirkpatrick, Josh Rosenberg, and the team at The Lyons Press always gave the impression that the book was in good hands. We are very grateful for their care in getting this labor of love out to the world.

And finally, to George Gmelch, who has godfathered the project and its authors and who generously shared his wisdom, his Rolodex, and even his own story—enormous thanks.

REFERENCES

While the majority of stories and information in *Haunted Baseball* derive from original interviews, the following sources provided valuable background information.

Adams, Charles J., III. 2006. *Haunted Berks County*. Reading, PA: Exeter House Books.

Antonen, Mel. "Baseball history lives at neighborhood stadium." *USA Today*. February 10, 2004.

Baker, Russell. "Observer." *New York Times*. October 6, 1962.

Baseball. DVD. 1994. Directed by Ken Burns. PBS Home Video.

Bernardoni, Brian. Unpublished manuscript. 2006 Wrigley Field Tour Narrative and Scrapbook.

Bishop, Gene. "Fan takes field to spread ashes; M's forbid action." *Seattle Times*. September 22, 2005.

Bosquet, Jean. "Lizard people's catacomb city hunted." *Los Angeles Times*. January 29, 1934.

Bradford, Rob. 2004. *Chasing Steinbrenner: Pursuing the Pennant in Toronto and Boston*. Dulles, VA: Potomac Books.

Caldwell, Alicia. "Dome parking project may unearth remains." *St. Petersburg Times*. July 22, 1990.

_____. "Graves might stall work on Laurel Park." *St. Petersburg Times*. July 26, 1990.

Canseco, Jose. 2005. *Juiced*. New York: Regan Books.

Condon, David. "In the wake of the news." *Chicago Tribune*, April 15, 1969.

_____. "In the wake of the news." *Chicago Tribune*, September 29, 1969.

Coyne, Kevin. "Ultimate sacrifice." *Smithsonian* magazine. October, 2004.

Cristodero, Damian. "Tropicana isn't a draw, but is it the problem?" *St. Petersburg Times*. March 7, 2005.

Curse of the Bambino, The. DVD. 2003. Directed by George Roy. HBO Video.

Daly, Dan. "Ashes lay where athletes play." *Washington Times*. December 1, 2005.

Dewey, Donald, and Nicholas Acocella. 2002. *The New Biographical History of Baseball*. Chicago: Triumph Books.

Eig, Jonathan. 2005. *Luckiest Man: The Life and Death of Lou Gehrig*. New York: Simon & Schuster.

"Ex-Tiger farmhand victim of WTC attack." *Michigan Daily*. September 20, 2001.

Fee, Gayle, and Laura Raposa. "Inside track." *Boston Herald*. July 10, 2002.

Francis, Bill. "Roberto Clemente Jr. shares memories of his legendary father." http://www.baseballhalloffame.org/news/2006/060609. htm. June 9, 2006.

Gatto, Steve. 2004. *Da Curse of the Billy Goat*. Lansing, MI: Protar House.

Grabowski, John F. 2003. *The Chicago White Sox*. Farmington Hills, MI: Lucent Books.

Harwell, Ernie. "Lone seagull a sentry for club's dying trainer." *Detroit Free Press*. September 4, 2002.

Hayes, Neil. "Plague of the plaque." *Contra Costa Times*. March 26, 2006.

Henderson, Joe. "Huff on DL? What the devil is going on!" TBO.com. http://www.tbo.com/sports/rays/MGBNQ1KIYLE.html. April 13, 2006.

Hill, Justice B. "Players praise Warfield's life." MLB.com. http://www.mlb.com/news/article.jsp?ymd=20020716&content_id =83826&vkey=news_cle&fext=.jsp&c_id=cle. July 16, 2002.

_____. "Trainer's passing hits Thome hard." MLB.com. http://www.mlb.com/news/article.jsp?ymd=20020719&content_id =85488&vkey=news_cle&fext=.jsp&c_id=cle. July 19, 2002.

Holway, John B. 2000. *The Baseball Astrologer and Other Weird Tales.* New York: Total Sports Illustrated.

Horrigan, Jeff. "Williamson hears boos: Ghost story a frighty for righty." *Boston Herald.* September 25, 2003.

Hoynes, Paul. "The Tribe lost their heart and soul yesterday." *Plain Deal Reporter.* September 17, 2002.

Johnson, Chuck. "Hard thrower, deep thinker." *USA Today.* April 27, 2004.

"Kenny Marino: a devout baseball fan." *New York Times.* October 20, 2001.

Ketchum, Don. "Miguel's mission." *Arizona Republic.* August 5, 2003.

Kirst, Sean Peter. 2003. *The Ashes of Lou Gehrig and Other Baseball Essays.* Jefferson, NC: McFarland & Company.

Lee, Bill. 1984. *The Wrong Stuff.* New York: Penguin USA.

Lieb, Fred. 1939. *Sight Unseen: A Journalist Visits the Occult.* New York: Harper Brothers Publishers.

_____. 1977. *Baseball as I Have Known It.* New York: Coward, Mc-Cann & Geoghegan.

Lindberg, Richard. 1983. *Who's on 3rd?* South Bend, IN: Icarus Press.

_____. 1997. *The White Sox Encyclopedia.* Philadelphia: Temple University Press.

Maraniss, David. 2006. *Clemente.* New York: Simon & Schuster.

McGrory, Brian. "Taking teeth out of curse?" *Boston Globe.* September 2, 2004.

Miller, Adam, and Cathy Burke. "Holiday at Shea." *New York Post.* September 22, 2001.

Murray, Jim. "O'Malley's Mahalley." *Los Angeles Times.* January 29, 1962.

New Voice of Fenway Park, The. Mini-DVD. 2003. Directed by Scott Hancock. A Wideshot Production. Hopkinton, NH. Mickley, Kara.

Nine Innings from Ground Zero. DVD. 2005. Directed by Ouisie Shapiro. HBO Video.

O'Leary, Ryan. " 'It had to be a UFO.' " *Northwest Indiana News.* August 2, 2003.

Olney, Buster. 2005. *The Last Night of the Yankee Dynasty*. New York: HarperCollins.

"Penthouse interview: Bill Lee." *Penthouse*. October 1979.

Pluto, Terry. 1994. *The Curse of Rocky Colavito*. New York: Simon & Schuster.

_____. 1995. *Burying the Curse: How the Indians Became the Best Team in Baseball*. Akron, OH: Akron Beacon Journal.

_____. 1999. *Our Tribe*. Cleveland, OH: Gray & Company Publishers.

Rasmussen, Cecilia. "L.A. scene: the city then and now." *Los Angeles Times*. July 22, 1996

Reaves, Joseph A. "Cubs' winning streak starting to get manager's goat." *Chicago Tribune*, April 30, 1994.

Ryan, Kelly. "Rays present city with practice field." *St. Petersburg Times*. December 12, 1999.

"74,200 see Yankees open new stadium; Ruth hits home run." *New York Times*. April 19, 1923.

Shaughnessy, Dan. 1990. *The Curse of the Bambino*. New York: Dutton.

Smith, Red. "Man who couldn't buy pennants." *New York Times*. July 12, 1976.

Spaceman: A Baseball Odyssey. DVD. 2006. Directed by Brett Rapkin. Hart Sharp Video. Dixon, Josh.

Stout, Glenn. "A 'curse' born of hate." ESPN.com. http://sports.espn.go .com/mlb/playoffs2004/news/story?page=Curse041005. Updated October 3, 2004.

Swanson, Harry. 2004. *Ruthless Baseball*. Bloomington, IN: Authorhouse.

Tomalin, Terry. "A medium, a stadium, a sad, sad situation series." *St. Petersburg Times*. June 9, 1999.

Topkin, Marc. "Curse of the Devil (Rays) series: What went wrong? 10 years of Devil Rays baseball." *St. Petersburg Times*. March 8, 2005.

"25 lost treasures." *Sports Illustrated*. Vol. 103, No. 2. July 18, 2005.

Walter, Patrick. "Coffins to bear logos of baseball teams." *Associated Press*. October 18, 2006.

"Warfield honored at private memorial service." ESPN.com. http://espn.go.com/mlb/news/2002/0718/1407462.html. July 18, 2002.

Whiting, Robert. 2004. *The Meaning of Ichiro*. New York: Warner Books.

Wulf, Steve. "The secrets of Sam." *Sports Illustrated*. Vol 79, No. 3. July 19, 1993.

INDEX

ABOUT THE AUTHORS

Mickey Bradley is a lifelong Yankee fan, named after the team's legendary centerfielder. He has been working as a freelance writer for more than a decade, both in Manhattan and Upstate New York. His diverse body of work covers topics ranging from sports to science to humor to entertainment and includes ghost-written books, corporate communications, magazine profiles, and hundreds of video/film projects.

Dan Gordon first experienced the magic of Fenway in the summer of 1975 when his father took him to his first game. With a Thomas J. Watson Fellowship, Gordon studied global baseball culture in Japan, the Dominican Republic, Cuba, and Nicaragua. His writings on baseball have appeared in numerous publications including the *Providence Journal* and *Fort Worth Star,* and he is the author of *Cape Encounters: Contemporary Cape Cod Ghost Stories* (Cockle Cove Press, 2004). He lives and dies with the Red Sox.